"This is a Tour de Force! Such an important book."
– Professor Rosie Flewitt, Manchester Metropolitan University, UK

"This book is informed by the outstanding scholarship and critical gaze of the authors. The focus on neo-liberalism, and its effects in early childhood education are relevant at a time of unprecedented policy intensification, and the intervention of Ofsted in professional development, curriculum, pedagogy, play, assessment, and school readiness. This book traces the evolution of neo-liberalism in ECE, taking into account the different circumstances compared to compulsory education.

This meticulous tracing draws on multiple sources of evidence within and beyond the UK to show the influence of supra-national discourses, and the particular interpretations of neo-liberalism within shifting UK government ideologies. The authors have revealed how neo-liberalism works at the level of systems and structures, and how it effects changes to the behaviour of individuals, including teachers, leaders, children and families. For this very reason this book should be compulsory reading for all ECE professionals, because neo-liberalism works on all levels and in many different ways to favour marketisation, competition, surveillance and regulation. As the authors rightly argue, these conditions produce a motivating stimulus of anxieties, fears and insecurities.

Another timely provocation for readers is the neo-liberal focus on what education must produce, and not what education is for. This stands as a rallying cry for the early childhood field to renew the democratic politics of education that has underpinned the work of the traditional pioneers and contemporary activists who link early childhood education to social justice and a more equitable society.

The authors do not shy away from controversial issues, and highlight many tensions between the marketised big business of childcare provision, and the failure to raise quality consistently across providers, or to achieve the claimed benefits of choice for families. Furthermore, the failure to address and ameliorate social and educational disadvantages stands as a rebuke to neo-liberal claims about raising standards and improving outcomes for children.

This book is essential reading for all early childhood specialists, at whatever stage of their careers. The authors provide a coherent framing of the socio-political conditions under which ECE has developed in the last thirty years, and will hopefully provoke deeper political engagement from the field."
– Professor Elizabeth Wood, University of Sheffield, UK

NEOLIBERALISM AND EARLY CHILDHOOD EDUCATION

Neoliberalism, with its worldview of competition, choice and calculation, its economisation of everything, and its will to govern has 'sunk its roots deep' into Early Childhood Education and Care. This book considers its deeply detrimental impacts upon young children, families, settings and the workforce. Through an exploration of possibilities for resistance and refusal, and reflection on the significance of the coronavirus pandemic, Roberts-Holmes and Moss provide hope that neoliberalism's current hegemony can be successfully contested.

The book provides a critical introduction to neoliberalism and three closely related and influential concepts – Human Capital theory, Public Choice theory and New Public Management – as well as an overview of the impact of neoliberalism on compulsory education, in particular through the Global Education Reform Movement. With its main focus on Early Childhood Education and Care, this book argues that while neoliberalism is a very powerful force, it is 'deeply problematic, eminently resistible and eventually replaceable' – and that there are indeed alternatives.

Neoliberalism and Early Childhood Education is an insightful supplement to the studies of students and researchers in Early Childhood Education and Sociology of Education, and is also highly relevant to policy makers.

Guy Roberts-Holmes is Associate Professor of Early Childhood Education at UCL Institute of Education, University College London, UK. His previous books include *The Datafication of Primary and Early Years Education* (Bradbury and Roberts-Holmes, 2017, Routledge).

Peter Moss is Emeritus Professor of Early Childhood Provision at UCL Institute of Education, University College London, UK. He co-edited the 'Contesting Early Childhood' series for its first ten years; his last book for the series was *Alternative Narratives in Early Childhood Education* (2018, Routledge).

CONTESTING EARLY CHILDHOOD
Series Editors: Liselott Mariett Olsson and Michel Vandenbroeck

This ground-breaking series questions the current dominant discourses surrounding early childhood, and offers instead alternative narratives of an area that is now made up of a multitude of perspectives and debates.

The series examines the possibilities and risks arising from the accelerated development of early childhood services and policies, and illustrates how it has become increasingly steeped in regulation and control. Insightfully, this collection of books shows how early childhood services can in fact contribute to ethical and democratic practices. The authors explore new ideas taken from alternative working practices in both the western and developing world, and from other academic disciplines such as developmental psychology. Current theories and best practice are placed in relation to the major processes of political, social, economic, cultural and technological change occurring in the world today.

Revisiting Paulo Freire's Pedagogy of the Oppressed
Issues and Challenges in Early Childhood Education
Edited by Michel Vandenbroeck

Neoliberalism and Early Childhood Education
Markets, Imaginaries and Governance
Guy Roberts-Holmes and Peter Moss

In Dialogue with Reggio Emilia
Listening, Researching and Learning (2e)
Carlina Rinaldi

For more information about this series, please visit: www.routledge.com/Contesting-Early-Childhood/book-series/SE0623

NEOLIBERALISM AND EARLY CHILDHOOD EDUCATION

Markets, Imaginaries and Governance

Guy Roberts-Holmes and Peter Moss

Routledge
Taylor & Francis Group

LONDON AND NEW YORK

First published 2021
by Routledge
2 Park Square, Milton Park, Abingdon, Oxon OX14 4RN

and by Routledge
52 Vanderbilt Avenue, New York, NY 10017

Routledge is an imprint of the Taylor & Francis Group, an informa business

© 2021 Guy Roberts-Holmes and Peter Moss

British Library Cataloguing-in-Publication Data
A catalogue record for this book is available from the British Library

Library of Congress Cataloging-in-Publication Data
Names: Roberts-Holmes, Guy, author. | Moss, Peter, 1945- author.
Title: Neoliberalism and early childhood education : markets, imaginaries and
governance / Guy Roberts-Holmes and Peter Moss.
Description: First Edition. | New York : Routledge, 2021. |
Series: Contesting early childhood | Includes bibliographical
references and index. |
Identifiers: LCCN 2020048164 (print) | LCCN 2020048165 (ebook) |
ISBN 9780367140823 (Hardback) | ISBN 9780367140830 (Paperback) |
ISBN 9780429030086 (eBook)
Subjects: LCSH: Early childhood education--Government policy. |
Child development--Government policy. | Neoliberalism. | Education and state.
Classification: LCC LB1139.23 .R62 2021 (print) | LCC LB1139.23 (ebook) |
DDC 372.21--dc23 LC record available at https://lccn.loc.gov/2020048164
LC ebook record available at https://lccn.loc.gov/2020048165

ISBN: 978-0-367-14082-3 (hbk)
ISBN: 978-0-367-14083-0 (pbk)
ISBN: 978-0-429-03008-6 (ebk)

Typeset in Bembo
by Taylor & Francis Books

For Pamela

CONTENTS

FIGURES

ACKNOWLEDGEMENTS

We would like to thank Karyn Callaghan, Rosie Flewitt, Jan Georgeson and Eva Lloyd for their valuable comments on the final draft of the book. Any errors, of fact or judgement, are entirely ours.

FOREWORD

Michel Vandenbroeck

Neoliberalism and Early Childhood Education: Markets, Imaginaries and Governance is a new landmark in the ground-breaking series of *Contesting Early Childhood*. There is little doubt that it will remain to be so for many years to come. Guy Roberts-Holmes and Peter Moss trace the origins of neoliberalism back to Mont Pèlerin, a small Swiss mountain resort, and they meticulously analyse how neoliberalism gradually pervaded many societal domains, including education in general and early childhood education in particular. They make us aware of the extent to which our present-day vocabularies and our thinking are influenced by neoliberal imaginaries as we commonly use concepts like 'human capital', 'social investment', 'public choice' or 'new public management'. By analysing and commenting on the origins and the meanings of such concepts, they confront us with implicit choices that need to be made more explicit. Indeed, if there is one reason why this book is a must-read for scholars and students as well as for policy makers, it is for how it shows that what we all too often take for granted in conceptualizing early childhood education is, in fact, a (political and ethical) choice. It is one of many choices that are possible, and it is an ideological choice that is closely related with a particular conceptualization of a capitalist society. Roberts-Holmes and Moss show how that choice is not only reflected in national policies, but also in international organizations, including the World Bank, UNESCO and particularly in the OECD, including in their early childhood policies. As Gramsci noted, discourses aspire to become and to remain hegemonic (Simon, 1991).

Yet, sadly, this is not only about discourses. As the authors aptly show, the neoliberal turn has a profound influence on the daily practices in early childhood education, on its funding mechanisms, on what data are produced, on inspection, performance and accountability, on the image of the child, the image of the parent and the image of the early childhood workforce. They illustrate this with many examples from English-speaking countries, including France and the Netherlands to the Middle East and Asia. To give but one example of how fast the marketisation and corporatisation of early childhood education has been spreading: in her well documented 2013 book on childcare markets, Eva Lloyd (2013, p. 5) described France as a country with 60 years of state-funded and state-provided ECEC and therefore at the opposite end of commodification. However, between 2013 and 2017, 25% (2013) to half (2017) of the growth in childcare places is due to 'micro-crèches', which are almost all private initiatives (Haut Conseil de la famille, de l'enfance et de l'âge, 2018) and to a very large extent owned by a handful of corporate for-profit organizations. In February 2020, the respected French journal *Le Monde Diplomatique* published an alarming dossier about how early childhood once was part of a successful public service that is now endangered (Shahshahani, 2020).

Roberts-Holmes and Moss delve deeply into how these evolutions have influenced our thinking and shaped a form of governmentality, borrowing the term from Foucault. Yet, there is another and maybe even more important reason why this book is a must-read. Through their precise and critical analysis, the authors show that it is possible to refuse the neoliberal imaginary. They carefully document what such 'politics of refusal' may look like and where the reader can turn to for inspiration (including Joan Tronto, Loris Malaguzzi and many others). Once it is clear that what appears to us as hegemonic is, in fact, a matter of choice and that other choices are possible, inevitably this becomes a discussion about the values of education. It becomes then impossible to think about what a pedagogy of the early years may look like without being explicit about these values and what we mean by 'the good life'. That is, according to the authors, about 'cooperating with and caring for others in a collective response to common needs and shared interests, rather than constantly competing in the untrammelled pursuit of their own self-interest'. Then, transformation becomes not only possible, but also inevitable. It is, after all in our own hands, to reject the neoliberal subject and if there is anything the Covid-19 crisis has clearly shown, it is the importance of collective and therefore public services. As this becomes increasingly clear, it may mean that we are at the verge of 'postcapitalism'.

In sum, with the present book, Guy Roberts-Holmes and Peter Moss have done what Foucault (1984) considered to be the task of an intellectual: through the analyses of their respective domains, question what seems to be evident, shake up the usual, the ways of being and of doing, and from this re-problematisation they participate in the formation of a political will. The task they have taken on cannot be missed and is an essential contribution to the *Contesting Early Childhood* series and to the early childhood community in general.

References

Foucault, M. (1984) 'Interview par Françoise Ewald'. *Magazine Litéraire*, May.
Haut Conseil de la famille de l'enfance et de l'âge (2018) *L'accueil des enfants de moins de trois ans. Synthèse du rapport.* Paris: HCFEA.

Lloyd, E. (2013) 'Childcare markets: An introduction', in E. Lloyd & H. Penn (eds), *Childcare Markets. Can They Deliver an Equitable Service?*Bristol: Policy Press, 3–18

Shahshahani, L. (2020) Le service public de la petite enfance, une réussite française en danger. *Le Monde Diplomatique*, February.

Simon, R. (1991) *Gramsci's Political Thought. An Introduction*. London: Lawrence & Wishart.

PREFACE

Stephen J. Ball

Neoliberalism, as Aiwah Ong (Ong, 2007) puts it, is a mobile technology that is structuring a new planetary geography. It migrates and is selectively taken up in diverse political contexts. It inserts itself differently into different local settings and into different spheres of social, economic and political life, but evinces a responsiveness to contingencies and is marked by strategic entanglements with politics – all of which this book vividly demonstrates. Neoliberalism is an insidious and seductive economisation of the social and depoliticisation of the political. It is a restless technology that is constantly seeking new market opportunities and to bring more subjects under its thrall. Neoliberalism now configures great swathes of our daily lives and structures our experience of the world – how we understand the way the world works, how we understand ourselves and others, and how we relate to ourselves and others. It constructs 'a regime of truth' that 'offers the terms that make self-recognition possible' (Butler, 2005, p. 22) or as Foucault puts it, neoliberalism is a 'principle of intelligibility and a principle of decipherment of social relations' (Foucault, 2010, p. 243).

That is to say, neoliberalism has become our 'discursive currency' (Prado, 2006, p. 80) – it frames and produces the possibilities for how we might make sense of our selves and what is important, how we make decisions about what to do, and how to behave. We are produced by it, animated, activated, 'made up'. It provides, for some, a sense of worth, purpose, success and improvement. For others, it is a distortion, a source of abjection – positing them as of little worth, as unproductive, in need for rectification. This, as Foucault puts it, is the face of truth which has been 'turned away from us for so long and which is that of its violence' (Foucault, 2013, p. 4). We count or not in relation to our outputs and our costs. We are encouraged to invest in ourselves, and to the extent we improve we may reap returns as income, esteem or reputation. Our use value is collapsed into exchange value. In other words, neoliberalism produces what Lazzarato (2006) calls our *state of being*. In many grand and mundane ways:

> both persons and states are construed on the model of the contemporary firm, both persons and states are expected to comport themselves in ways that maximize their capital value in the present and enhance their future value, and both persons and states do so through practices of entrepreneurialism, self-investment, and/or attracting investors.
>
> (Brown, 2015, p. 22)

Neoliberalism is 'out there', in the form of the structures and processes of the market and competition, and 'in here' – in our heads, hearts and souls. We become what we are at the nexus between the production of a particular conception of human nature, a particular formation of subjectivity, and a particular political ideology. This is our anthropology, we are commodified as *homo economicus*, as heroes of enterprise, and as *homo calculus*, representing ourselves and others in terms of economic value. Neoliberalism is not just a manner of governing states or economies, but is intimately tied to the government of the individual, to a particular manner of living. Perhaps we are all neoliberals now.

As this book demonstrates in relation to early childhood education in particular, the metier and modalities of neoliberalism, both its *modus operandi* and *modus vivendi*, are visibility, accountability, transparency, measurement, calculation, comparison, evaluation, ratings, ranking, indicators, metrics and indices. These now infuse, inform and construct large parts of our social life, and the life of the early years classroom, of the nursery and parenting, producing particular forms of our relation to ourselves and to others. We interact with others, make decisions and think about ourselves in these terms and instil these values in our children. We govern, represent and improve ourselves through these media of calculation. They are invested in a myriad of practices and technologies and in multiple points of contact between government and self government, they work to make 'government possible and to make government better' (Rose, 1996, p. 45). The dry, soulless grids and techniques that report and represent us, elicit a range of often, unhealthy emotions – fear, anxiety, envy, despair, humiliation. Our emotions are linked to the economy through our anxieties and pleasures and our concomitant efforts of self-management and self-improvement. What *counts* is 'bare' numbers rather than a life well lived or an idea well thought.

The body and the emotions are the object and the vehicles of neoliberalism, it is a visceral technology, it inscribes itself on our life and labour. Within the logic of neoliberalism the population is a resource to be garnered and nurtured in relation to 'the mundane objectives of the administrative state – social order, economic prosperity, social welfare' (Hunter, 1996, p. 153). This is a particular economy of power that operates by raising, enhancing, improving and maximising capabilities and the production of particular modes of *subjectification*, in which individuals can be brought to work on themselves, under certain forms of authority, in relation to truth discourses, by means of practices of the self. This is what Foucault terms *governmentality,* a manner or mentality in which people are governed and govern themselves. As Lemke (2000) argues, neoliberalism is a political project that attempts to create a social reality that it suggests already exists, stating that competition is the basis of social relations while fostering those same relations

The new economy of power, this *governmentality* is made practical in changes to the form and modalities of the state. The economy is an ensemble of 'regulated' activities, which is constantly instituted and reordered (Lazzarato, 2009), supported and monitored by the state. The state manages and makes malleable the definition and boundaries of the economy, so that almost anything is now subject to economic relations, to 'investment', to profit. At the same time the state divests itself of certain responsibilities, practical and moral, but takes on new forms of power relations – funding, contracting, target setting, monitoring and measurement – although in practical terms the work of these forms of governance can also be outsourced. The state is a 'market maker'. In other words, 'the "economic politics" of enterprise appears to know no boundaries either in terms of where it might be applied' or to whom (du Gay, 2004, p. 40).

Neoliberalism then is a *dispositif*. It is made up of discourse, practices, relationships, organisation forms, ethics and subjectivity – a machine 'which make[s] one see and speak', and a 'regime of lights … distributing the visible and the invisible, giving birth to objects which are dependent on it for their existence' (Deleuze, 1986, p. 160).

All of this begs very difficult questions about the possibilities of opposition to neoliberalism, or its refusal – that is the refusal of what it is that we have become. Thinking about the politics of refusal solely in terms of economic abstractions is disempowering and debilitating, but when we recognise the immediacy of the processes of *neoliberalisation*, its presence in our quotidian practices, our social relations, and our relation to ourselves, then perhaps we can begin to struggle against it and meet it on its terrain – that of the production of subjectivity, freedom and possibility. Such a struggle begins with our relation to ourselves and to *others*, and the truths we tell about ourselves and to ourselves. What this involves is a challenge to everything that makes us what we are, without any of the comforts of another way of being. This is modest yet momentous, in the sense that it requires us to question our own validity, to give up on essentialism and fixity and 'restore to things their mobility, their possibility of being modified', (Foucault, 2016, p. 129). This book creates possibilities and necessities for such questioning. It creates discomfort, it makes things intolerable and not as necessary as all that. It clears a space in which it is possible to think differently about early childhood education and care, and about ourselves.

Stephen J. Ball
Emeritus Professor, Institute of Education University College London, UK
Catalunya, May 2020

References

Brown, W. (2015) *Undoing the Demos: Neoliberalism's Stealth Revolution.* Cambridge, MA: MIT Press.

Butler, J. (2005) *Giving an Account of Oneself.* New York: Fordham University Press.

Deleuze, G. (1986) *Foucault* (trans Sean Hand). Minneapolis: University of Minnesota Press.

du Gay, P. (2004) Against 'Enterprise' (but not against 'enterprise', for that would make no sense), *Organization*, 11(1), 37–57.

Foucault, M. (2010) *The Birth of Biopolitics: Lectures at the College de France 1978–1979*. Basingstoke: Palgrave Macmillan.

Foucault, M. (2013) *The Will to Know: Lectures at the College de France 1983–84*. Basingstoke: Palgrave MacMillan.

Foucault, M. (2016) *About the Beginning of the Hermeneutics of the Self: Lectures at Dartmouth College, 1980*. Chicago: University of Chicago Press.

Hunter, I. (1996) 'Assembling the school', in A. Barry, T. Osborne and N. Rose (eds), *Foucault and Political Reason: Liberalism, Neo-liberalism and Rationalities of Government*. London: UCL Press.

Lazzarato, M. (2006) Biopolitics and bioeconomics. *Multitudes*, 23.

Lemke, T. (2000) *Foucault, Governmentality, and Critique*, paper presented at the Rethinking Marxism Conference, University of Amherst (MA), 21–24 September 2020. www.thoma slemkeweb.de/publikationen/Foucault,%20Governmentality,%20and%20Critique% 20IV-2.pdf

Ong, A. (2007) 'Neoliberalism as a mobile technology', *Transactions of the Institute of British Geographers*, 32 (1), 3–8.

Prado, C. G. (2006) *Searle and Foucault on Truth*. Cambridge: Cambridge University Press.

Rose, N. (1996) 'Governing "advanced" liberal democracies', in A. Barry, T. Osborne and N. Rose (eds), *Foucault and Political Reason: Liberalism, neo-liberalism and rationalities of government*. London: UCL Press.

1

NEOLIBERALISM'S MOMENT

There's a lot of talk in early childhood education and care (ECEC) today about 'outcomes' and 'quality', 'testing' and 'assessment', 'interventions' and 'programmes', 'evidence-based' and 'best practice', 'investment' and 'human capital', 'preparation' and 'readyness', 'markets and marketing'. But why do we talk like this about ECEC, in such technical, instrumental and economistic terms? Why have we come to accept such language so unquestioningly as the normal and obvious way to discuss the education of young children? What are the consequences of this language and the thinking behind it? What is going on?

Our attempt to answer these questions is the subject of this book. In a nutshell, we contend that, like so much else in our lives, ECEC has over the last 40 or so years been drawn into the gravitational field of a powerful force, a political ideology that has become increasingly influential across the world since the 1980s: the ideology of neoliberalism. The way we talk so often today about young children and services for them is the language of neoliberalism. This book is an exploration of how neoliberalism, with its distinctive worldview and signature, has not only 'sunk its roots deep into everyday life' (Mirowski, 2013a, p. 28) but also into ECEC; of how it has come to influence the ways in which we think about, talk about and do ECEC with, in Margaret Sims's words, 'a devastating impact on the early childhood sector with its focus on standardisation, push-down curriculum and its positioning of children as investments for future economic productivity' (Sims, 2017, p. 1).

To propose a relationship between neoliberalism and education is not, as we shall see, original; much has been written about the deep penetration of neoliberalism into this field. Most of this work, though, has focused on compulsory and higher education, neoliberalism in the school and the university. Some, too, have acknowledged neoliberalism's implication in ECEC, but less has been written on this subject. We aim, therefore, to go more deeply and more broadly into neoliberalism and its impact on the early childhood sector, to make the existence and effects of this ideology more visible, more believable, and in doing so to emphasise the significance of the political and economic for early childhood education.

This is a book of exploration, but as we explore and, hopefully, show more clearly the neoliberal environment and the way it governs and shapes contemporary early childhood education and care, we also want to avoid some traps. One of these traps is reductionism, to end up implying everything is determined by one cause, in this case neoliberalism. There are, of course, other forces and influences bearing on early childhood services, and these will vary from place to place. Moreover, while the influence of neoliberalism is pervasive, how far it has sunk its roots also varies from place to place; as Stephen Ball observes in his foreword to this book, neoliberalism 'migrates and is selectively taken up in diverse political contexts. It inserts itself differently into different local settings'. Another trap is to treat neoliberalism itself as a homogeneous thing: it may have 'become omnipresent but it is a complex, mediated and heterogeneous kind of omnipresence, not a state of blanket uniformity' (Mirowski, 2013a, p. 52). So those who subscribe to neoliberalism will not all sing from exactly the same hymn sheet, context and culture always having a part to play.

Last but not least, while we want to argue that neoliberalism is a very powerful force, impacting on ECEC in substantial and varied ways, and while we agree with Margaret Sims's assessment that '[n]eoliberalism has become so entrenched in our thinking that for many, there is no alternative: it is simply the way the world operates' (Sims, 2017, pp. 1, 2), we do not want to treat it as all powerful, an irresistible and inevitable force, 'a kind of biological law, like Darwin's theory of evolution (Monbiot, 2017, p. 31)', before which all must submit and to which 'there is no alternative' – a refrain much used by Margaret Thatcher, the former British Prime Minister who, as we shall see, played an important part in establishing neoliberalism as a dominant ideology. This, Joan Tronto argues, is a trap into which it is easy to fall:

> Many articles and books have been written that see neoliberalism as a problematic way to organise human societies.... Yet, the main response of scholars to neoliberalism has been either to treat it as the new normal or to think of it as invincible. Among the first group, what is surprising is that scholars continue to accept this state of affairs rather than to react against it
>
> *(Tronto, 2017, p. 27)*

Neoliberalism is certainly a powerful force and it has a big impact. But it is, as we shall discuss, resistible and is resisted. There are alternatives in theory and in practice. Nor is neoliberalism dominant and invincible in perpetuity. Indeed, arguably neoliberalism has at least peaked and may be starting to enter the phase of decline and fall: as the newspaper columnist John Harris observes, 'a great deal of the free-market, laissez-faire ideas that have dominated the last four decades [are] being criticised and contested, perhaps as never before' (Harris, 2018). While economist Kate Raworth argues that putting blind faith in markets – while ignoring the living world, society, and the runaway power of banks – has taken us to the brink of ecological, social and financial collapse. It is time for the neoliberal show to leave the stage: a very different story is emerging.

(Raworth, 2017, p. 61)

It is important, though, to keep this talk of decline in perspective. For neoliberalism is by now deeply entrenched – it has 'become part of the mental furniture of the political elite' (Marquand, 2004, p. 118) – and reluctant to relinquish its leading role. Despite being subject to increasing criticism and scepticism, despite being seriously undermined by the 2008 financial crisis and its aftermath, neoliberalism has shown itself to be resilient, revealing considerable powers of recovery. It is far from finished.

One reason for this staying power is the failure of critics to develop and clearly articulate alternatives to neoliberalism: to not only argue another world is possible but to provide convincing and detailed accounts of what that world might be like and how we might get from here to there. The moral is clear. It is more important than ever for work to be undertaken on developing new ideas, for example about ECEC, and new policies to enact those ideas. The last thing we need now is to throw our hands up in despair, when so much needs to be done and can be done to prepare for post-neoliberalism.

The focus of this book is neoliberalism and early childhood education and care. But before homing in on this stage of education, we think it useful to review and reflect on some of the considerable body of work that has been done on neoliberalism and the wider world of education, in particular in primary and secondary schooling, some of which will certainly resonate with those in the field of early childhood. That is the theme of Chapter 2.

Competition, choice and calculation are central themes of neoliberalism, and these operate through the medium of the market and transactions in it between buyers and sellers. So, in Chapter 3, we examine how neoliberalism's belief in this mechanism has been enacted in ECEC and the place of the market in the delivery of services for young children; we consider, too, what evidence there is about the consequences of delivering early childhood services in this way. In Chapter 4 we consider neoliberalism's imaginary of ECEC: the images of the child, the parent, the early childhood centre and the early childhood worker, as seen through the neoliberal lens, and how these images are productive of the subjectivities or identities of these individuals and institutions. Then in Chapter 5 we turn to the governing of ECEC under neoliberalism, in particular how it is intensively controlled through the principles and techniques of new public management.

In these three chapters, our focus is on neoliberalism and how its ideas have been brought into and applied to early childhood education and care. Our focus is critical, but the focus nevertheless is on this particular perspective or worldview, and its consequences, including whether it seems to work in its own terms – does it do what it says on the tin? This focus does not mean that we think neoliberalism normal, invincible or, indeed, desirable. On the contrary, we view neoliberalism as deeply problematic, eminently resistible and eventually replaceable. In the final chapter, therefore, we go further into why we think neoliberalism has little or no future and turn to alternatives; for if the neoliberal mantra has been 'there are no alternatives', ours is 'there are alternatives'. We adopt a hopeful note (at least for those who, like us, find neoliberalism unpalatable), arguing that this worldview, so powerful for the last 30 years, is faced by growing scepticism and disenchantment, and entering an inevitable period of decline and fall – and that now is the time to develop and propagate different ways of thinking, talking and doing ECEC. The danger facing neoliberalism is, in Michel Foucault's words, that 'as soon as one can no longer think things as one formerly thought them, transformation becomes both very urgent, very difficult, and quite possible' (Foucault, 1988a, p. 155).

That was where we originally intended to finish. But just as we were ready to send this book to the publisher, the world was struck by a global pandemic, impacting on the lives of everyone. While it is too soon to comprehend the full impact and future consequences of Covid-19, we felt the need to acknowledge its significance to our narrative, so have added a last minute 'pandemic postscript'. One of the themes of this postscript chimes with Chapter 6: after the pandemic passes, do we go back to where we were before, to a continuation of neoliberalism, or will our current experience provide an impetus, a desire, a determination to pursue alternatives in a world where thinking differently is not only a possibility but a necessity?

But first we turn in this chapter to offer a short introduction to neoliberalism – what it is, how it has emerged as such a powerful force in the world today, and what have been some of its main effects on that world. We finish the chapter by introducing three important concepts that are closely related to neoliberalism: human capital, public choice and new public management.

What is neoliberalism?

Before seeking to answer the question 'What is neoliberalism?', we should first acknowledge that it is a contentious term 'that has attracted a remarkable degree of frustration and fury, in politics, the media and within academia' (Davies, 2016), being dismissed by some as vacuous or useless or a delusion that does not really exist. Others still write it off 'as a boo-word signifying only the users' opposition to capitalism' (Barnett, 2020, np). For many more, the term is either unknown or meaningless. As Philip Mirowski puts it, 'even at this late hour, the world is still full of people who believe neoliberalism doesn't really exist' (Mirowski, 2013a, p. 28). While for George Monbiot, neoliberalism has 'become almost invisible to us: we cannot stand far enough back to see it (Monbiot, 2017, p. 29). It might be said that neoliberalism hides itself in full view, 'almost to the point of passing as the "ideology of no ideology"' (Mirowski, 2013a, p. 28).

We disagree with those who dismiss neoliberalism as vacuous, useless or a delusion, siding with the many writers who have argued that the term describes a meaningful body of thought and action propagated by what Mirowski (2014, p. 2) terms 'a thought collective and political movement combined' that has come to operate and exert influence on a global scale. Far from being a 'boo-word', the term neoliberalism 'is essential for an understanding of where we have got to', including 'why there has been such a stand-out failure by the US and Britain in their responses to the coronavirus' (Barnett, 2020). David Harvey, in his book 'A Brief History of Neoliberalism', argues that neoliberalism has, in fact, had 'pervasive effects on [our] ways of thought to the point where it has become incorporated into the common-sense way many of us interpret, live in, and understand the world' (2005, p. 3); while Monbiot describes 'a vicious ideology of extreme com-petition and individualism that pits us against each other, and weakens the social bonds that make our lives worth living...[and that] has seeped into our language, our understanding of the choices we face and our conception of ourselves' (2017, pp. 29–30). Most people today may not be able to name or describe neoliberalism, which 'contributes to its influence and success – just try to oppose something that you cannot name' (Barnett, 2020, np). Yet most people, also, recognise its signs and symptoms, including an increasingly competitive, individualised, unequal and insecure world. By making neoliberalism and its effects visible, by naming and describing it, by revealing its presence in the full light of day, it can be seen to be neither a neutral force or a biological law – but the consequential result of human choices and actions, and therefore contestable and changeable.

So, if we argue there is such a thing as neoliberalism, what is it? Neoliberalism has been variously described as a 'theory of everything' (Mirowski, 2013a, p. 23); 'a hegemonic ideology' (Gormley, 2018, p. 4) and a 'political ideology, a set of ideas that offer a coherent view about how society should be ordered' (Tronto, 2017, p. 29); 'an intellectual and political movement for concrete social and economic change'; and a successful narrative or story (Monbiot, 2016a; Raworth, 2017), that 'like many successful political narratives, provides not only a set of economic or political ideas, but also an account of who we are and how we behave' (Monbiot, 2017, p. 30). It can also be understood as what the French philosopher Michel Foucault calls a 'dominant discourse'. 'Dominant discourses' are narratives or stories that have a decisive influence on a particular subject, by insisting that they are the only way to think, talk and behave, that they are the only reality, that they represent *the* Truth.

Such discourses seek to impose, in Foucault's words, a 'regime of truth'. They do this by exercising power over our thoughts and actions, directing or governing how we construct the world or weave reality and, therefore, what we see as 'the truth'. Typical of dominant discourses is how they make 'assumptions and values invisible, turn subjective perspectives and understandings into apparently objective truths, and determine that some things are self-evident and realistic while others are dubious and impractical' (Dahlberg and Moss, 2005, p. 17). Or as Elizabeth St. Pierre comments, 'it is difficult to think or act outside [a dominant discourse] … other statements and others' ways of thinking remain unintelligible, outside the realm of possibility' (2000, p. 485). In dominant discourses, fictional stories claim to be non-fictional statements, presenting themselves as natural, unquestionable and inevitable, the common sense of everyday life, just something we take for granted. This is simply how things are, the dominant discourse asserts; no need to add any qualifications, to say 'in my opinion' or 'it seems to me' or 'from my perspective' or 'some might say'.

What is captured by these various terms to describe neoliberalism is the idea of a particular way of thinking, a particular worldview, a particular utopian (or dystopian, depending on your point of view) vision that has laid claim to understand how human life on earth works and what needs to be done to bring about an ideal future – and that, for reasons we will discuss later, has achieved a position of dominance, not only in areas like the economy and government, but more insidiously in our language, our understandings and even our conception of ourselves and others. What are the basic tenets of this powerful theory, movement, ideology, story?

Neoliberalism is based on certain strong values and beliefs, starting with the three Cs: competition, choice and calculation. Many would see competition as neoliberalism's first principle, its core value, ranging from the environmental activist George Monbiot to the French philosopher Michel Foucault to the International Monetary Fund (IMF), a mainstay of the global economic establishment, which has described increasing competition as one of the 'two main planks' of the Neoliberal agenda (the second plank, according to the IMF, is 'a smaller role for the state', to which we shall return later in this chapter). Susan George (1999) puts it this way: 'competition is central [to neoliberalism] because it separates the sheep from the goats, the men from the boys, the fit from the unfit'.

The second C is choice, not the collective choice of a community engaging in participatory democracy, but an ideal of individual choice where autonomous individuals choose between competing offers, to find the product (broadly defined) that best suits their needs, preferences and pockets: competition improves choice, and choice stimulates competition. While for this synergy to work well requires the third C, calculation, to come into play. In each transaction, both buyer and seller, the one who has something to offer and the one who wants something, must be able to calculate as accurately as possible what terms are in their own best interests, what will maximise their benefits and minimise their costs. To do this they need information, preferably reduced to the form of numbers – complexity is hard to calculate!

This basic relationship of competition, choice and calculation requires certain conditions to perform as it should and to become embedded in all aspects of life. First and foremost, it needs the establishment and effective functioning of markets, places where sellers and buyers can be brought together and where competition, choice and calculation can work their magic. Neoliberals have a strong faith in markets as the best means of maximising efficiency by ensuring the optimal allocation of resources; the argument goes that 'by discovering a natural hierarchy of winners and losers, the market creates a more efficient system than could ever be devised though planning or design' (Monbiot, 2017, p. 30).

This faith in the virtue of markets calls not only for '"market" society [to] be treated as a natural and inexorable state of mankind' (Mirowski, 2013a, p. 55), but for extending marketisation to all parts of the economy – and beyond, to the rest of society. Indeed, the market is seen as the basis for all social relations. This means the commodification in principle of everything, 'the systematic conversion of common goods into private and tradeable property, that makes possible the reduction of everything to a calculus' (Venn, 2018, p. 42). In this way, everything has a price and is tradable in the market place, to be bought and sold for a profit.

Wendy Brown uses the term 'economization' to describe this insertion of economic rationality into every nook and cranny of life and the subsequent collapse of everything into the economic:

> One crucial signature of neoliberalism is its extension of … 'economization' – the conversion of non-economic domains, activities and subjects into economic ones – to all spheres of life…. [This is] the ascendency of a form of normative reason that extends market metrics and practices to every dimension of human life; political, cultural, personal, vocational, educational…. [T]his form of reason displaces other modes of valuation for judgment and action, displaces basic liberal democratic criteria for justice, with business metrics, transforms the state itself into a firm, produces everyday norms of identity and conduct that configure the subject as human capital, and configures every kind of human activity in terms of rational self-investment and entrepreneurship
>
> *(Brown, 2016, pp. 3, 5, 8)*

In sum, neoliberalism reduces everything to the economic.

This spread of neoliberal reasoning, beliefs and practices 'from the state to the soul' (Brown, 2015a), and 'into every form of human activity', is important to understand, marking out, as it does, neoliberalism as a totalising theory and project, a meta-narrative that encompasses everything and everyone and shows 'total blindness to non-economic forms of activity or experience' (Davies, 2015a). Everything, therefore, is reducible to economics and to the logic and practice of the market place, with market relations becoming the basis for all social relations and almost every single aspect of our lives (Shamir, 2008); everything can be allocated a value, its worth rendered measurable and calculable. Competition and choice, self-interest and calculation are applicable even to the most intimate of settings and human relationships, including marriage and parenthood; indeed, the economist Gary Becker received the 1992 Nobel Prize in Economics for his work in applying market principles to human behaviour, including an attempt to use market logics to understand household dynamics (Becker, 2004), such as marriage and parenthood. Not only should the market 'be the organizing principle for all political, social and economic conditions' (Giroux, 2004, p. 495), but market exchange is valued in neoliberalism as an ethic, 'acting as a guide to all human action' (Harvey, 2005, p. 3). We delve further into the role of the market in early childhood education and care in Chapter 3.

Neoliberals believe that private businesses are the best way to deliver products and services, offering more choice, efficiency and innovation through the discipline of competition in the market place; as a consequence, 'needs formerly met by public agencies on a principle of citizen rights, or through personal relationships in communities and families, are now to be met by companies selling services in a market' (Connell, 2013, p. 100). This calls for privatisation of formerly public utilities and public services, either selling off public assets or opening up previously publicly-run services to private competition. Taken to its extreme, society itself 'should be run in every aspect as if it were a business, its social relations reimagined as commercial transactions' (Monbiot, 2017, p. 30). This process of privatisation is not just about who provides utilities and services, but about their very nature: as Brown (2015a, np) observes, 'public institutions and services have not merely been outsourced but thoroughly recast as private goods for individual investment or consumption'. In short, they are commodified, traded in the marketplace as commodities.

The other side of the coin is a deep distaste for public provision of services, which must, neoliberals believe, inevitably be less efficient and innovative than private counterparts. Where it continues to exist, such public provision should be run as competing businesses, with private businesses often allowed in to further augment competition. This inevitably means a smaller role for the State, identified by the International Monetary Fund as the second main plank of the neoliberal agenda. Neoliberalism sees no need or case for a strong 'welfare state', providing collective responses to protect citizens against risks and enhance their well-being, indeed this can only undermine the workings of the market and the autonomy and responsibility of the individual.

In his foreword, Stephen Ball highlights this changing role of the State, which 'divests itself of certain responsibilities, practical and moral'. But a smaller and changing role for the State does not mean no role for the State. Neoliberals should not be confused with their 19th century cousins, *laissez-faire* liberals; while sharing many ideas with their 20th century descendants, including a belief in market relations and an abhorrence of dependency, these 19th century liberals sought to exclude the State entirely from the workings of markets and private businesses. Today's neoliberals seek to control the State, redefining its role, not destroying it; that role is reconfigured, away from being a provider of services and a guarantor of citizen rights, to being an enabler of a market-friendly culture and guarantor of other conditions needed for a neoliberal society. The State, Stephen Ball writes, 'takes on new forms of power relations – funding, contracting, target setting, monitoring and measurement'. As Mirowski explains,

> conditions for [neoliberalism's] existence must be constructed and will not come about 'naturally' in the absence of concerted political effort and organisation.... What is 'neo' about neoliberalism ... [is] the remaking and redeployment of the state as the core agency that actively fabricates the subjectivities, social relations and collective representations suited to making the fiction of the market real and consequential.

> [Neoliberals want] to explore new formats of techno-managerial gov-
> ernance that protect their ideal market from what they perceive to be
> unwarranted political interference.... [Democracy] must in any case be kept
> relatively impotent to ensure citizen initiatives rarely are able to change
> much of anything.... One way to exert power in restraint of democracy is
> to bend the state to a market logic, pretending one can replace 'citizens'
> with 'customers'.
>
> *(Mirowski, 2013a, pp. 53, 54, 56, 57)*

This last point about customers brings us to a final part of the neoliberal story. Competition, choice, calculation, commodification, markets, the respective roles of the private and the public – all these depend, to deliver the neoliberal utopia, on the last piece in the puzzle: the subject. For neoliberalism has the ambition to re-construct subjectivity, identity, the sense of who one is; as Margaret Thatcher put this goal, 'economics are the method, the object is to change heart and soul'. Neoliberalism 'thoroughly revises what it means to be a human person' (Mirowski, 2013a, p. 58), calling forth a very particular subject, an individual with a very particular subjectivity. All of us must change how we think of ourselves.

The shift from 'citizen' to 'customer' is just one part of a much larger forging of personal identity: the neoliberal subject as *homo economicus*, economic man (or woman). This neoliberal subject is self-interested and competitive; a capable market trader and informed consumer, independent and self reliant, thus able to 'self manage according to market principles of discipline, efficiency, and competitiveness' (Ong, 2006, p. 4); and able, too, to calculate what is in his or her best interests – so also, in Stephen Ball's words, *homo calculus*. She or he is an autonomous self-manager, taking responsibility for her or himself without expecting the solidarity or support of others, focused on finding individual solutions to life's challenges, while eschewing criticism of the system or making demands for any form of social protection.

This subject is responsible for competing successfully in a competitive labour market. This means being an entrepreneur of the self, seeking to maximise returns, 'being for himself his own capital, being for himself his own producer, being for himself the source of [his] earnings' (Foucault, 2008, p. 226). For this individual, 'every kind of human activity [is reconfigured] in terms of rational self-investment and entrepreneurship' (Brown, 2016, p. 5). She or he must be infinitely flexible and responsive to the changing needs of the market, in a state of constant readying, perpetually prepared for whatever turns up, for whatever new twist or turn takes place in the economy and employment, ever responsive to signals from the market. As such, she or he is 'malleable rather than committed, flexible rather than principled – essentially depthless' (Ball, 2012, p. 31). Last but not least, the neoliberal subject, *homo economicus*, flexible and ever ready, is a quantum of 'human capital', a concept we shall explain later in this chapter.

We explore further this neoliberal subject, both as child and adult, in Chapter 4.

A short history of neoliberalism and its spread

In 2016, three members of the Research Department at the International Monetary Fund (IMF), using 'a composite index that measures the extent to which countries introduced competition in various spheres of economic activity to foster economic growth', concluded that '[t]here has been a strong and widespread global trend toward neoliberalism since the 1980s' (Ostry, Loungani and Furceri, 2016, p. 38). Most studies would agree with these authors that the 1980s was when neoliberalism became a big hit, gaining an influential following and widespread influence. The historian Tony Judt captures that sense of a watershed decade when he wrote that

> [m]uch of what appears 'natural' today dates from the 1980s: the obsession with wealth creation, the cult of privatization and the private sector, the growing disparities of rich and poor. And above all, the rhetoric which accompanies these: uncritical admiration for unfettered markets, disdain for the public sector ... the delusion of endless growth.
>
> *(Judt, 2010, pp. 1–2)*

But the story has its origins well before then.

This is not the first time that a liberalism of 'unfettered markets' has figured as a dominant regime of political economy, at least in Europe. As previously mentioned, there was a former manifestation that thrived in the early stages of industrialisation in the 19th century, sometimes referred to as an age of *laissez-faire* capitalism. This was followed by the rise of the 'social state' from the early years of the 20th century, in part in response to the growing power of working-class movements, and which brought in a greater regulation of free-wheeling capitalism and a greater recognition of the importance of social protection and collective security. Nikolas Rose has written about this earlier turn from rampant free market capitalism – epitomised by the widespread and unrestrained use of child labour in factories and mines – to a more regulated and socially responsible form:

> In the face of rising political unrest and evidence of the malign effects of irregular employment, poor living conditions and squalor, socialists and social liberals were now demanding more extensive social intervention to mitigate what were now seen as the inevitable social consequences of capitalist economic arrangements. Whatever their differences, in each case the term 'social' implied a kind of anti-individualism: the need to conceive of human beings as citizens of a wider collectivity who did not merely confront one another as buyers and sellers on a competitive market. Hence at least some aspects of the economy required to be politically governed in the name of the social, in order to dispel a whole range of conflicts ... and to ensure social order, social tranquillity, perhaps even social justice.
>
> *(Rose, 1999, p. 118)*

The 'social state', with the limits it placed on the economic, reached its high point, at least in the West, in the 30 years or so after the end of the Second World War, as welfare states with their collective sharing of risk, progressive taxation and protection of workers' rights contributed to a more equal balance being struck between public and private interests, labour and capital (Venn, 2018). But times change, as they always do – a point worth remembering today. The age of the 'social state' has been superseded by the age of neoliberalism, the social swallowed up by the economic, the 'wider collectivity' deposed by the autonomous and self-interested subject.

Neoliberalism, based on free markets, deregulation, and limited government first emerges in the inter-war years, in a reaction, on the one hand, to New Liberalism, Progressivism and the American New Deal and, on the other, to the onset of Nazi and communist totalitarianism. It picked up again after the Second World War, with a meeting in 1947 of free market economists in the Swiss resort of Mont Pelerin. This group, who became the Mont Pelerin Society (MPS) – a closed, members-only debating society, backed by businesses and billionaires – subsequently expanded in numbers (from an initial 39 to 500, at which point membership was capped) and in geographical coverage, to become 'the premier site of the construction of neoliberalism' (Mirowski, 2013a, p. 29), and a key part of what Mirowski (ibid.) terms the 'Neoliberal Thought Collective'. This 'Collective' built out from the MPS, adding university departments that neoliberals came to dominate (e.g. in the University of Chicago, the London School of Economics, the 'Virginia School'); foundations for education in and promotion of neoliberal doctrines, examples including those run by the Coors and Koch families; and think tanks and other organisations in the United Kingdom and the United States, where neoliberal ideas and how they might be implemented were spawned, hatched and spread (Mirowski, 2014). With more than 80 MPS-affiliated think tanks by the 1990s, 'think tanks were the preferred vehicle of neoliberal thinkers' (Stedman Jones, 2014, p. 336). Alive and well today, they include the Heritage Foundation, the American Legislative Exchange Council and the Ayn Rand Institute in the United States, and the Adam Smith Institute and the Institute of Economic Affairs in the United Kingdom.

Led by key figures such as Friedrich Hayek and Milton Friedman, a huge international network was thus spun, a network that developed multiple contacts with politicians, businessmen and other sympathisers: 'a web of institutions and people grew up to spread and popularize neoliberal ideas so that eventually they seemed the natural alternative to liberal or social democratic policies' (ibid., p. 153). But to get to the next stage, to be able to put ideas into practice, needed opportunities for radical political change to open up. The first of these appeared in 1973 in Chile, when a military coup led by the right-wing General Pinochet overthrew the government of President Salvador Allende. The new authoritarian regime, alongside systematic human rights abuses and the merciless eradication of opposition, initiated a turn towards neoliberalism, a new economic direction subsequently pursued by other Latin American regimes, 'though with less consistency; and [they] were soon followed by policymakers in other developing countries such as Turkey' (Connell, 2013, p. 100).

Other opportunities also came in the 1970s, with the increasing failure in that decade of the dominant post-war economic regime, social democratic or Keynesian, 'the system of regulated capitalism and state-supplied services that was dominant in the generation from 1945 to 1980' (Connell, 2013, p.101). This failure was marked by a toxic combination of anaemic growth and high inflation, so-called 'stagflation'. But as Raworth (2017, p. 67) comments,

> the big time came at last in 1980 when Margaret Thatcher [Prime Minister of the United Kingdom [UK] from 1979–1990] and Ronald Reagan [President of the US from 1980 to 1988] teamed up to bring the neoliberal script to the international stage … [and] the neoliberal show has been playing ever since, powerfully framing the economic debate of the past thirty years.

The 'neoliberal show' gained increasing audiences not only from the performance of the Thatcher-Reagan double act, but through the backing of influential international organisations; '[Neoliberals] learned to appreciate that suitably staffed international institutions such as the WTO [World Trade Organisation], WB [World Bank], the IMF, and other units are better situated [than pure market discipline] to impose neoliberal policies on recalcitrant nation-states' (Mirowski, 2013a, p. 62). With the help of the hefty leverage that such Western-based institutions could exert on national governments globally, for example through the dispersal of large loans with strings attached, 'neoliberal policies were imposed – often without democratic consent – on much of the world' (Monbiot, 2017, pp. 34–35): policies including marketisation, privatisation of public services and utilities, deregulation of business, weakening of trade unions, and tax cuts for the rich. Among those imposed neoliberal policies was a portfolio for education, including early childhood education and care, as Amita Gupta observes:

> When translated into educational policy and pedagogy [neoliberal] ideas reflect a distinct shift from a group-orientation to an individual-orientation; education pivots from being a social, not-for-profit enterprise to a consumer-based, for-profit movement.
>
> In Asia, a '…shared trend of making a "right" turn through neoliberal policies to reform preschool education' (Lee, 2012: 31) has been observed. This shift is manifested in increased privatization of schools, standardization of curriculum, regulation of institutions through stricter licensing procedures, increased hierarchical control over teachers with a corresponding decrease in teacher autonomy, and a policy narrative that is couched in the language of dominant 'Western' ECE discourses.
>
> *(Gupta, 2018, p. 14)*

This neoliberalising of education is explored in more detail in subsequent chapters.

It was an impressive achievement. The unimaginable had become the new normal; for as George (1999, np) so aptly puts it, '[i]n 1945 or 1950, if you had seriously proposed any of the ideas and policies in today's standard neo-liberal toolkit, you would have been laughed off the stage or sent off to the insane asylum'. What had once been the vision of a fringe group drawn from one part of the world had, by the end of the 1980s, become global and dominant. Neoliberalism had transformed the political landscape not only in the UK and the US, but worldwide, so that at 'the dawn of the 21st century, the triumph of the free market was almost universally accepted by mainstream politicians, public officials, and civil servants' (Stedman Jones, 2014, p. 329). From local beginnings, emerging from a particular spatial and temporal context, to be precise from the English-speaking world in the 1970s and 1980s, the story of neoliberalism has been borne far and wide in a process of what has been called hegemonic globalisation, 'the successful globalisation of a particular local and culturally-specific discourse to the point that it makes universal truth claims and 'localises' all rival discourses' (Santos, 2004, p. 149).

Such globalisation has owed much to taking advantage of crises when they have arisen, what Naomi Klein calls 'The Shock Doctrine' (Klein, 2008) to describe how crises have provided opportunities for the implementation of neoliberal policies. But the point to emphasise is that the neoliberals created a highly effective and disciplined movement and did their homework, so were ready when crises came along, ready with well-developed ideas and with plans for enacting them, ideas and plans that had germinated in that burgeoning network of individuals and groups, and which had grown out of that first meeting in a small Swiss mountain resort.

Some consequences of neoliberalism's hegemony

Neoliberal proponents will point to its benefits, such as raised living standards and reduced poverty levels in many countries over the last 30 years; indeed, 'never before in human history have so many people been lifted out of poverty so quickly' (Banerjee and Duflo, 2020, p. 22). As Oxfam notes in its 2019 report 'Public Good or Private Wealth?', '[o]ne of the great achievements in recent decades has been the huge reduction in the numbers of people living in extreme poverty, defined by the World Bank as $1.90 per person per day'. Though the same report goes on to record that in 2018 'just under half the world's population – 3.4 billion people – [were] subsisting on less than $5.50 a day' (Oxfam, 2019, p. 11).

But others will agree with Raworth's assessment that, taken overall, 'it has become increasingly clear that the Neoliberal economic plot … has whipped us into a perfect storm of extreme inequality, climate change and financial crash' (Raworth, 2017, p. 63). Political scientist Sheri Berman comes to a similar conclusion:

> Over recent years, the negative consequences of neoliberal capitalism have become impossible to ignore. It contributed to such traumatic events as the 2008 financial crisis as well as such destructive long-term trends as rising inequality, lower growth, increasing monopsony [a market with only one buyer] and growing social and geographic divides. Moreover, its impact has not been limited to the economic sphere: these events and trends have negatively influenced western societies and democracies as well.
>
> *(Berman, 2019, np)*

As Berman indicates, the 2008 financial crash and the subsequent period of wide-spread economic recession and austerity were due in large part to the failure of neoliberal beliefs, especially in the virtue of deregulation and the perfection of self-regulating market. While climate change, and other gathering environmental catastrophes, have been fuelled by neoliberalism's espousal of ceaseless growth, driven by the constant stimulation of consumption and an ethos of competition. In her book on climate change, Naomi Klein argues neoliberalism, or 'market fundamentalism' as she calls it, 'has become the greatest enemy to planetary health … we have an economic system that fetishizes GDP growth above all else, regardless of the human and ecological consequences' (Klein, 2015, pp. 26, 88). This commitment to growth has created what Tim Jackson calls a 'profound dilemma' for all human societies: 'To resist growth is to risk economic and social collapse. To pursue it is to endanger the ecosystems on which we depend for long-term survival' (Jackson, 2009, p. 102). A further profound dilemma arises from the need for collective action and public intervention if there is to be any hope of effectively tackling the environmental emergency confronting humankind – both anathema to neoliberal doctrine (Klein, 2015).

Even the International Monetary Fund, no enemy of neoliberalism, has argued that some of neoliberalism's claimed benefits have been overstated, while drawing particular attention to the first part of Raworth's 'perfect storm' – inequality, a problem acknowledged by the IMF's own researchers:

> there are aspects of the neoliberal agenda that have not delivered as expected.… An assessment of these *specific* policies [i.e. removing restrictions on movement of capital and austerity] (rather than the broad neoliberal agenda) reaches three disquieting conclusions:
>
> - The benefits in terms of increased growth seem fairly difficult to establish when looking at a broad group of countries.
> - The costs in terms of increased inequality are prominent. Such costs epitomize the trade-off between the growth and equity effects of some aspects of the neoliberal agenda.
> - Increased inequality in turn hurts the level and sustainability of growth. Even if growth is the sole or main purpose of the neoliberal agenda, advocates of that agenda still need to pay attention to the distributional effects.
>
> *(Ostry et al., 2016, pp. 38, 39)*

Indicators of growing inequality are shocking. Here are some about wealth inequality taken from Oxfam's 2019 report:

- In the 10 years since the financial crisis, the number of billionaires has nearly doubled.
- The wealth of the world's billionaires increased by $900bn in the last year alone [2018], or $2.5bn a day. Meanwhile the wealth of the poorest half of humanity, 3.8 billion people, fell by 11%.

- Billionaires now have more wealth than ever before. Between 2017 and 2018, a new billionaire was created every two days.
- Wealth is becoming even more concentrated – last year 26 people owned the same as the 3.8 billion people who make up the poorest half of humanity, down from 43 people the year before. The world's richest man, Jeff Bezos, owner of Amazon, saw his fortune increase to $112bn. Just 1% of his fortune is the equivalent to the whole health budget for Ethiopia, a country of 105 million people.

(Oxfam, 2019, p. 12)

Income inequality has also increased in recent years in nearly all countries, but at different speeds and varying from region to region. It has, for example, grown rapidly in the United States since 1980, but moderately in Western Europe; levels were similar in 1980,

> but today [2016, they] are in radically different situations. While the top 1% income share was close to 10% in both regions in 1980, it rose only slightly to 12% in 2016 in Western Europe while it shot up to 20% in the United States. Meanwhile, in the United States, the bottom 50% income share decreased from more than 20% in 1980 to 13% in 2016
>
> *(Alvarado, Chancel, Piketty, Saez and Zucman, 2018, p. 6)*

Some of the reasons for this divergence are summarised below, and we will return to this subject later in the book when we consider, and cast doubt upon, some of the extravagant claims made (often by American researchers) for early childhood education and care as a high returning investment.

> The income-inequality trajectory observed in the United States is largely due to massive educational inequalities, combined with a tax system that grew less progressive despite a surge in top labor compensation since the 1980s, and in top capital incomes in the 2000s. Continental Europe meanwhile saw a lesser decline in its tax progressivity, while wage inequality was also moderated by educational and wage-setting policies that were relatively more favorable to low and middle-income groups. In both regions, income inequality between men and women has declined but remains particularly strong at the top of the distribution
>
> *(ibid., p. 6)*

To which might be added another underlying trend driving rising inequality. After being largely stable for many years, the share of national income paid to workers (labour) has been falling since the 1980s, from about 54% in 1980 to about 40% in 2015 in advanced economies. This means that the share going to capital has risen. Since, as the IMF researchers have noted, 'capital tends to be concentrated in the upper ends of the income distribution, falling labor income shares are likely to raise income inequality' (Dao, Das, Koczan and Lian, 2017, np). Underlying this shift has been the unequal distribution of the benefits of technological advancement and global economic integration, capital having taken the major share, along with the weakening of trade unions undermining the capacity of labour to resist this trend. Note in the examples cited above how change in the direction of increased inequality sets in around the early 1980s, coinciding with the onset of the era of neoliberalism.

We could give many more examples, since the theme of increased inequality under neoliberalism recurs; we hope, though, that the relationship between neoliberalism and inequality is clear. But this should hardly come as a surprise. For inequality lies at the very heart of neoliberalism. It is not just some unfortunate by-product, but a key driver of economic efficiency and a necessary condition for the ideal market system (Mirowski, 2013a), a system of competition in which all may have an equal right to compete but in which, too, there must always be winners and losers; for neoliberals, 'inequality has the capacity to sharpen appetites, instincts and minds, driving individuals to rivalries' (Lazzarato, 2009, p. 117). So, while some may express concern at the worldwide trend of recent years towards concentrations of income and wealth, such inequality is, to the neoliberal story teller, simply 'the playing out of a neoliberal script to produce a more efficient and vibrant capitalism' (Mirowski, 2013b, p. 8).

Growing inequality has been partnered by growing insecurity, not least in employment with the spread of temporary and zero-hour contracts, of enforced self-employment and low paid jobs; in the United Kingdom now, most poor families have at least one member in employment. Again, this should not come as a surprise. Insecurity is the other side of the coin to flexibility, providing a ready pool of labour available to respond to the ebb and flow of the market, an efficient allocation of resources as a neoliberal would argue – but a source of fear and stress for those on the receiving end. Both growing inequality and insecurity have been further enabled by the decline of trade unions (trade union membership in high income OECD member states fell from 30% in 1985 to just 16% in 2018 (https://twitter.com/OECD/status/1123875322653442048)), an early target for neoliberals as an 'inimical force in society … whose main effect was to "distort" the labour market' (Stedman Jones, 2014, p. 331), and of collective agreements, anathema to the neoliberal belief in the virtues of untrammelled individualism and individualised incentives (payment by results). This decline in trade unions and consequent changes in bargaining power have played a major part in the significant decline in the share of wages in GDP in both developed and developing countries since the 1980s, referred to above (Onaron, 2018).

Insecurity has not been confined to more marginalised and lower income workers. Albena Azmanova (2019) contends that, under neoliberalism, there is a 'precarious multitude' and not just a 'precarious class': economic insecurity has 'come to afflict not only the low-skilled, poorly-educated, precariously-employed and under-paid working classes in exposed industries – the so-called "losers of globalisation". It is increasingly affecting also highly-skilled, well-educated and solidly-remunerated professionals'. And while the pressures of profit-driven capitalism have always generated economic insecurity, she argues that these pressures have 'intensified in the age of neoliberal capitalism', and further that 'insecurity, more so than inequality, is the social question of our time'.

If neoliberalism has contributed to growing inequality and insecurity, it has contributed also to a weakening of democracy. Put bluntly, neoliberalism has little time for democracy, whether in politics, governance or everyday life. Indeed, neoliberalism is 'profoundly suspicious of democracy' (Harvey, 2005, p. 66), which is viewed, at best, as an irrelevance, at worst as a potential hindrance to markets and their efficient functioning, and hence to economic performance and high returns. In this scenario, the democratically active citizen fades away to be replaced by the market savvy consumer; democratic politics gives way to the rule of experts, technicians and managers.

True, some neoliberals would argue that markets provide the purest form of democracy, through the unrestricted working of individual preferences, equating democracy with the exercise of consumer choice and redefining citizens as consumers 'whose democratic choices are best exercised by buying and selling' (Monbiot, 2016b). Viewed from this perspective, the exercise of individual calculation and choice in the market place is lauded over public deliberation and collective choice, private interest extolled over public good. But for those who disagree with this understanding of democracy, siding with Gerd Biesta when he says that

> the behaviour of consumers in a market where their aim is to satisfy their needs … should not be conflated with democracy, which is about public deliberation and contestation about the public good and the just and equitable (re)distribution of public resources
>
> *(2010, p. 54)*

then neoliberalism has been bad news. In mainstream politics, democracy has been undermined by an electorate increasingly disillusioned and angry with democratic institutions that seem unwilling or unable to tackle discontents arising from inequality and insecurity; while growing inequality has gone hand-in-hand with the growing influence of money on policy-making. Governments of any party have too often appeared to collude with corporate interests and against the public good: as a result, 'whereas the power of elected governments in the postwar period was exercised in part to balance that of corporations and markets, its main role today has become to enforce the latter's power in many settings' (Rustin, 2016, p. 15).

In these circumstances, democratic politics has seemed unable to tell and enact alternative stories, stories that connect with the lives of many people, contributing to what Monbiot claims is the dominant condition of the age: alienation.

> Alienation means many things. Among them are people's loss of control over the work they do; the loss of connection with community and society; their

loss of trust in political institutions and in the future; their loss of a sense of meaning and of power over their own lives; and a convergence of these fissures into psychic rupture. In the political sphere, alienation leads to disengagement, and disengagement opens the way for demagogues.

(Monbiot, 2017, p. 54)

As Monbiot suggests, one important symptom of alienation is a widespread sense of powerlessness in the face of impersonal and unstoppable economic forces, forces that seem uncontrollable and to which all we can seemingly hope to do is adapt, doing our best to hang on to the Juggernaut of inexorable change as it races heedlessly ever onwards. Such powerlessness allows what Roberto Unger calls 'the dictatorship of no alternative' (Unger, 2005, p. 1) to become established in neoliberalism's 'regime of truth', and with it a failure of imagination, an impoverishment of ambition and a fading of hope in the future.

As if this was not bad enough, democracy has also been undermined by a further consequence of the rise of neoliberalism: the process of 'economization' already referred to, the conversion of non-economic domains, activities and subjects into economic ones. In this process, the social, the cultural, the aesthetic and the political all collapse into the economic, and so are reconceptualised along purely economic lines, being reduced to 'calculative actions undertaken through the universal human faculty of choice' (Rose, 1999, p. 141). Edgar Morin recognises this when he says that politics has become 'reduced to technology and economics, and economics is reduced to growth … the civic spirit is weakened, and people find escape and refuge in private life' (Morin, 2001, p. 92). In this situation, political questions, with no one right answer but only alternative and often conflicting answers, the essence of democratic politics, are recast in economic terms to be decided by economic and other technical experts, and then left to management to ensure performance, without any semblance of democratic input or of meaningful choices. Societies, thus, become increasingly depoliticised, with contestations about ends (what do we want?) replaced by technical assessments of means (what works?), active citizens re-cast as calculating consumers.

The weakening of civic spirit that Morin writes of can be seen as part of a deeper decay, the weakening of social bonds, relationships described and valued by Nancy Fraser as

the ties between the generations – so, birthing and raising children and caring for the elderly … [and also] sustaining horizontal ties among friends, family, neighborhoods, and community. This sort of activity is absolutely essential to society. Simultaneously affective and material, it supplies the 'social glue' that underpins social cooperation. Without it, there would be no social organization – no economy, no polity, no culture.

(Fraser, 2016a, np)

Fraser goes on to argue that what she calls the 'financialized capitalist regime', or neoliberalism, is undermining people's capacity to sustain these social bonds, 'between the need for increased working hours and the cutback in public services'. One consequence, she contends, is a 'crisis of care', due to 'financialized capitalism's rapacious subjugation of reproduction to production', which in turn is 'one aspect of a "general crisis" that also encompasses economic, ecological and political strands, all of which intersect with and exacerbate one another' (Fraser, 2016b, pp. 117, 99).

A final consequence to be noted in this opening chapter is the negative effect neoliberalism has had on a whole range of public services, not least the undermining of the concept of 'public'. Stedman Jones, the historian of neoliberalism, argues that the long-term effects of this regime are

> arguably even more problematic [than the short-term effects]: a legacy of financial deregulation and the wholly inappropriate importation of free markets into the provision of public services such as health care provision, education and housing. These policy areas were classic examples of market failure. It was rarely profitable to provide high-quality services for poorer people.... The obsession with the market corroded the idea of the public realm and ate into its foundations.
>
> *(Stedman Jones, 2014, pp. 268, 279)*

We will explore this issue in more detail in later chapters, when we focus our attention on education in general and early childhood education and care in particular.

Three sub-plots in the story of neoliberalism

In the final part of this chapter, we bring in three sub-plots in the meta-narrative of neoliberalism, each with their own storyline, but each closely entwined with the main storyline of neoliberalism, each sharing that story's instrumental rationality, technical approach and economistic worldview.

Human capital

Human Capital Theory, first articulated in the 1950s, has become enormously influential today, not least as we shall see in subsequent chapters in education, including early childhood education and care. It has

> developed into one of the most powerful theories in modern economics ... [and] lays considerable stress on the education of individuals as the key means by which both the individual accrues material advantage and by which the economy as a whole progresses.
>
> *(Gillies, 2011, pp. 224–225)*

It is closely related to neoliberalism. One of Human Capital Theory's initial proponents, Gary Becker, was part of that original group of neoliberal thinkers and
advocates, the Mont Pelerin Society. Becker, himself, has described the essence of
Human Capital Theory and its importance in the contemporary world.

> Human capital refers to the knowledge, information, ideas, skills and health of
> individuals. This is the 'age of human capital' in the sense that human capital is
> by far the most important form of capital in modern economies. The eco-
> nomic successes of individuals, and also of whole economies, depend on how
> extensively and effectively people invest in themselves.
>
> *(Becker, 2002, p. 3)*

Human capital, which as well as competencies and attributes includes attitudes such as
reliability, self-reliance and individual responsibility, adds up therefore to what economists would consider to be marketable skills acquired through investment in education
and training (Bernheim and Winston, 2008). The focus then of Human Capital Theory
is on the capacities needed for economic success by the individual, by employers and by
national economies. Investment in education – by parents, by the state and by the self –
is the main way to fully realise this essential economic resource: 'In a simple equation,
the more and better education individuals possess, the better their returns in financial
rewards and the better the national economy flourishes' (Gillies, 2015, p. 1).

Human Capital Theory provides powerful reinforcement to the neoliberal image
of the essentially economic subject, that *homo economicus* we have discussed above.
This has major consequences. As Mirowski puts it,

> [n]eoliberalism thoroughly revises what it means to be a human person.…
> Foucault correctly identifies the concept of 'human capital' as the signal neo-
> liberal departure – initially identified with the MPS [Mont Pelerin Society]
> member Gary Becker – that undermines centuries of human thought that
> parlayed humanism into stories of natural rights.… Neoliberalism reduces the
> human being to an arbitrary bundle of 'investments', skill sets, temporary alli-
> ances (family, sex, race) and fungible body parts.
>
> *(Mirowski, 2013a, pp. 58–59)*

This revised human being, this subject of neoliberalism, is not only focused on
maximising her or his advantage in the market place and operating as an entrepreneur of the self; he or she is conceived in Human Capital Theory as a unit of
economic potential, to be developed and deployed to maximise economic returns.
As such Human Capital Theory is based on certain assumptions about human
behaviour: in particular that human beings are seeking to maximise their own
economic interests, through for example investing in education and training in the
hope of getting a higher income in the future.

It is a sign of how times have changed that back in the 1960s, when the term
'human capital' was first being used by academics, 'it was considered too debasing

to be used publicly … [being seen] correctly, as objectifying people and only suitable to refer to anonymous "others"' (Holborow, 2012, p. 101). Theodore Schultz, an early theorist of human capital, was aware of the term's 'offensiveness to some', not least because of its evocation of slavery. In his 1961 article 'Investment in Human Capital', he raised its potentially 'offensive' connotation: 'Our values and beliefs inhibit us from looking upon human beings as capital goods, except in slavery, and this we abhor' (Schultz, 1961, p. 2). Even today, despite the apparent wide acceptance of the term,

> it is, in practice, only used in official documents and hardly at all in ordinary conversation (Who, indeed, would spontaneously describe themselves as human capital?).… *Capital,* as applied to individuals, invites identification with guaranteed returns on a fixed sum of money.… The metaphor erases social relations.
>
> *(Holborow, 2012, p. 101; original emphasis)*

Human Capital Theory, therefore, contributes to the economisation of life under neoliberalism, that collapsing of the social, the cultural and every other facet of life into the economic, for in Human Capital Theory, 'human beings act for economic reasons only' (Robyns, 2006, p. 72).

But there are other problems with Human Capital Theory. It has been critiqued as not only dehumanising, desocialising and hyper-instrumental, valuing the individual and education only in so far as both contribute to economic competitiveness and productivity, but also as politically reactionary. It is closely associated with methodological individualism, the doctrine that the roots of all social phenomena can be found in the individual's behaviour (Tan, 2014), so letting structural injustices, such as inequality and insecurity, off the hook. From a similar perspective, Steven Klees argues that

> *contrary to the hype, the human capital discourse, and offshoots of it, like the 'Knowledge Economy',* have been, at least in one way, some of the most destructive ideas of the modern era. Solving the triple challenge of poverty, inequality, and jobs has been unproductively directed to lack of individual skills and education instead of to capitalist and other world system structures whose very logic makes poverty, inequality, and lack of employment commonplace.
>
> *(Klees, 2018, p. 14; original emphasis)*

So, rather than bearing down on poverty and inequality through redistribution of income and wealth, Human Capital Theory deflects attention to solutions that enhance human capital development, solutions that emphasise the individual taking responsibility for improving themselves through, for example, undertaking more education or training (Leary, 2019).

A further problem is that recent experience casts doubt on whether the individual and national cultivation of 'human capital' does actually pay off in the economic terms predicted by the theory. Investment in human capital through education may not, in fact, be delivering its expected returns. While Kleess acknowledges that abilities that contribute to human capital, such as numeracy, literacy and problem solving, may pay off in the labour market, he argues they will only do so when they are valued; the more 'useful and important question is the demand-side one, usually ignored by human capital theorists, regarding how we can create good jobs that require valuable skills' (Klees, 2018, p. 14). In fact, young people entering adulthood today have invested in education as never before, yet many struggle to find employment that is secure, satisfying and well remunerated; as a result generational progress, the expectation that every generation should enjoy higher living standards than the one before, has ground to a halt (O'Connor, 2018). Margaret Stuart, too, in her thesis on 'Human Capital Theory and Early Childhood Education in New Zealand', casts doubt on 'the expectation that ECEC policies based on the principles of HCT [Human Capital Theory] will be able to achieve what they promise' referring to 'the unfulfilled promise of HCT … [and how] HCT acts as a modern-day form of alchemy in contemporary Western societies' (Stuart, 2011, pp. 210, 211, 213).

Despite such gathering problems, the influence of Human Capital Theory and the primacy attached by governments and international organisations to the promotion of human capital continues unabated, unruffled by criticism. What should be a fundamental political question – what is your image of the human being? – has been cast aside in favour of dwelling on the technical question: what technologies are best able to augment the human being as human capital?

Public choice

Accompanying the rise of neoliberalism has been a declining belief in the dependability and efficacy of government and public services; the public sector and the state have fallen out of favour, losing trust, as the private sector and business have risen. This onslaught on public services and the public sector has been further fuelled by the development and adoption of public choice theory, closely associated with another Nobel prize-winning economist, James Buchanan, and his colleague Gordon Tullock. Also a member of the Mont Pelerin Society, Buchanan believed that 'people were primarily driven by venal self-interest … [wanting] to control others and take away their resources', in a society which he saw as 'a cutthroat realm of makers (entrepreneurs) constantly under siege by takers (everyone else)' (Parramore, 2018, np). With this dismal view of human nature, Buchanan set himself to protect the wealthy from the demands made on them by democratic societies, through for example sowing mistrust of government institutions. At the 50th anniversary of the Mont Pelerin Society in 1997,

> Buchanan and his associate Henry Manne, a founding theorist of libertarian economic approaches to law, focused on such affronts to capitalists as environmentalism and public health and welfare, expressing eagerness to dismantle Social Security, Medicaid, and Medicare [government schemes in the USA

that help some groups with the costs of health care] as well as kill public education because it tended to foster community values. Feminism had to go, too: the scholars considered it a socialist project.

(ibid.)

Extreme as many may find these views, Buchanan had

huge impact, especially in America and in Britain. In his home country, the economist was deeply involved in efforts to cut taxes on the wealthy in 1970s and 1980s and he advised proponents of the Reagan Revolution in their quest to unleash markets and posit government as the 'problem' rather than the 'solution'.... In Britain, Buchanan's work helped to inspire the public sector reforms of Margaret Thatcher and her political progeny.

(ibid.)

Public choice theory, based on Buchanan's work, has refined and sharpened neoliberalism's attack on the public sector. With its 'dismal view' of human nature, 'primarily driven by venal self-interest', it dismisses the idea of dispassionate public servants, whether politicians or officials, who are committed to and motivated by ideals of public service and the public good. It recasts them instead in the mould of *homo economicus*, seeking to further their own interests and maximise their own personal advantage, just like everyone else. Indeed, in this scenario the public sector has come to be viewed not only as inherently inefficient but also as inescapably self-seeking, in sharp contrast to the private sector, viewed as inherently efficient and with the adverse effects of self-interest curbed by the discipline of the market.

Public choice takes the same principles that economists use to analyze people's actions in the marketplace and applies them to people's actions in collective decision making. Economists who study behavior in the private marketplace assume that people are motivated mainly by self-interest. Although most people base some of their actions on their concern for others, the dominant motive in people's actions in the marketplace – whether they are employers, employees, or consumers – is a concern for themselves. Public choice economists make the same assumption – that although people acting in the political marketplace have some concern for others, their main motive, whether they are voters, politicians, lobbyists, or bureaucrats, is self-interest.

(Shaw, nd)

At least three important consequences flow from this sceptical and distrustful view of the public sector and its servants. First, it further undermines the public provision of services, building on the general hostility to an active 'social state' embedded in neoliberal thinking. Far better, the argument goes, that provision is provided privately, where it benefits from the discipline of the market place and escapes the malign influence of so-called 'producer interests'.

Second, it assumes no-one, least of all those working in the public sector, can be trusted, since ideals such as public service and the public interest count for nothing in practice. Institutions and organisations instead should be seen and treated as chains of low-trust relationships in which performance depends on incentives or sanctions. James Buchanan's and Gordon Tullock's Virginia school public choice theory 'undermined the basis for a public sector that was defined by public service rather than by self-interest and profit.... [Under this theory] the particular interests of the bureaucrat or bureaucracy supposedly displaced the public interests of citizens they were supposed to serve' (Stedman Jones, 2014, pp. 332, 334)

Third, it follows from this that remaining public involvement in policy and provision should be subject to market principles and disciplines, and strongly managed to curb self-interest and tackle inherent inefficiency – which brings us to our third sub-plot.

New Public Management

New Public Management (NPM) has been described as the neoliberal way of governance (Vabø, 2009, p. 2), the way in which organisations and systems are governed under this regime. New Public Management refers to the reform of the public and non-profit private sectors based around the importation and application of management methods from private business, inscribed with the ethos of competition, the logic of the market and the demands of customers.

> [A]t the ideological heart of the new public management was the conviction that the public sphere of services, organisations and institutions would be improved by the application of public choice theory, business values, microeconomics and market mechanisms ... the extension of business practices to the public sector ... in an attempt to make [public sector organisations] more like firms.
>
> *(Norris and Kuschner, 2007, p. 3)*

The term 'New Public Management' first emerged in the 1970s, evolving from the Public Choice discourse, with its concern to curb self-interest in the public sector and its supposed interference with the public interest (Widmalm, 2016), but also as a response to economic crises and fears about the growing costs of public services and welfare. New Public Management got taken up by neoliberal think tanks and governments, notably in the United Kingdom, Australia and New Zealand, in their desire to modernise public services, reduce spending and improve efficiency, effectiveness and excellence. But it became widespread during the 1990s, 'on account of an international booming consultancy industry, [and] finance institutions such as the World Bank, the International Monetary Fund and above all OECD through their Public Management (PUMA) reports' (Vabø, 2009, p. 8). In many respects, therefore, the history and spread of NPM parallels that of Human Capital Theory and Public Choice theory, and of neoliberalism itself.

Christopher Hood, who first coined the term 'New Public Management', identified seven overlapping principles that often figured in discussion (Hood, 1991): 'Hands on' professional management in the public sector; explicit standards and measures of performance; greater emphasis on output control; a shift to dis-aggregation of units in the public sector; a shift to greater competition in the public sector; stress on private sector styles of management practice; and stress on greater discipline and parsimony in resource use. Underpinning these principles, and picking up again on the issue of trust, or the lack of it, Dunleavy and Hood (1994) describe one of the key features of the shift from 'old public administration' to New Public Management as coming to view organisations as 'a chain of low trust principal/agent relationships' (Norris and Kuschner, 2007, p. 4).

But rather than a uniform and coherent programme, defined by the standardised application of common principles, New Public Management should be seen as taking diverse forms in different countries and policy areas:

> NPM is a loose term and the different elements suggested under this umbrella [of seven principles] do not occur in every case.... [C]haracteristic mixtures vary from country to country.... [NPM is] an umbrella concept used to label a shift from traditional public administration to public management characterised by use of market-type mechanisms and business styles of management.... [Both] marketization and business-style management have continued to co-exist as the common core of NPM.
>
> *(Vabø, 2009, p. 3)*

New Public Management was 'born of a technocratic mindset. It has been driven by the demand for increased efficiency and accountability, rather than the need to maximise other values, such as fairness, equity, due process and public participation' (ibid., p. 2). But it is more than just a technique of managing better, in a more business-like way. It is a vital element in the depoliticisation and economisation of life, and the fundamental transformation of society through neoliberal reason:

> It is through governance practices that business models and metrics come to irrigate every crevice of society, circulating from investment banks to schools, from corporations to universities, from public agencies to the individual. It is through the replacement of democratic terms of law, participation, and justice with idioms of benchmarks, objectives, and buy-ins that governance dis-mantles democratic life while appearing only to instill it with 'best practices'.
>
> *(Brown, 2015)*

What New Public Management has represented, therefore, is not only the spread of private business management techniques into the public sector (in which we include the non-profit private sector), but also a way of thinking about the sector in economic terms, wholly consistent with neoliberalism's 'economisation' agenda. All public services are commodified, construed as private businesses competing in the market place, and needing to be strongly and systematically managed to max-imise returns on investment through high performance. This new imagery displaces all others, including those that envisage public services as democratic institutions at the service of and involving participation by local communities and their citizenry.

New Public Management also serves another purpose for neoliberalism – it dis-ciplines or governs people to behave in neoliberal ways, and eventually to come to embody them. Jeremy Gilbert argues that most people do not want to be subject to neoliberal norms: 'Teachers want to teach and students want to learn because teaching and learning are fundamental to any fulfilled human existence, and not just so that the corporations that students will work for can make money' (Gilbert, 2020, p. 65). But New Public Management coerces teachers, and others, to adopt neoliberal norms, and is supported in this task by the emergence over the last few decades of a new class of managers:

> Their main job, unlike that of old managers of business or government agen-cies, is not to make sure that the organisation runs efficiently and effectively. Their job is instead to discipline other workers within the organisation, to force them to follow neoliberal norms such as meeting targets and fulfilling competitive criteria. A complex and oppressive bureaucracy has grown since the 1970s, in corporations and in the public sector, the purpose of which is to monitor, audit and direct the behaviour of citizens constantly, forcing them to comply with neoliberal codes.
>
> *(ibid., p. 66)*

New public managers for the era of new public management, a powerful group with a strong commitment to the neoliberal project and its way of thinking, and focused on results, on the achievement of predetermined goals, on performance.

We conclude this brief discussion of New Public Management with three observations. First, NPM has given great impetus to the importance of numbers in public services, including education. In a competitive market (which we dis-cuss in Chapters 2 and 3 in the case of education), consumers need some way of assessing the performance of competing providers, to enable them to make informed choices. Similarly, governments funding such services, whether pro-vided publicly or privately, and doing so to deliver particular policy goals need some way of judging performance – to know if they are getting what they are paying for. The answer to both needs has been the introduction of ever more quantitative measures, as NPM introduced a culture to the public sector 'that was characterised by constant monitoring and the construction of targets and league tables for every public service' (Purdue, 2005, p. 123). Spurred on by distrust of professional judgement and the ideology of consumer choice, the result has been what Jerry Muller terms 'metric fixation … the seemingly irresistible pressure to measure performance, to publicize it and reward it, often in the face of evidence that this just doesn't work very well' (Muller, 2018, p. 4). We shall see this pro-cess at work in ECEC in Chapter 5.

Second, New Public Management, with its commitment to standardised measures to assess and manage performance (on the principle that what can't be measured can't be managed), epitomises neoliberalism's close relationship with the paradigm of positivism, the paradigm supplying neoliberalism with a necessary epistemological foundation. Those adopting this paradigm believe in the possibility of producing, through the application of systematic methods, knowledge that is value- and context-free, universal and replicable – in short, an objective Truth, *the* Truth. Such knowledge holds out the prospect of being able to reach a final and correct conclusion, free of context and perspective, untroubled by positionality or other complexities.

Positivism is not, therefore, a paradigm at ease with social context or complexity, inter-connectedness or life's irreducible messiness. As St. Pierre has argued:

> Many of these ideas [associated with positivism] illustrate an age-old desire to get below the messy, contingent surface of human existence to a pristine, originary foundation, a bedrock of certitude … [which persists] because of the romance of an orderly, progressive, predictive empirical science based on fact devoid of value as the final arbiter.
>
> *(St. Pierre, 2012, p. 493)*

This, of course, is exactly the kind of epistemological foundation that neoliberalism, and 'professional management', needs. Both crave knowledge that can act as 'a bedrock of certitude', and so enable accurate calculations and correct decisions in the market place, as well as effective management in particular through measurement of performance. Business, we are constantly reminded, dislikes uncertainty; positivism holds out the prospect of avoiding it through the generation of objective, stable and certain knowledge based on measurement and numbers.

Third, neoliberalism pays high regard to individual choice and freedom, individual responsibility and self-management. Yet New Public Management is about strong and hierarchical control of the individual. This apparent paradox is not really a paradox. For neoliberalism is about achieving the best deals and the highest returns, based on achieving the greatest efficiency in performance – and that requires strong management of others. Individual choice and freedom are fine as far as they go, but there are places they cannot go, including the rejection of individual choice and freedom when, for example, someone may wish to settle for less efficiency in favour of, say, more job security and satisfaction: *homo economicus* cannot choose to be someone else.

New Public Management is subject to extensive academic and public criticism today, for example 'for providing perverse incentive structures, overwhelming and ineffective evaluation structures, a dehumanizing work environment, and for deprofessionalizing a number of occupations in the health, education, research and administration sectors' (Widmalm, 2016, p. 128). Doubts have also grown about its over-reliance on measurement and numbers, with the consequent denigration of personal judgement based on experience and the attendant risk of simplification: 'the problem is not measurement, but excessive measurement and inappropriate measurement' (Muller, 2018, p. 4). Yet despite this growing questioning and disenchantment, New Public Management and its 'metric fixation' remain forces to be reckoned with.

A note on terminology

Any book about formal services for young children (i.e. those below compulsory school age) has to struggle with how to label these services. Our preferred choice would be 'early childhood education', because we think that these services should be conceptualised and organised as primarily educational and as the first stage of the education system – though we recognise that this begs many questions about the meaning and purpose of 'education', and the many other functions that early childhood services do or could perform. For example, in our view, all mainly educational services *should* have a strong element of care (expressed both as an 'ethic of care' and by having opening hours that take account of carers' working hours); and should also be multi-purpose, acting as 'public forums situated in civil society in which children and adults participate together in projects of social, cultural, political and economic significance' (Dahlberg, Moss and Pence, 2013, p. 73).

In practice, though, many existing educational services do not match this ideal. We have decided, therefore, to use the more common term 'early childhood education and care', sometimes 'ECEC', so there can be no mistaking that we are covering both services described as mainly educational or pedagogical and those described as mainly for 'childcare' (understood to be primarily for children with employed parents). As very few countries have fully integrated early childhood services, the Nordic states being the main exceptions, this education/care split is still unfortunately the norm globally. When we refer specifically to mainly educational or pedagogical services (e.g. those in schools or kindergartens), we use the term 'early education', and when referring specifically to 'care' services we use the term 'childcare'.

We have used this chapter to set out the aims of the book and introduce its contents. We have also set the broad scene that provides the context for our more focused study of education, and in particular early childhood education and care, in subsequent chapters. That broad, neoliberal scene, we have argued, is dominated by a set of inter-connected beliefs, assumptions and practices, inscribed with an economic understanding of life expressed in an assemblage of economic images, values and relationships. At its centre is the economisation of life, which to quote Mirowski again 'has sunk its roots deep into everyday life'.

This is a scene in which the language we introduced at the start of this chapter, so prevalent today in early childhood education and care, begins to make perfect sense. It is significant, too, that this language is in the English language, since the epicentre of the story of neoliberalism, and its associated sub-plots, has been the English-speaking world, and in particular the UK and the USA. This is a language that bears concepts and ways of thinking that are particularly at home in this cultural context.

We turn now to consider how the story of neoliberalism, with its sub-plots, has impacted the world of education, starting first with an overview of compulsory schooling and higher education.

2

NEOLIBERALISM AND THE WIDER WORLD OF EDUCATION

The main purpose of this book is to explore the relationship between neoliberalism and early childhood education and care. But before homing in on that particular relationship, we want to look at the wider educational context, and the way neoliberalism has impacted on compulsory education. As we shall see in subsequent chapters, there is much here that is in common with the experience of early childhood education and care. Perhaps the main difference concerns the challenge confronting neoliberalism.

In most high-income countries, a public system of compulsory education existed for many decades before neoliberalism's rise to power in the 1980s, with an acknowledged public responsibility for providing a service for all children and with well-established institutions and professions. Neoliberalism faced, therefore, the challenge of transforming this universal and embedded public service and replacing it with one based on neoliberal principles, including 'market logic'. By contrast, ECEC in the 1980s was less extensive and well-established, especially in the English-speaking world. The system, such as existed, was with few exceptions split between 'childcare' (assumed to be primarily for children of working parents) and 'early education', the former commonly seen as an essentially private responsibility, something that parents should pay for, the latter a public responsibility but less developed in the Anglophone world than in Continental Europe. As demand has subsequently grown for 'childcare', often preceding substantial policy involvement by government, these services were initially left to private providers and 'market logic', in particular in Anglophone countries. Neoliberalism has, in short, had a head start and found favourable conditions for spreading in the early childhood field.

Neoliberalism and compulsory education have been the subject of a large literature, far more than for early childhood education and care. We intend to take only a brief and broad look at this literature, sketching out some of the main features identified in this vast array of material that have led to

[t]hings that at one time seemed unthinkable becom[ing] over time the common sense and the obvious of policy, as 'what works' and as 'best practice'; they become embedded in a 'necessarian logic', most commonly in relation to the necessities of international economic competitiveness.

(Ball, 2016a, p. 1048)

We will come across many of these features again, and go into them in more detail, in subsequent chapters focused on ECEC. We have organised the remainder of this chapter under three headings: how neoliberalism has manifested itself in compulsory education; how neoliberalism's influence has spread; and some consequences of neoliberalism.

How neoliberalism has manifested itself in compulsory education

Pasi Sahlberg, a Finnish educator and author, has coined the term 'Global Education Reform Movement', or GERM for short. GERM, he writes, 'has emerged since the 1980s and has increasingly become adopted as an educational reform orthodoxy within many education systems throughout the world, including in the U.S., England, Australia and some transition countries [countries formerly in or dominated by the Soviet Union]' (Sahlberg, 2012a). GERM can be seen as the manifestation of compulsory education's contamination by neoliberal thinking, one consequence of the neoliberal hegemony that, as we described in the previous chapter, asserted itself in the 1980s. These neoliberal reform policies have now become dominant in many countries, 'infecting schools around the world' (Sahlberg, 2012b), though some countries such as Japan, South Korea, Denmark, Norway, Belgium and Finland have remained relatively immune to GERM, at least until recently (Verger, Parcerisa and Fontdevila, 2019).

National systems of compulsory education were made susceptible to contamination by GERM as a result of arguments that public education was in 'crisis' and needed major reform to make it fit for purpose in a competitive world – a variant of Naomi Klein's 'shock doctrine' that we met in Chapter 1. For example, in the US, the 1983 report 'Nation at Risk: The Imperative for Educational Reform' blamed poor quality teachers and schools for the low standing of American pupils on international tests and compared the purported 'failures' of the public educational system to an attack from an unfriendly nation; a flood of criticism of public schools has followed (Lightfoot-Rueda and Peach, 2015). Similarly, in England 'a discourse of derision' (Kenway, 1990, p. 201 in Ball, 2017) circulated regarding 'failing' teachers who were not to be trusted because of their left-wing politics and self-interested professionalism.

With public education systems, their schools and teachers, on the defensive, the way was opened for neoliberal market and business style education policy 'solutions' and reforms (Ball, Juneman and Santori, 2017, p. 142), advocated to hold so-called 'self-interested' teachers and schools to account and to make them more efficient. These solutions and reforms soon gelled into a global education reform movement. This GERM manifests itself in five closely linked symptoms, neoliberal educational reform policies that were originally developed in the 1980s in the US, the UK and Australia and have become a 'new educational orthodoxy', a 'global policyspeak' as Stephen Ball terms it, that holds out the prospect of improved quality and overall educational performance worldwide.

At the heart of GERM is the neoliberal belief that education should be governed and managed primarily using commercial and market principles (Murgatroyd and Sahlberg, 2016): 'whatever problem exists, market logic can fix it' (Connell, 2013, p. 101). The *first symptom* of the GERM infection, therefore, is the spread of *market logic*, with its corollary of 'the logic of competition between students, teachers, schools and writ large between nations' (Ball, 2017, p. 23). As Raewyn Connell describes the process in her native Australia

> Once a neoliberal policy regime had been established around the mid-1990s, a cascade of 'reforms' followed which brought every institutional sector under the sway of market logic. Education is a major example.... [P]olicy changes all move in the same direction – increasing the grip of market logic on schools, universities and technical education
>
> *(Connell, 2013, p. 102)*

Central to this increasing grip is the introduction of parental choice of schools, to provide a scenario where schools compete in a market for pupils and the custom of their parents. Such marketisation is further enabled by reconfiguring existing schools (or groups of schools) as autonomous institutions, no longer managed by public bodies but managing themselves, acting as businesses seeking customer-parents, who in turn are intended to act as informed consumers exercising choice through accessing increasing amounts of information about the performance of competing schools. To boost competition, the market may be opened to a plethora of private (but publicly-funded) schools – for example, charter schools in the US, academy and free schools in England, and free schools in Sweden. Parent choice between competing schools drives market logic into education systems so that 'parents choose schools like they shopped for shoes, schools advertised their services and school boards acted as though they were managing a stock portfolio' (Ravitch, 2010, p. 244).

This process is supposed to lead to enhanced 'quality', productivity and efficiency by freeing schools from the restrictive control of government and creating incentives to innovate and improve, such as raising test scores, which leads to more pupils and greater funding (Murgatroyd and Sahlberg, 2016). As well as working to improve performance, schools must act entrepreneurially, engaging in promotion and marketing activities to attract prospective customer-parents, whilst also achieving internal cost savings and generating new income streams (Ball, 2017). In this Darwinian version of education, schools' survival depends upon attracting sufficient parents and children to sustain themselves and their income because 'inefficient and unproductive schools will lose pupils and be forced to improve or shut down' (Murgatroyd and Sahlberg, 2016, p. 10). In short, the market determines which schools will live and which will die.

Accompanying marketisation has been the privatisation of education, not only through the growth of schools operating as essentially private entities, autonomous businesses competing in the education market place, but through the sub-contracting of services to businesses and the insertion of private finance to fund the provision of basic educational services.

The *second symptom* of GERM is the *standardisation of education*, with the specification of performance standards for pupils, schools and, as we shall see in our discussion of the Organisation of Economic Cooperation and Development (OECD), countries. Standardisation draws on the inclusive premise that all students should be educated to attain the same centrally determined performance targets. Externally prescribed standardised testing and school evaluation systems ensure that all schools adhere to standards-driven education policies; all, too, can be judged against the same criteria and norms. The promise of standardisation, that it will provide 'significant gains in efficiency and quality of education, has been widely accepted as a basic ideology of change, both politically and professionally' (Sahlberg, 2016, p. 119).

The *third symptom* of GERM is a focus on the *core subjects* of literacy, numeracy and sciences to the exclusion or marginalisation of other curriculum subjects. Within GERM these core subjects become the prime goal of education and performance on this core becomes the indicator of 'quality' educational systems; they come to 'dominate what pupils study, teachers teach, schools emphasise and national educational policies prioritise in most parts of the world' (ibid., p. 117). International large-scale student assessments, such as OECD's PISA, looked at later in this chapter, reinforce the emphasis upon these core subjects.

The *fourth symptom* of GERM is the transfer of *corporate and business management models* into public education systems; leadership and performance become key concepts. This turn towards New Public Management provides the total institutional and cultural shift that transforms schools to become 'business-like and like a business' (Ball, 2017, p. 57) and reshapes and reconfigures them into competitive 'profit seeking firms' (Connell, 2013, p. 101). Underpinning the creation of 'new organisational ecologies, with much greater emphasis on forms of management modelled on business' (ibid., p. 90), has been a deep distrust, by politicians, policy makers and the media, of teachers and their claims to professionalism, and a belief that they need to be brought within systems of strong managerial control – shades of public choice theory.

This means in practice a greater emphasis on output control through establishing explicit standards and measures of performance; and the importation from business of management tools such as 'content management systems' and 'workload management systems' for the daily management of schools and universities (Castañeda and Selwyn, 2018). With this new culture, performance, productivity and efficiency have become the main drivers of organisational change, while chains of low trust relationships are manifested in 'databases, appraisal meetings and annual reviews; report writing, quality assurance visits, the regular publication of results, inspections and peer reviews' (Ball, 2017, p. 58); and 'an infrastructure of organisation, processes and subjects [develops] in whose relations market exchanges become a sensible and necessary form for the production and consumption of education' (Ball, 2018a, p. 587).

Within this business management model schools are transformed into auditable entities and drawn in to 'ever-expanding systems of measuring, costing, monitoring and ranking' (Shore and Wright, 2015, p. 25). So, for example, attainment data becomes a 'currency' to be used within a competitive market in which pupil outcomes 'are "consumed" in the service of the competitive market environment' (Pratt, 2016, p. 897). Education and schools become reimagined as calculable commodities in an 'economics of results based management' (Murgatroyd and Sahlberg, 2016, p. 10). Digital 'platform' performance management systems are bought from business and industry (Castañeda and Selwyn, 2018) to solve and maximise schools' results-based performance management. Schools, teachers and pupils are constantly measured and compared through a proliferating dataveillance of test results, performance management and efficiency progress in ever greater depth and across ever wider spaces. A business-style language of 'targets', 'accountability', 'competition and choice', 'leadership', 'entrepreneurism', 'performance-related pay' and 'privatisation' becomes expected and normalised and justifies so-called educational 'winners' and 'losers'.

Closely related to this is the *fifth symptom* of GERM, *Test Based Accountability* (TBA), which operates as yet another tool to construct competitive educational markets. TBA enables Governments to steer and regulate the market from a distance, often through decontextualised numerical data presented as competitive rankings in league tables. Such visualised TBA data creates a competitive 'race' of winners and losers that operates at both global and national levels, often focusing on literacy and numeracy. TBA makes schools and teachers responsible for pupils' attainment in national curricula through external standardised tests. The performance of schools in these tests is tied to the evaluation, inspection and rewards or punishments that schools receive; in this way, schools are managed and governed.

The same applies to individual teachers. TBA can link the test scores of individual students to individual teachers and so creates a visible business style 'bottom line' to hold teachers, as well as schools, to account. In short if children's test scores go up, the teacher is considered to be 'effective', but if the scores go down the teacher is deemed 'ineffective'. Such crude simplistic and business style labelling of teachers has led to press headlines such as 'We must fire bad teachers' (Newsweek, 2010 in Ravitch, 2013, p. 99). Teachers' pay, as well as school budgets, can be determined by test scores and poor test results can result in teachers losing their contracts and schools closing down (Sahlberg, 2016) – so-called 'payment by results' or 'performance-related pay' (discussed later in this chapter). With such dire consequences hanging over schools and teachers, TBA has been termed 'high stakes testing'.

These separately described symptoms of GERM are, in fact, inter-connected. Test Based Accountability focuses on core subjects and measurement of performance against externally imposed standards. Performance, in turn, produces school league tables, which enable effective management of schools and teachers, as well as being a key market making strategy by driving competition into education systems through parents making choices based on schools' league table positions.

England: a case study of the neoliberalising of education

GERM's neoliberal symptoms have appeared in many countries. In Australia, for example, the 'National Assessment Program – Literacy and Numeracy' (NAPLAN), an example of TBA, was introduced in 2008 and is a series of national standardised tests set against prespecified outcomes focused on basic skills in literacy and numeracy that are administered annually to Year 3, 5, 7 and 9 students. NAPLAN is used to compare and rank all Australian schools' average performance. Test results are directly linked to federal funding agreements with the states. They are also used to stimulate parental choice of school. The 'My School' website (www.myschool.edu.au), provided by the Australian Curriculum, Assessment and Reporting Authority, is advertised as 'a resource for parents, educators and the community to find information about each of Australia's schools'. It includes performance on NAPLAN for each school in Australia, colour coding schools by attainment to help parents make a choice, in exactly the same way as England's 'Find and Compare Schools' website (see Chapter 5). And in the same way, the 'My School' website negates clear differences in context between, for example, 'the Northern Territory's large remote highly disadvantaged Indigenous communities and the Australian Capital Territories relatively small, homogenous population many of whom are well educated and work in the public service' (Thompson, 2016, p. 216). Connell notes that NAPLAN 'signalled the consolidation of the market in schooling, the triumph of competitive testing and consumer choice as the basis of policy, and the end of a concept of public education' (2013, p. 104).

National testing regimes have also been introduced into the United States through 'No Child Left Behind' (NCLB, 2001) and 'Race to the Top' (RTTT, 2009), federally mandated programmes that advocated accountability measures, school choice and merit pay (payment by results) as necessary and the only 'reforms' to improve schools. NCLB and RTTT decreed by law that all states must test every child annually in Grades 3 to 8 in reading and maths, and that by 2014 all pupils should achieve high proficiency results on standardised tests known as Common Core State Standards. These 'high stakes' tests link evaluation of teachers to pupils' test scores and penalise public schools that are persistently unable to meet the progress targets, handing them over to state control or private management or turning them into charter schools, an independently run school granted greater flexibility in its operations, in return for greater accountability for performance:

> between school years 2000–01 and 2016–17, the percentage of all public schools in the United States … that were charter schools increased from 2 to 7 percent, and the total number of charter schools increased from approximately 2,000 to 7,000.
>
> *(National Center for Education Statistics (US), 2019, np)*

Neoliberal education reforms have, however, gone furthest in England, which

> has played a particular role in the development and dissemination of the edu-
> cation 'global policyspeak' as a social laboratory of experimentation and
> reform. Policies like school-based management, parental choice, information
> and accountability systems, contracting out of education services and public-
> private partnerships ... are now being 'exported' round the world by English
> education businesses and policy entrepreneurs. These are key features of what
> Pasi Sahlberg calls GERM, the Global Education Reform Movement
>
> *(Ball, 2017, p. 3)*

The ground was first prepared for the laboratory in October 1976 when then
Labour Party prime minister, James Callaghan, stated in a speech that the education
system had to change and be guided more by work and economic imperatives –
teachers' professionalism and the curriculum should be opened up for critical
scrutiny and be more directed by the central state (Jones, 2016, p. 75). The
laboratory itself opened with the 1988 Education Reform Act (ERA), the culmination of a narrative of 'crisis' in English education, supported by the use of
international league tables, which enabled a public 'discourse of derision' (Ball,
2017, p. 103) aimed at supposedly failing schools and at allegedly self-interested
teachers who could not be trusted and whose 'working habits were slow to
respond to policy initiatives' (Jones, 2016, p. 197).

The ERA emerged in this hostile environment. It 'changed the institutional
pattern of schooling and reshaped its values, meanings and objectives' (Jones, 2016,
p. 138), turning away from a welfare state public education service and towards a
neoliberal schools market in which competition and choice for parents became the
core values of education. The marketisation process was set in train by:

- offering parents a degree of choice about schools;
- introducing 'local management of schools', which increased school autonomy
  by allowing all schools to be taken out of the direct financial control of local
  authorities, so breaking the power of local education authorities and creating
  schools as autonomous units with control over budget, staffing and enrolment,
  their income dependent on their ability to attract parental custom; and
- increasing the diversity of school provision by allowing schools to 'opt out'
  totally of local authority control and become central government controlled
  Grant Maintained Schools and City Technology Colleges, effectively 'independent' private schools in a direct contractual relationship with the English
  government's Department for Education.

At the same time, the introduction of a national curriculum paved the way for
stronger central managerial control and standardisation of compulsory education. This
was a detailed, prescriptive and standard-setting curriculum for all students aged between
5 and 16 years in publicly-funded schools, specified by government-appointed

committees and approved by the Minister of Education (ibid., p. 138). The national curriculum was central to market making because pupil 'progress through the curriculum would be monitored by national tests, which would enable measurement of the performance of individuals and schools' (ibid.).

The ERA laid the foundations of a new educational system: 'market managerialism', a mix of quasi-markets and tightly governed and regulated schools and teachers – or put another way, diversity and competition between schools combined with uniformity and centralised control of content. The legislation

> combined decentralized operational management and detailed central regulation … what counted as achievement would be determined not simply by consumer demand, but also by government decision. It would be central government that set the criteria for success, that measured progress towards them, and that rewarded or punished institutions. Thus market regulations were interwoven with state regulation of a stronger and more intrusive kind.
>
> *(ibid., p. 120)*

Subsequently, marketisation has gone much further. Grant Maintained Schools and City Technology Colleges were the precursors of today's so-called 'academy' and 'free schools', similar to privatised 'charter schools' in the US, which now account for nearly half of all English pupils (47%) (National Audit Office (England), 2018). Many of these schools, publicly funded but essentially independent, are managed by school academy chains or multi-academy trusts – MATs, run by private and charitable organisations; MATs have become 'the educational equivalent of Tesco and Sainsburys, Aldi or Lidl [supermarket chains] to parent consumers all over England' (Millar, 2018, p. 47).

Managerialism has also developed apace since 1988. Central government has adopted a variety of tools for more closely controlling a host of autonomous schools. These include the creation in 1990 of a national education inspectorate, the Office for Standards in Education (Ofsted); the introduction of football style league tables showing schools' results for national examinations for 16- and 18-year-olds (GCSEs and A Levels); and the implementation of a new national system of testing (Standard Attainment Tests – SATs), based on the national curriculum, for 7-year-olds (1990), 11-year-olds (1994) and 14-year-olds (1994, but scrapped in 2009) (Curtis, 2008). Other tests have been or are being introduced for younger children, discussed in Chapter 5.

This whole edifice of measurement has served the dual purpose of tightening management and increasing competition by providing parents with market information about schools, and by doing so encouraging 'parents to vote with their feet using the knowledge they [have] gleaned from new inspection reports and football-style "league tables" ranking every school in an area by results' (Millar, 2018, p. 8). However, these league tables are offered 'without reference to such crucial factors as the social class composition of the school in question.… [S]chools now became like shops, with league tables, a kind of shorthand indicator of desirability … [and] league-table talk came to dominate the anxious chatter of the middle-class state-school parent' (Benn, 2012, p. 70) who had the financial and cultural capital to move house and access higher performing schools.

To add to the armoury available for the central management of education, the English Minister of Education's powers over schools has increased vastly since 1988. Tim Brighouse, a leading figure in English education over several decades, has observed that before 1988, '[m]ost influence was with local education authorities (LEAs) and the schools: the minister had only three powers', but today Education ministers 'have over 2,000 powers and seem increasingly unaccountable, while local authorities have lost most educational functions, with expert staff not being replaced' (Brighouse, 2019, np). Brighouse argues that, while there may have been too little accountability pre-1988, today there is too much; now 'very little of what goes on in schools is free of central government interference, from the centrally devised national curriculum, centrally regulated exams and centrally devised accountability measures in the form of league tables and inspections' (Millar, 2018, p. 12).

Management powers have also become stronger at local level, within schools themselves. An egregious example, an instance of new public management, has been the spread of 'performance-related pay' (PRP). Introduced by the English government in 2013, PRP creates a direct link between pupil grades and potential pay rises for teachers; teachers, it is assumed, need to be consistently motivated and disciplined by financial rewards or sanctions imposed upon them. Automatic pay progression based on length of service has gone to be replaced with PRP, as explained in this government guidance to school governance bodies:

> Decisions about teachers' annual pay uplift and pay progression are linked to performance. All individual pay awards need to take account of performance and be objectively justifiable based on evidence. There is no need for a school to award an increase to an individual unless it is merited by performance in accordance with their pay policy. Performance-related pay progression enables schools to recognise and reward a teacher's performance through an increase in pay. It can act as an incentive for continuous improvement
>
> *(Department for Education (England), 2019c, p. 16)*

PRP has meant, in the words of the then senior minister for education, that 'school leaders are now free to reward their best teachers more than ever before – with more autonomy to attract, retain and reward those teachers who have the greatest impact on their pupils' performance' (Gove, 2013, in Pratt, 2016, p. 898). This performance-based management approach has become widespread in a short time, symptomatic of a wider turn to management through performance data. Analysis of the OECD's 2015 PISA study found not only that more than 90% of English school headteachers used data to judge the effectiveness of their school but also that they were far more likely to use data to judge teachers' effectiveness than the OECD average. Indeed 'schools in England make extensive use of education data – much more so than other education systems across the world' (Jerrim, 2019, np).

On the one hand, therefore, the 1988 ERA and subsequent legislation have given schools greater autonomy and control over their financial budgets, staffing and enrolment; but on the other hand, schools and their performance have been subjected to a prescriptive centralised regime of management deploying a national curriculum, a national inspection agency and a national system of testing. Ball (2017, p. 51) notes that the ERA began 'a process of *reregulation* ... set within the constraints and requirements of "performance" and "profitability"'. While Benn (2011, p. 70) suggests that the ERA prescribed 95% of what goes on in schools so that 'overnight teachers became the most controlled − and oppressed − group of professionals in the country'.

What has emerged in compulsory schooling in England over the last 30 years is the personification of GERM, combining a market of competing providers of education, battling it out to attract customers for their products, together with a highly centralised system of content control and performance management. A strange mix of market forces, autonomous schools and centralised direction!

How neoliberalism's influence has spread in compulsory education

Sahlberg (2012), as we have seen, coined the term Global Education Reform Movement or 'GERM' to explain the global exchange and 'policy borrowing' of 'best educational practices' between nations that has led to the spread of neoliberal thinking into many compulsory school systems. Within GERM's deterritorialised and policy networked world, international, national and local educational boundaries have collapsed into a global marketised space. Moving through this space, GERM 'is like an epidemic that spreads and infects education systems through a virus. It travels with pundits, media and politicians. Education systems borrow policies from others and get infected. As a consequence, schools get ill, teachers don't feel well, and kids learn less' (ibid., p. 3).

The neoliberalisation of education has followed in the wake of neoliberalism itself, and like neoliberalism has taken deepest root in the Anglosphere, in particular England, Australia and the United States. It has been aided and abetted, therefore, from the global reach of the English language, which has proven a powerful means of disseminating neoliberal ideas that are so deeply embedded in the culture and politics of Anglophone countries. Unfortunately, native English-speakers rarely seem to appreciate the power their language exerts and the specific cultural meanings it carries.

But the spread of neoliberalism's influence on education, 'beyond the boundaries of the nation state', has not depended simply on a change in the political climate. It has been furthered by the actions and interplay of particular 'global actors':

> like multinational businesses and multilateral agencies such as the World Bank, World Trade Organisation (WT) and OECD; regional states and organisations like the EU or Association of Southeast Asian Nations and Japan; and, latterly, global philanthropists like the Bill and Melinda Gates Foundation [who] are

becoming increasingly influential and having policy impacts independently of governments. Policy is being done in new places, by new actors, beyond the boundaries of the nation-state.

(Ball, 2017, pp. 32–23)

Such individuals, non-profit organisations, businesses and others have formed networks of advocates for change, for 'the spread and take-up of neo-liberal practices rests upon a great deal of political and ideological work that is highly organised and well-funded' (Ball, 2012, p. 18). If neoliberalism has created a political climate, these actors have played a lead role in forming the neoliberal education weather.

Together they have created an educational 'global policyscape' (Carney, 2012) by means of which they are able to influence national education agendas (Verger et al., 2019, p. 7) through their fast moving 'globalising policy networks' (Ball, 2018a). These are networked global players (Ball, 2017, 2019), with 'sprawling assemblages of actors, events, materials, money and technologies' (Williamson, Rensfeldt, Player-Koro and Selwyn, 2018, p. 705), who seek to transform public education into 'an entrepreneurial sector of the economy' (Ravitch, 2013, p. 19). With their entrepreneurial capacities, technical expertise, massive economic capital, and political aspirations these global actors are 'funding, catalyzing and incubating the global educational space as a market' (Ball, 2018a, p. 587), as they reimagine schools 'as sites for the generation of profits' (Apple 2016, p. ix, in Hursh, 2016).

Ball has illustrated how this global process of spreading neoliberal ideas and experience has worked by constructing maps showing the relationship of a cast of global actors in complex policy networks (an example from this work is given in Figure 2.1). We will consider here the contribution of three troupes of these actors – philanthrocapitalists, business corporations, and international non-governmental organisations, while also noting that these new educational influencers have risen to prominence at the expense of 'some established policy actors and agencies like educational researchers and local authorities [being] marginalised or disenfranchised or circumvented' (Ball, 2012, p. 112). New dominant stories have brought with them new dominant story tellers.

Philanthro-capitalists

Various individuals have played supporting roles in the spread of neoliberal ideas through education. Some are what Stephen Ball calls neo-liberal 'policy entrepreneurs', paying particular attention to the work of James Tooley, whom he describes as

> a card-carrying Hayekian, an academic, a 'thought leader' and businessman. His work has won a series of 'prizes' awarded by 'pro-market' think tanks and advocacy groups. He directs, serves on the boards, is trustee, published by, speaks at a variety of inter-connected 'pro-market' organisations.... He performs all three of the functions of a policy entrepreneur (Mincrom and Vergari, 1996). He has

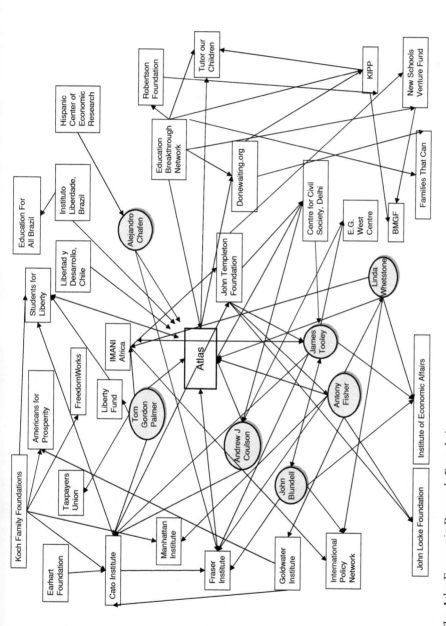

FIGURE 2.1 The Atlas Economic Research Foundation

Source: Ball, 2012, p. 20. Permission granted from Informa UK Limited.

identified particular educational needs and offers innovative means to satisfy them; he is willing to take financial and emotional risks in pursuing change where consequences are uncertain, albeit it with very substantial financial support from others; and has been able to assemble and coordinate networks of individuals and organisations, local and transnational, with the capabilities and resources needed to achieve change.... He is a policy traveller, he animates global circuits of policy knowledge, and is a co-constructor of infrastructures that advocate, frame, package and represent policy ideas.... He takes his policy ideas, or perhaps more accurately the authoritative discourses of neo-liberal economics, into influential and exclusive 'global microspaces'.

(ibid., pp. 38–39)

In addition to such 'policy entrepreneurs', there are a further group of individuals who are influential on account of the huge resources they command: these are the philanthro-capitalists. A global elite of the financial super-rich use their immense wealth to breathe life into the global educational market making process. Diane Ravitch (2013) notes how GERM is in fact a 'corporate reform' movement funded by Wall Street private finance and investment firms, global edubusinesses such as Pearson, and increasingly super-rich philanthro-capitalists engaged in what has been called 'new philanthropy'. Ball writes that

[w]hat is 'new' in 'new philanthropy' is the direct relation of 'giving' to 'outcomes' and the direct involvement of givers in philanthropic action and policy communities. This is a move from palliative to developmental giving.... The 'new' philanthropists want to see clear and measurable impacts and outcomes from their 'investment' of time and money. In this way the business perspective is brought to bear upon social and educational issues and problems

(Ball, 2012, pp. 69–70)

By far the most significant of this new breed of philanthropists are Bill and Melinda Gates and their Foundation, leading Hursh (2016) to suggest that Bill Gates has more power over education policy than the US Secretary for Education. For example, the $2.3 billion donated by the Gates Foundation enabled President Obama to pursue his competitive test-based accountability programme, 'Race to The Top'. Working in collaboration with the Pearson corporation (discussed below), and the US Department of Education, the Foundation ensured delivery of the programme's online standardised tests in every US classroom.

Other philanthro-capitalists include Wall Street hedge fund managers, the Walton Family Foundation (owners of Walmart), Facebook's Mark Zuckerberg, Netflix's Reed Hastings and Amazon's Jeff Bezos, as well as Silicon Valley-based 'computer-savvy venture capitalists' and 'angel investors' (Selwyn, 2016, pp. 114–115). Such neoliberal entrepreneurial players reimagine schools in their own image as competitors in a market and 'inject billions of dollars into public education systems in the United States and, to a lesser extent, in some other countries...[and] by doing so promote the viral spread of GERM globally' (Sahlberg, 2011, p. 99). For example, when announcing a $2 billion fund to help homeless families and build a network of preschools, Jeff Bezos, the owner of Amazon, stated that 'We'll use the same set of principles that have driven Amazon. Most important among these will be genuine intense customer obsession. The child will be the customer'. Within this way of thinking, teachers and pupils become reimagined as neoliberal market products who will experience education as an 'intense' consumer-style Amazon profiling (Levin, 2018).

Philanthro-capitalists are also actors in the school system in England, albeit on a smaller scale than the United States. For example, a study in 2016 found that nearly £20 million in charitable donations had been handed over to just 12 academy trusts in the preceding two years:

> The largest donation by some way was from the Absolute Return for Kids (Ark) charity to the trust it sponsors [in England], Ark Schools. Ark, set up to distribute donations from hedge fund financiers to improve the life chances of disadvantaged children across the world, donated £3.6 million to Ark Schools in 2015, on top of £4.7 million in 2014.... The David Ross Education Trust, which runs 33 schools, received £4.2 million in the past two years from its sponsor, the David Ross Foundation. The charity was set up by philanthropist David Ross, the co-founder of Carphone Warehouse.... Alan Howard, the co-founder of one of the world's richest hedge funds, donated £5 million to the United Learning Trust, which runs 42 schools.
>
> *(Dickens, 2016, np)*

Business corporations

GERM, Sahlberg (2012) notes, is 'often promoted through the interests of international development agencies and private enterprises through their interventions in national education reforms and policy formulation.' Neoliberalism has opened up increasing opportunities for the involvement of such private enterprises in education, 'edu-businesses', creating an expanding educational market potentially worth $30 trillion by 2030 (HolonIQ, 2018).

> The [education] market is enormous, since all countries use a substantial amount of the national spending for schools and education. Commercial, private and for-profit providers take an increasing slice of this cake. Edu-business has become a blooming global market, often fueled [sic] by the results of the large-scale international studies, in particular PISA. The World Yearbook of Education in 2016 had 'The Global Education Industry' as its main topic. Large portions of what used to be public services are out-sourced to commercial providers.
>
> *(Sjøberg, 2019, p. 41)*

Under neoliberalism, therefore, education has become big business for big business. In this favourable climate, 'edu-businesses' have grown rapidly and become increasingly influential, selling a range of products and services. Such businesses have inserted themselves into a wide range of activities related to education, from providing schools and colleges (and indeed universities) to the provision of many ancillary services: consultancy, training, test development and preparation, data analysis, remedial programmes, support and improvement, management and back office facilities, and so on.

There is more. These businesses have begun participating in 'national and international policy communities and in the work of policy mobility' [i.e. the global circulation of policy prescriptions and knowledge] (Ball, 2012, p. 93). This has led to what has been termed the 'privatisation of policy' (Mahony, Menter and Hextall, 2004). As Ball (2012, p. 139) observes, '[i]n the interface between education policy and neo-liberalism, money is everywhere…. [P]olicy is now bought and sold, it is a commodity and profit opportunity, there is a growing global market in policy ideas.' In the neo-liberal environment, policy work is increasingly outsourced to businesses, which involves

> the production by education and consultancy companies of policy 'texts' and policy ideas *for* and *within* the state, that is, the export of 'statework' to private providers and 'agencies', and the formation and dissemination of new policy discourses arising out of the participation of these companies in report writing, evaluation, advice, consultancy and recommendations…. This involves a new generation of *knowledge companies* and consultants, from whom governments are purchasing 'policy knowledge'…. [For example, Matrix Knowledge Group] produces 'evidence-based' policy knowledge using indicators of performance and value and offers the possibility of 'improvements' in these terms. Policy itself is rendered into a commodity in both senses. Policy solutions are for sale, and these solutions render policy into a set of measurable outcomes.
>
> *(ibid., p. 99)*

As another example, 'the most cited sources of evidence in educational policy documents around the world are the reports published by McKinsey's, an American worldwide management consulting firm' (Morris, 2016, p. 5). Moreover, this firm has, especially throughout the Middle East,

> been contracted to plan, evaluate, and deliver educational reform. Their work is linked with a large network of private companies sub-contracted to deliver reform. For instance, in many Gulf states, McKinsey reviewed the education system, recommended a massive reform exercise, and was contracted to deliver and evaluate it. This was undertaken by hiring a range of subcontractors such as Nord Anglia, Pearson, and Capita.
>
> *(ibid., p. 9)*

Amongst the many national and international edu-businesses, Pearson stands out as the largest supplier of educational services in the world, describing itself as the 'world's learning company with more than 24,000 employees operating in 70 countries' (www.pearson.com/about-us.html). It provides a wide range of education services and products, including being a 'leader in the advancement of low-cost private for-profit schooling throughout Africa and Asia' (Riep, 2017, p. 361), and (as we will discuss below) playing a major role in the world's largest international assessment project. But its involvement in education goes further, for it now 'sees itself as part of the international education policy community alongside governments and multi-laterals and seeks to be an active participant in national education policy conversations' (Ball, 2017, p. 44).

International non-governmental organisations

Over the last 30 years international non-governmental organisations (INGOs) such as the World Bank, UNESCO, WEF (World Economic Forum) and the OECD (Organisation for Economic Cooperation and Development) have been major players in the creation of an educational 'global policyscape', through which they have been able to influence national education agendas (Verger et al., 2019, p. 7). They have come to play an active role in policy networks, receiving, generating and distributing policy information and ideas. Such influential INGOs, in particular those whose main purpose is economic, have justified their growing involvement in the field of education on grounds of the vital importance of education to economic performance and growth.

A prime example is the Organisation for Economic Cooperation and Development (OECD), a Paris-based intergovernmental economic organisation. Founded in 1948 as the Organization for European Economic Cooperation to promote and support a free market, capitalist economic system in war-torn Europe, it changed its name and broadened its membership and scope in 1961. The OECD today consist of 36 mostly high income member countries, from across the globe, committed to the market economy and who coordinate both domestic and international policies.

The OECD has become the most influential of these global INGO policy actors, and its technical approach and economistic worldview has been central to the development of the neoliberal Global Education Reform Movement. The rationale for the organisation's move into education was primarily economic, and in particular a concept and theory we introduced in Chapter 1 – human capital:

> The importance of human resources as prime drivers in the modern economy was the main reason for the OECD to focus on education. The theoretical underpinning of this is often referred to as Human Capital Theory. The competencies of the work-force in contemporary economy are considered to be even more important than other forms of capital, like machines, buildings and infrastructure. Hence, the efficient development of a productive work-force becomes a key concern for development of the economy.
>
> *(Sjøberg, 2019, p. 38)*

The OECD's educational work has taken various forms and emerged during the 1960s. In 1968, it established a Centre for Educational Research and Innovation (CERI). Today, CERI is still active: in its own words, it 'draws together international research and expertise, identifies effective practices across different countries and develops new approaches across a range of topics towards the frontiers of education policies, practices and outcomes' (www.oecd.org/education/ceri/brochure.pdf). Current projects include trends shaping education, measuring innovation in education, strategic education governance, teacher knowledge, smart data in education and 21st century children. It also publishes 'Education at a Glance', an annual book described by the OECD as 'the authoritative source for information on the state of education around the world' (OECD, 2020) that brings together indicators and statistics from many sources, and is used by policymakers and researchers world-wide.

But perhaps OECD's best known and most influential work is its battery of international large-scale assessments (ILSAs), which it has used 'to create a standardised global definition of the purpose of schooling – portraying it primarily as an investment in human capital through the inculcation of "21st Century skills" – and its goal is to align education systems with that vision (Auld and Morris, 2019, p. 13). Foremost among these ILSAs is the 'Programme for International Student Assessment', commonly known as PISA. PISA is a triennial international programme of testing 15-year-olds in reading, maths and science, which began in 2000 and is now into its seventh round; results from this 2018 round of testing were published in December 2019. It involves the testing of a sample of half a million students who represent 28 million 15-year-olds in 80 countries and economies. PISA is now firmly established, with wide participation and high levels of interest in its results from politicians, policy makers and the media.

PISA is a deliberately decontextualised exercise, transcending culture and independent of national curricula. Instead, the OECD claims that it is a measure of globalised 21st century skills situating the project within a broader framing of the world situation that 'centres on the emergence of a hyper-competitive global knowledge economy' (Auld and Morris, 2019, p. 15). This world-view is expressed in one of its reports:

> Rapid globalisation and modernisation are posing new and demanding challenges to individuals and societies alike.… In a globalised world, people compete for jobs not just locally but internationally. In this integrated worldwide labour market, highly-paid workers in wealthier countries are competing directly with people with much the same skills in lower-wage countries. The same is true for people with low skills. The competition among countries now revolves around the quality of their human capital.… This is not a description of one possible future, but of the economic dynamics that are now in play.… The implication is that the *yardstick for educational success is no longer simply improvement against national standards, but against the best performing education systems worldwide.*
>
> (OECD, 2014, p. 18; emphasis added)

To help each country easily compare their students' performance against other countries', OECD publishes league tables of results (Figure 2.2) and a comparison website at www.compareyourcountry.org/pisa/country/GBR?lg=en. Figure 2.3 provides an example from this website comparing 2018 maths results between England and China – or rather students from just two Chinese cities, Beijing and Shanghai, and two provinces, Jiangsu and Guangdong, since the Chinese students included in PISA are only drawn from these selected areas rather than being a national sample, as is the case for England and most other participating countries,

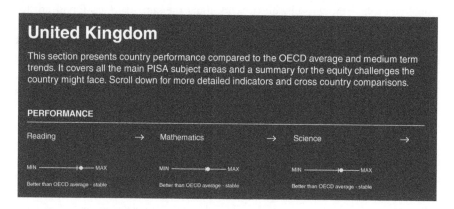

FIGURE 2.2 Showing the PISA 2018 Country Overview results compared to OECD average with decontextualised traffic light colours
Source: www.compareyourcountry.org/pisa/country/gbr?lg=en

Average performance

The headline indicator for the three subject areas: science, mathematics and reading. Average performance refers to all 15-year-old students in a country/economy regardless of the school type and grade attended. Small differences between countries and over time may be statistically insignificant.

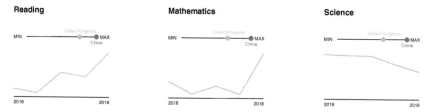

FIGURE 2.3 UK and China PISA 2018 results in comparison
Source: www.compareyourcountry.org/pisa/country/gbr?lg=en

and further are drawn only from the best schools and students (Sands, 2017). In Chapter 5 we explore the remarkably similar English Government's 'Find and Compare' schools' website, which allows users to manipulate and create competition between local English schools in exactly the same way that PISA creates national competition.

PISA, according to the OECD's own account, has a vital part to play in improving education performance and hence national competitiveness and economic success. Improved PISA results, it claims, mean improved economic productivity and output. The OECD cites a study by Hanushek and Woessman (2010, 2015) to support this central rationale – though subsequent work using the same data-sets found no significant correlation between PISA scores and economic growth rates, describing the claims underpinning the OECD's cognitive-economic model as based on 'flawed statistics' (Komatsu and Rappleye, 2017). It is worth noting that despite this and many other critical studies, 'PISA's hold on policy makers' imaginations has, if anything, strengthened.... [G]lobal enthusiasm for PISA remains undimmed. And policy makers continue to pursue a goal that, in the end, will give them nothing but bragging rights' (Morrison, 2020, np).

PISA links the OECD with the edu-business of Pearson, working together in a close cooperation. Pearson won the contract for important parts of the 2015 PISA testing and was even more closely involved in the 2018 PISA, winning the contract to develop the frameworks which 'define what will be measured in PISA 2018, how this will be reported and which approach will be chosen for the development of tests and questionnaires' (Pearson, 2018, np). As a result, Pearson organise and administer the process. Pearson continues to forge personal links with countless academics in key positions and numerous representatives for national educational authorities. This contract is of course a most valuable strategic investment for Pearson. The cooperation is already in place for several bi-products, like a video series about 'Strong Performers and Successful Reformers in Education' (Sjøberg, 2019, p. 41).

PISA is not the extent of the OECD's ambitions. It has added or is developing other ILSAs, to build on the success of PISA. These include:

- *PISA-based Test for Schools*: a 'PISA-like' test that may be used to 'benchmark' how well an individual school or school district compares with others or with those countries that are 'PISA-winners'.
- *PISA for Development* (PISA-D): a version of PISA that is meant to be used by low- and middle-income countries. It will do this using 'enhanced PISA survey instruments that are more relevant for the contexts found in middle- and low-income countries but which produce scores that are on the same scales as the main PISA assessment' (www.oecd.org/pisa/aboutpisa/pisa-for-development-background.htm). The primary goal of PISA-D is to incorporate low- and middle-income countries into PISA by making the testing instruments accessible and relevant to these countries, while maintaining the comparability of the findings with the PISA standard. The report on an initial study involving seven countries was published in late2018.

- *International Early learning and Well-being Study*: an assessment of 5-year-olds discussed further in Chapter 5.
- *Study on Social and Emotional Skills*: an assessment of social and emotional skills among 10 and 15-year-old children across the 'big five' domains – task performance, emotional regulation, collaboration, open-mindedness and engaging with others. After field testing in 2018, the main study, to be undertaken in ten cities in nine countries, is scheduled for 2019–2020.
- *Programme for the International Assessment of Adult Competencies* (PIAAC): a programme of assessment and analysis of adult skills, including a Survey of Adult Skills that measures 'adult proficiency in key information processing skills – literacy, numeracy and problem solving – and gathers information and data on how adults use their skills at home, at work and in the wider community' (www.oecd.org/skills/piaac/). The first cycle collected survey data between 2011 and 2018 in 38 countries/economies, with data collection for a second cycle scheduled for 2021–2022 in 30 countries.

This expanding collection of ILSAs adds up to a growing global web of educational measurement, assessing national performance on a range of educational standards by applying common and decontextualised indicators. This is the standardisation of education on a global scale, focused on core subjects, and a hugely ambitious exercise in test-based accountability conducted (with the exception of the PISA-based Test for Schools) at the national rather than the school level. It is an exercise, too, in creating competition between countries, in which climbing the PISA rankings is formulated as the main goal for schools in many countries, striving for improvement 'against the best performing education systems worldwide'.

But it is also an exercise in New Public Management on a global scale, with the OECD acting to define, measure and assess the outputs of participating countries. The ambition is global governance of education, to be achieved, as Svein Sjøberg explains, by 'soft power', underpinned by the use of comparisons, statistics and indicators:

> Neither PISA nor its 'owner', the OECD, has any formal, legal power. They exert influence by [sic] through a range of instruments and actions, collectively often labeled 'soft power'. A key role is played by the provision of numbers and indicators. Over the years, the OECD has become a key global provider of statistics, not only for the economy, but also in the education sector. The OECD statistics is increasingly being used by other global actors, including the European Union, the World Bank and gradually also UN-organizations like UNESCO.
>
> *(Sjøberg, 2019, p. 42)*

Through PISA, the OECD offers metrics for countries to use in assessing relative performance and formulating policies. This is a test-based accountability system that acts, too, as a powerful stimulus for change with the improvement of test scores as 'the only sound basis for undertaking educational reform' (Lingard, Sellar and Savage 2014, p. 725). So poor performance on PISA 'creates a "policy window" through which ideas, which previously seemed extreme or outlandish, can enter national policy discourses and attract attention and support' (Ball, 2016a, p. 1048).

PISA, its director Andreas Schleicher has declared, has 'globalized the field of education that we usually treat as an affair of domestic policy'; the aim, via the implementation of PISA-D, is to extend PISA from its current limited global coverage of mainly affluent countries to a comprehensively global coverage of 170 countries by 2030. An OECD Education Working Paper details the normative effects of PISA, itemising the supposed impact that PISA has had on all OECD countries. PISA, the report proclaims,

> has been adopted as an almost *global standard*, and is now used in over 65 countries and economies. [...] PISA has become accepted as a reliable instrument for *benchmarking* student performance worldwide, and PISA results have had an *influence on policy reform* in the majority of participating countries/economies.... [Even] high-performing countries such as Korea and Japan have *enacted reforms* in response to a large range of PISA results.
>
> *(Breakspear, 2012, p. 5, emphasis added)*

Global standards, benchmarking, reforms – the PISA machine is a management tool of awesome power. But not a solitary one. For alongside PISA, a whole raft of ILSAs, whether in the OECD fold or administered by other organisations (e.g. Progress in International Reading Literacy Study or PIRLS; Trends in International Maths and Science Study or TIMMS), form

> a complex apparatus of global neoliberal policies that, by mobilising diverse methods of assessment, classification, comparison, ranking and categorising, have become the key techniques of modern governing and strategic devices in the reform of education systems around the world and the production of new kinds of subjects – head teachers (school leaders), teachers, students and families.
>
> *(Collet-Sabé and Ball, 2020, p. 124)*

This is governing by numbers on an awesome scale.

Some consequences of the neoliberalism of compulsory education

The impoverishment of education

Under neoliberalism, education has become increasingly standardised, with a 'widely accepted – and generally unquestioned – belief among policy-makers and education reformers ... that setting clear and sufficiently high performance standards for schools, teachers, and students will necessarily improve the quality of expected outcomes' (Sahlberg, 2012a). This has led to a homogenisation of education, and also a narrowing, internationally and nationally, with an emphasis upon the core subjects of reading, maths and science entering into education policies and curricula. Sahlberg notes that GERM has brought a

> *focus on core subjects* in school, in other words, on literacy and numeracy, and in same [sic] case science. Basic student knowledge and skills in reading, writing and mathematics are elevated as prime targets and indices of education reforms. As a consequence of accepting international student assessment surveys, such as PISA, TIMSS [Trends in International Mathematics and Science Study] *and PIRLS* [Progress in International Reading Literacy Study], as criteria of good educational performance, reading, mathematical and scientific literacy have now become the main determinants of perceived success or failure of pupils, teachers, schools, and entire education systems. This is happening on the expense of social studies, arts, music and physical education that are diminishing in many school curricula.
>
> *(Sahlberg, 2012a, np)*

As an example, England's PISA inspired educational reforms have led to 'a serious narrowing of the curricula provided to pupils' (Morris, 2016, p. 6), including a reduction in creativity, art and music.

Sahlberg further argues that an emphasis on predetermined standards and core subjects also impoverishes education through minimising experimentation and the use of alternative pedagogical approaches: 'The higher the test-result stakes, the lower the degree of freedom in experimentation and risk-taking in classroom learning' (2011, p. 178). Instead, competitive ranking leads to schools adopting 'safe' and narrow pedagogies such as 'teaching to the test'. In this sense GERM is antithetical to teacher's professional autonomy and decision making as fear of market failure closes down educational alternatives and possibilities.

António Nóvoa (2018) also takes a critical view of the consequences of homogenisation and uniformity in education, referring to a 'solutionist drift' in recent decades entailing a belief in 'global solutions imposed by data and evidence on "what works" and "where the best results are" … [an approach] based on the false idea of consensus on the aims of education and the paths to achieving them' (ibid., p. 4). Comparative education, he argues, has increasingly moved towards a phase of prescription, with 'a celebration of "big data", allowing experts to prescribe the best solutions for the different educational systems'; perhaps, he adds, 'we can call it "dataism", the religion of data' (ibid., p. 5). Instead 'of yielding to comparisons transformed into "modes of governance"', Nóvoa urges us to 'value and reinforce difference', since there is 'no single solution for educational issues and politics'; this means 'to build a science of difference, rather than a "solution" that tends to homogenise educational directions throughout the world' (ibid., pp. 5, 11). In sum, we are in danger of losing the richness of educational diversity, stifled by an impoverishing search for a common approach to service neoliberalism's global demands.

The process of impoverishment affects not only content, pedagogy and policy solutions, but also the most fundamental ideas about what education is for and our understandings or images of pupils, teachers and schools. Under neoliberalism, education has been increasingly framed as having a primarily or even exclusively economic rationale, with the production of human capital at its core as providing the secret to economic success and growth in an increasingly competitive world. Fazal Rizvi and Bob Lingard (2009, p. 10) write that

> [As a result of the almost universal shift from social democratic to neoliberal orientations] educational purposes have been re-defined in terms of a narrower set of concerns about human capital development, and the role education must play to meet the needs of the global economy and to ensure the competitiveness of the global economy.

While David Labaree makes the same argument in blunter terms:

> From the Global Education Reform Movement (GERM) to its policy apparatus in the OECD and its policy police in the PISA testing program, we have seen one goal trump the others. Nowadays the uniform message is human capital uber [sic] alles.
>
> *(Labaree, 2017, p. 281)*

Sjøberg seconds Labaree's argument that PISA is deeply implicated in this re-purposing, narrowing and reduction of educational purpose, concluding in his essay – 'The PISA-syndrome – How the OECD has hijacked the way we perceive pupils, schools and education' – that the most fundamental and serious influence of PISA is that

> it redefines the very purpose of schooling and education. PISA claims to measure skills and competencies that are important for the future economy and employability. It thereby ignores that schools serve the much broader purpose of contributing to the personal, human and social development of the child with an overall aim to help them become well-informed and well-functioning individuals and citizens. In all countries, the obligatory school is the key socializing agent. The school provides the induction in the nation's culture, values, history and norms, and the school is a place where the developing child is exposed to a broad variety of disciplines and ways of thinking and acting. PISA assumes that this complex set of purposes of the school can be reduced to one common, standardized and measurable metric, independent of country, culture and context. It is this basic postulation that is the most serious objection to the whole PISA undertaking. PISA reduces the purpose of schooling to be what can be measured on a single dimension in a single test at a particular time in a sample of 15-year olds in school.
>
> *(Sjøberg, 2019, p. 43)*

What has happened, therefore, under neoliberalism is the economisation of education, to the exclusion of other purposes and rationales: social, cultural, aesthetic, moral and political. As Connell observes, 'neoliberalism has a definite idea about education, understanding it as human capital formation ... the business of forming the skills and attitudes needed by a productive workforce' (2013, p. 104). Under this logic, 'education is reduced to an "investment" that should be judged on the same basis as other financial investments – through future financial gain or loss ... determined by the productivity of future labour markets' (Lightfoot-Rueda and Peach, 2015, p. 7).

But perhaps the most fundamental and disturbing consequence of the impoverished environment that has followed from the neoliberalisation of compulsory schooling is the way it treats education, first and foremost, not only as an economic activity but also as a technical practice, a matter primarily of means, management and measurement. Understood in this way, education has been reduced to how best to produce and measure predefined and standardised outcomes, with one right solution, to be determined by unaccountable organisations such as the OECD supported by a battery of measures and an array of experts. This brave new world has also provided a welcoming environment for business, opening up education as a new market for its products and services and as a new source of profit and influence, and exposing education to business values and influence. This begs the question posed by Diane Ravitch: 'Are we prepared to hand over our children, our teachers, and our definition of knowledge to Pearson?' (Ravitch, 2012, np).

But education is, arguably, first and foremost a rich political practice, built upon asking political questions, questions with no one right answer, questions such as: What is our image of the child and of the school? What do we want for our children? What is education for? What are the fundamental values of education? Stephen Ball writes of the loss of this political dimension under neoliberalism, sacrificed to the pursuit of technical practice:

> in the heat and noise of reform, of initiatives and fixes and of 'what works', the issue that is neglected or ignored, or simply just pre-empted within the processes of reform, is 'what for'. Any sense of the values of education is lost in the maze of policy hyperactivity, and goals and purposes are foregone by the demands of fast policy – that is, processes of intensification and compression, new ideas, fads, and fashions moving at social-media speed (Peck & Theodore 2015). What counts as education is in the current policy context, to a great extent, formed and produced by its measurement – that is, quality in education is defined in terms of performance, and what are referred to as educational standards are rendered as performance outputs.... Educational substance is reduced to indicators or outputs.
>
> *(Ball, 2018b, p. 234)*

Political questions of image, purpose and values should generate a democratic politics of education, in which alternative answers to such questions are recognised, valued and deliberated upon, creating an education in which ends come before means, in which technical practice is subsumed to political practice. Neoliberalism, with its impoverished view of education, has stifled any signs of such a democratic politics of education.

Changed subjectivities and images

We will discuss at length in Chapter 4 how neoliberalism works not just to change behaviour but also to produce subjectivity, how we think of ourselves, as well as the images we hold of others and the institutions in our society. For now, though, we will confine ourselves to noting that neoliberalism, in the words of Sjøberg when writing about the OECD and PISA, 'hijacks the way we perceive' pupils and schools, to which we might add parents and teachers. For, under its gaze, pupils become defined in economic terms as future human capital, being prepared or readied to participate productively in the labour market as flexible and compliant workers. Parents are re-imagined as consumers, seeking to purchase the commodity of education through informed choices between competing providers in the schools market place. While teachers are no longer professionals, applying knowledge, reflection and judgement, but are reduced to technicians, whose task is to efficiently deliver prescribed and standardised outcomes by applying 'best practice', all the while being subjected to performance management; in such circumstances, 'experience is nothing, productivity is everything' (Ball, 2016b, p. 1054).

Such performance management, including tools like PRP, moves teachers away from thinking and acting professionally, instead constraining and forcing them to adhere to a performativity agenda, focused on achieving externally imposed outcomes, and learning 'to discipline themselves, as marketized, managed, and performative' (Holloway and Brass, 2018, p. 380). The results can be profound.

> For anyone not associated with education in English schools it may be hard to appreciate just how much of a hold this assessment-driven culture has over the lives of those who work in them; to a large extent it dominates the way they think and talk about their work, with assessment data being used as a proxy for the overall standard of education in a highly politicised landscape.
>
> *(Pratt, 2016, p. 892)*

Changed subjectivity reaches to the top of the school hierarchy. As neoliberalism has led to a more powerful and aggressive approach to management (Stevenson and Wood, 2013, p. 52), school principals and other senior staff

> are being re-shaped in the neoliberal imagination as a managerial class, exactly parallel to corporate managers in the private sector. With schools being redefined as firms competing with each other in a market, of course the firms need entrepreneurial managers to run them – not educators. They need managers

who control a budget, hire and fire staff, attract corporate funding, market
their product through advertizing and so on.

(Connell, 2013, p. 107)

The headteacher becomes the CEO, leading the school that has become a business,
purveying the commodity of education, striving for customers in a competitive
market place, seeking to emulate the profit-seeking corporation. This importation
of business management from profit-seeking businesses into education forces a
wholesale change in the values, cultures and practices of schools away from notions
of public service and towards a competitive market-based logic. As businesses they
operate as processing plants producing standardised outcomes or as 'exam factories',
whose worth and competitive advantage are judged in terms of test performances.

This re-imagining of schools as competitive businesses has had the consequence
of undermining any semblance of democracy in their management or everyday life,
with less participation by parents and pupils. Academy trust boards in England
recruit members who have professional business skills rather than local parents
leading to 'a fundamental shift of power away from parents. This is a reduction in
local democracy that has gone largely undetected, yet has resulted in half the student population no longer having the right of a voice in decision making' (Male,
2019, p. 2).

Inequalities, exclusions and social segregation

For both Diane Ravitch, writing about the United States, and Stephen Ball, writing about England, inserting marketisation and parent choice into education has
proved to be highly problematic. Ravitch writes that

Choice does not produce equality; choice exacerbates inequality, as a free market
produces winners and losers. Both choice and high-stakes testing erode equity by
encouraging self-segregation and by ranking that reifies socioeconomic status

(Ravitch, 2013, p. 320)

While Ball points out the way that the 'the education market is rife with gaming
and allows agile and well-resourced middle-class parents to seek out and maintain
social advantage in educational settings leading to multiple forms of social segrega-
tion' (Ball, 2018b, p. 226)

What both draw our attention to is the workings of the Matthew principle of
accumulated advantage – to those who have shall be given, or the poor get poorer
and the rich get richer. In an environment of markets and consumer choice,
middle-class parents are better able to work, and sometimes game, the system,
entrenching patterns of social advantage; they prove adept at exploiting school
admissions criteria such as religious faith, academic ability, aptitude, primary feeder
schools, and arbitrary catchment areas to ensure their children gain admission to the
'best' schools (Millar, 2018). These advantaged schools, in turn, in the face of strong

demand also know how to work the system, using their increased market power to choose which pupils they will admit. In this way, social stratification is perpetuated, and parental choice of school becomes school choice of pupils (and parents).

Greany and Higham (2018) found worrying evidence of how these processes work in England. In their study, schools sought to maintain or improve their position in the 'local status hierarchy', in particular by improving their Ofsted inspection rating. The researchers noted some of the practices adopted to achieve this goal: 'These ranged from gradual, authentic work to enhance the quality of learning and engage parents, through to aggressive marketing campaigns and "cream skimming" aimed at recruiting particular types of students' (p. 13). The obverse meant shunning children who qualify for free school meals and whose parents receive state help, i.e. the more disadvantaged members of society. The analysis by Greany and Higham showed a relationship between Ofsted inspection grades and the changing socioeconomic composition of a school's student body. Schools that sustained or improved their Ofsted inspection rating to 'outstanding' in the 2010–2015 period saw, on average, a reduction in the percentage of students eligible for free school meals, while schools downgraded to a 'requires improvement' or 'inadequate' rating saw, on average, an increase in such eligibility.

But there is more, not just selection but de-selection. A competitive economy of student worth has led to 'the widespread practice of illegitimately removing children to climb league tables' (Adams, 2019, np) in a practice known as 'off-rolling', witnessed by 25% of England's teachers. In these illegal exclusions 'schools are playing the system and getting rid of children who might do badly in their GCSEs [national exams taking by 15- and 16-year-olds in England] and compromise the school's performance in league tables' (Weale, 2018, np). Pupils with special educational needs (SEN), eligible for free school meals, looked after by local authorities and from some minority ethnic groups are more likely to leave their school just ahead of GCSEs. Within this competitive schools' market economy of student worth, headteachers and governors protect and prioritise their school's performance outputs and league table positioning over the rights of vulnerable families and children.

Neoliberalism is a mutually reinforcing system of winners and losers. Middle-class children getting into 'best' schools are among the winning pupils; off-rolled children among the losers. The same dichotomy applies to schools. For Millar (2018) the competitive schools market has a 'dark side' leading to winner and loser schools. 'Winner schools' benefit from the schools' market as they can attract and choose to admit more aspirant, advantaged and supportive families, due to their enhanced socio-economic location and because they use some form of selective entry criteria. Over time they become more popular as they constantly improve and sustain strong performance in the competitive environment. The schools market compounds problems for schools located in poor socio-economic areas who are struggling in league tables and finding it hard to recruit teachers. For example, schools serving the most disadvantaged communities are less likely to be successful in Ofsted inspections (Hutchinson, 2016), leading to further problems of recruitment and retention of teachers, in turn leading to poorer results. These virtuous and vicious circles have led to greater polarisation of performance between the best schools and the worst and the creation of 'local status hierarchies'.

This 'academic stratification is always closely linked to social stratification' (Whitty, 2000, p. 7), and the English education system continues 'to be decisively marked by very clear relations between performance and social class, and poverty and access' (Ball, 2018, p. 23). Hence despite the 1988 Education Reform Act, 'it would take fifty years to close the attainment gap between England's most disadvantaged pupils and their wealthier peers' (ibid.). Indeed, the schools' market has served to compound and exacerbate differences between schools located in different socio-economic contexts so that 'in some areas there is an even steeper hierarchy than it was in 1988' (Millar, 2018, p. 106). For example, Ofsted have noted the existence of a small group of schools in England that have been rated as 'inadequate' or 'requires improvement' consistently since 2005. These schools have been described as 'intractable' and are predominately located in poorer socio-economic areas, accounting for 10% of all secondary schools in the North East, Yorkshire and the Humber and the East Midlands, and 7% of secondary schools in the North West, but just 3% in the South East and South West, and 2% of those in London (Whittaker, 2018).

Though neoliberalism, through its reliance on markets and individual choice, exacerbates inequality and exclusion, it translates these deep-seated structural problems into individual failings. Those children and families who are cast into the role of 'losers' in this highly competitive environment have no-one to blame but themselves; the fault is individual not societal, a failure to be a savvy consumer, an effective entrepreneur of the self, a high performing business. In this way, neoliberalism turns its own adverse consequences back on the victims of its harsh regime.

The 'terrors of performativity'

This haunting phrase has been coined by Stephen Ball (2003), who uses the term 'performativity' to 'refer to systems of performance management or the deployment of performance indicators' but also to 'the complex and powerful relationships between such indicators and management systems and teacher identity and professionalism' (Ball, 2016b, p. 1052); it is a form of steering or managing at a distance which 'replaces intervention and prescription with target setting, accountability, and comparison' (Ball, 1998, p. 123), deploying technologies such as performance indicators, league tables, result-oriented management, monitoring systems and performance auditing (Schwandt, 2003). In regimes of performativity, everything and everyone is focused on achieving high performance as measured against externally defined standards or, put another way, performativity is 'a technology that relates effort, values, purposes and self-understanding directly to measures and comparisons of output' (Ball, 2003, p. 1053).

In this context, the 'terrors of performativity' refer to an assemblage of negative effects of neoliberalism on the health and well-being of those on the receiving end, namely teachers and pupils, both of whom share neoliberal contexts that privilege individual competition, accountability and management, and that rely on the motivating stimulus of anxieties, fears and insecurities. These negative effects take various forms. Teachers work longer and more intensely: for example, full-time secondary teachers in England report they spend almost as much time on management, administration, marking and lesson planning (20.1 hours a week) as they do teaching (20.5 hours), while a quarter of all teachers work more than 60 hours a week during term-time, far in excess of their counterparts elsewhere in the world (Allen, Benhenda, Jerrim and Sims, 2019).

The prospect of failing to perform as required – to miss targets set, to contribute to a poor Ofsted rating – generates fear: the fear of job loss or a school's forced 'academisation'. Indeed, fear is an integral part of managing performance, for to be effective such management needs to be 'threaded together by narratives of failure, fragmentation and fear' (Stevenson and Wood, 2013, p. 53). Fear takes its toll on well-being. Teachers show 'growing levels of stress and anxiety … within top-down low-trust performativity cultures and [research studies] show a strong negative (unintended) outcome for the well-being of the teaching profession' (Simmie, 2014, p. 189). A literature review of 'teacher well-being in neoliberal contexts' concludes that

> neoliberal policy regimes are deeply problematic for establishing a sense of professional wellbeing in teachers. These ideologies are enacted through policies of accountability and managerialism and performativity technologies such as NAPLAN and My School; the resulting work intensification and exclusion of the emotional labour of teachers opposes what is indicated as necessary for supporting wellness and professional flourishing. These impositions shape teachers' work and can be seen as incompatible with the themes identified in wellbeing literature of valuing emotional work, collegiality and collaboration and establishing a workplace climate that respects teachers' professional decisions and encourages a healthy work-life balance.
>
> *(Acton and Glasgow, 2015, p. 110)*

The wear and tear of performativity also shows itself in teacher retention – teachers voting with their feet in the face of often intolerable conditions. In the United States, 44% of teachers leave teaching within five years of qualifying (Will, 2018). In England, the retention rates of early career teachers are

> lower now than they were a few years ago. Around 87% of teachers who enter teaching remained in the profession at the end of their first year, which is a figure that hasn't changed since 2010, until this year [2017] when it decreased to 85%. Worse still, the three-year retention rate has dropped from 80% in 2011 to 73% in 2017 and the five-year rate has dropped from 73% in 2011 to 67% in 2017.
>
> *(Worth, 2018, np)*

In 2016, the equivalent of 10.4% of the secondary school teaching workforce in England left teaching in publicly funded schools. The number of teachers going 'out of service' (that is, not retiring) rose from 25,260 in 2011 to 34,910 in 2016, a 38% increase (Ball, 2018b, p. 232). Ball blames these losses on neoliberalism's restless 'policy hyperactivity' in which 'the teacher is defined by and tied to systems of performance-related pay and positioned as part of what Barber (2007) calls the delivery chain and its necessarian logic' (ibid., p. 235). In short, it's the price of the neoliberalising of education.

The 'terrors of performativity' are not confined to teachers. During the past 30 years or so of neoliberalism, pupils have become 'children of the market' (Keddie, 2016, p. 109). Their educational experiences have been forged in an environment of competitive individualism, which pupils have come to experience as natural, normal and taken for granted; pupils unquestionably 'live a "performative" and entrepreneurial existence of calculation that involves organising themselves in response to targets, indicators and evaluations' (Keddie, 2016, p. 115). These children of the market speak about themselves in terms of measuring, comparing and evaluating their worth against external tests and in competitive relation to other pupils' performance. But this relentless performative pressure, for academic excellence and improvement, comes at the price of anxiety, self-doubt and dissatisfaction as pupils struggle to maintain their success or worry that they are not good enough. As this Year 5 primary school pupil (aged 9–10 years), Sophia, explains

> I do try hard but I hope it's hard enough.... I still get As but the thing is … I'm still not amazing. The thing is now I'm having tuitions [for] Maths and Science … sometimes I wonder if, I really want to be one of the top students … I don't think … I don't put enough pressure on myself, that's the point. I don't push myself as I could do.
>
> *(Keddie, 2016, p. 115)*

Rebecca, in Year 6 (aged 10–11 years), expresses similar dissatisfaction at her performance in a maths competition aimed at pupils in Year 8.

> I got a Bronze medal and I was annoyed because I didn't get the Silver, if I had got Silver I would have been annoyed because I didn't get Gold. If I got Gold I would have been annoyed because I hadn't got into the Europe Championship, if I got into the Europe Championship I'd be annoyed because I didn't win. If I did win … I would be annoyed because my handwriting wasn't neat enough. It's like I appreciate it but then I think about all the stuff I could have done better and then I just end up annoyed.
>
> *(ibid., p 108)*

Both children in Amanda Kiddie's study had learnt to be entrepreneurial and that success or failure in tests was an individualised and personal responsibility that they took seriously. The fear of failure was real, most of the young children in the study noting 'quite simply, [that] working or studying hard were key to getting a good education, a good job and a good future, the absence of which would mean a life of menial jobs or even living on the streets' (Keddie, 2016, p. 118).

English primary school pupils, such as these, are subject to regular testing (discussed in Chapter 5). Many headteachers are concerned about the effects on children; in a study of primary school headteachers, 83% agreed that 'SATs have a negative impact on pupils' wellbeing', the main concerns being about stress and anxiety, and the impact on pupils with SEND and those seen as 'vulnerable' (Bradbury, 2019). Referring to Year 6 SATs (for 11-year-olds), this primary school headteacher thought

> it causes a lot of mental health, being stressed, especially for vulnerable children. [...] I mean, the first year they introduced the new papers, was the first year in this school we had kids in tears. And that breaks your heart – kids sitting SATs in tears. And what's worse.... What's worse than the kids in tears is you thinking I still want them to finish the frigging paper, even though I don't really, because I love that child and I don't want to put them through it.
>
> *(ibid., p. 30)*

Hutchings (2015) in a national report on the impacts of school tests and accountability described England's schools as 'Exam Factories'. She noted that

> teachers complain that low achievement at tests or exams is resulting in low pupil motivation and low self-esteem. One secondary school teacher at an unnamed school said 'self-harming is rife' at key stage 4 (14- to 16-year-olds) and reported that a pupil was hospitalised for three months in a psychiatric ward following a suicide attempt, another nearly starved herself to death and numerous other students 'suffered from symptoms that are on the questionnaires that the NHS uses to diagnose depression'.
>
> *(Hutchins, 2015, p. 59)*

Similarly, a recent study has noted how, due to a number of overlapping factors including exam stress, one in five young women have self-harmed (Campbell, 2019). Given the above, it is not surprising that the 2015 PISA survey found that 'schoolchildren in Britain are more likely to be miserable and less likely to think that their lives have meaning compared with children in other countries' (Adams and Barr, 2019, np).

This overview has shown how far neoliberalism has reached into compulsory education, especially but not only in the Anglophone world, and in the process changed its structure, purpose, ethos and identity, as well as bringing a wide range of often adverse consequences. It is no exaggeration to say that what has occurred over the last 30 years has been revolutionary – but a revolution not from below, rather a top-down transformation that has been scripted and fuelled by powerful actors deploying their substantial resources. We turn now to look at how neoliberalism has shaped and influenced early childhood education and care, bearing in mind the qualification with which we started this chapter about the different circumstances of early childhood, compared to compulsory education, when the neoliberal age dawned in the 1980s; the effect for ECEC, it might be said, has been more evolutionary than revolutionary. We will look in particular at neoliberalism's impact on image or subjectivity and on governance and management, but first at how that cornerstone of neoliberal thinking, market logic, has manifested itself.

3

NEOLIBERALISM AND MARKETS

Markets are at the heart of neoliberalism. They are where neoliberalism's virtues – commodification, competition, calculation, choice – are enacted and honed, to achieve neoliberalism's great goal, the efficient allocation of resources, 'a state in which all goods and services are produced and consumed at socially optimal levels such that individual and societal well-being are maximised' (Harbach, 2015, p. 677). Put another way, from a neoliberal perspective markets are the perfect way to achieve a range of valued outcomes: meeting consumers' needs and preferences while protecting them from the self-seeking behaviour of providers; driving down prices while driving up quality; and eliminating unresponsive and inflexible services while stimulating innovation through producing solutions to the requirements and demands of consumers. In neoliberalism's world-view, therefore, introducing and expanding markets is the answer to every social, economic and political problem – including the provision and improvement of early childhood education and care. 'Market logic' pervades this sector as much as other sectors of education.

Markets can form of their own accord, as buyers and sellers come together to trade products (though usually such markets move to some form of external regulation). But the process can be actively promoted and supported by governments through deliberate acts of public policy. This process of 'marketisation' refers to 'government measures that authorise, support or enforce the introduction of markets, the creation of relationships between buyers and sellers and the use of market mechanisms to allocate care' (Brennan, Cass, Himmelweit and Szebehely, 2012, p. 379) – or any other commodity.

Marketisation has been pursued across a wide range of services, for people of all ages.

> The use of markets and market mechanisms to deliver [childcare and eldercare] is one of the most significant and contentious ways in which welfare states have been transformed.... In the last quarter of the 20th century, enthusiasm

for neo-liberal ideas about competition and choice, together with increasing pressures on public finances, have led many governments to adopt policies that foster markets in care and encourage for-profit providers

(ibid., pp. 377–378)

England has been at the forefront of this process of marketising services, including eldercare, universities, compulsory education – and early childhood education and care. For many years after the end of the Second World War, 'childcare services' for young children (or 'daycare' as they were commonly referred to then) were provided mainly by childminders, individuals offering a service in their own homes. An informal market operated, with low demand and minimal official oversight. Then from the end of the 1980s, demand for childcare services rose rapidly, as more women with young children returned to full-time employment (Brannen and Moss, 1998). The result was an explosive growth in private childcare provision in England. The number of places with childminders doubled between 1989 and 1997 (from 186,500 to 365,000), but this rate of increase was outpaced by private day nurseries, where places nearly quadrupled (from 46,500 to 173,500) (Department of Health (England), 1997); in less than a decade a large market in private and mainly for-profit childcare centres had emerged.

It was only in 1997 that government made ECEC a policy priority, with a 'new Labour' government now actively seeking to support employed parents; beforehand, successive national administrations had treated parental employment and the provision of 'childcare' as primarily a private responsibility, with the regulation of private providers left to local authorities. Marketisation was a central strategy of this new policy priority. The existing market in 'childcare' was supported and enhanced: subsidies, via the tax system, were made available to lower income parents to help them enter and purchase services in the market, so-called demand-side funding (as opposed to supply-side funding, made direct to providers); a national and uniform system of inspection replaced the previous local and more varied approach, with reports of inspections of individual services made publicly available, to increase market information for consumers; while a duty was placed on local authorities, not to provide services themselves but to manage their local childcare market to ensure sufficiency of private supply.

The result of this active support of marketisation of 'childcare' services is celebrated in this report on the market by a private consultancy:

Despite the economic downturns in 2001 and 2008, the childcare market [in the United Kingdom] has demonstrated remarkable resilience and has continued to grow year on year. This growth in overall market size will continue at a possibly even faster rate in the coming years as further government intervention and funding becomes inevitable.... The UK market for formal childcare is valued at £5.5 billion in 2018. This represents faster value growth than market volumes would suggest as settings and places have decreased.... Overall, there is increasing interest in the UK nurseries market from both UK and international private equity groups and financial investors. However, genuine growth platforms of scale remain scarce.

(*LaingBuisson, 2019, np*)

Marketisation of early childhood provision in England has not been confined to 'childcare' services. It has also been actively pursued in 'early education', following the post-1997 introduction of a part-time, free entitlement for all 3- and 4-year-olds. Delivery of this entitlement was not restricted by government to schools, with their nursery classes; delivery was also opened up to any early childhood provider who could meet certain conditions. Not only were schools competing between each other for children (a feature of the English school scene since 1988, when the market was first introduced into compulsory education), but schools were competing with day nurseries, childminders and other private 'childcare' providers.

Today, the market in childcare and early education is so deeply embedded in England that it has become taken-for-granted; few find it cause for comment and public policy refers to a market in services for young children as if it was the most natural thing in the world, as if there were no alternatives. To take just three examples. In 2015, the English Department for Education, with the support of Deloitte (which describes itself as 'a leading global provider of 'audit, consulting, financial advisory, risk management, tax, and related services' (www2.deloitte.com/ru/en/pages/about-deloitte/articles/about-deloitte.html)), produced a report sub-titled 'An economic assessment of the early education and childcare market and providers' costs'. The Department describes the purpose of the report in the following terms: 'As a major purchaser in the childcare market, government also wanted a better understanding of the state of the market, its strengths and weaknesses and to learn about the business practices of the most efficient providers in the market' (Department for Education (England), 2015a, p. 4). What follows includes a section on 'market strengths' and 'market weaknesses', while altogether the word 'market' appears 152 times in a 96-page document: but never once is the concept of 'childcare' or the aptness of marketisation questioned.

Three years later, the Treasury Committee of the UK House of Commons, undertook an enquiry into 'Childcare', its brief including:

> how well the [English] Government's childcare schemes address the stated overarching policy aims of: 'delivering an efficient childcare market, which is getting good value for money, high-quality and affordable for parents, helping with child development, and helping parents into work, particularly focused on the lowest-income parents'.

While the Committee's report covers such issues as 'the economic impact of child-care', 'the design of Government's childcare schemes', and 'identified problems within childcare policy implementation', once again neither the concept of 'childcare' itself nor the goal of 'delivering an efficient childcare market' is questioned (House of Commons Treasury Committee, 2018).

The third example is the way market language has become widely accepted in discussing early childhood education and care. It is not just the incessant use of the term 'market' itself, but a whole vocabulary of associated trading language, 'market speak' we might say: terms such as 'value growth', 'private equity', 'financial investors', 'growth platforms', 'portfolio platforms', 'premium multiples'. For us, we must admit, this language grates, being totally at odds with how we think and talk about early childhood education and care; yet obviously for others it is a perfectly natural way to think and talk, an unexceptionable usage that needs no justification or apology.

Markets are not necessarily confined to private services. As the example of England's early education entitlement shows, public services, such as schools, can be made to compete with each other and with private service providers through marketisation. But in practice, marketisation usually comes with privatisation, the stimulation of private providers to enter the market; and while this process can include not-for-profit providers (and in some countries, such as Germany and Norway, these providers are in the majority), in countries where neoliberalism is rife the main entrants are more likely to be for-profit businesses; for example, 'the UK is out on a limb in Europe in the extent to which it has deliberately and successfully promoted the for-profit private sector' (Penn, 2014, p. 454), which in 2019 accounted for 82% (by value) of the 'day nursery market' (Gaunt, 2020c) This association of marketisation and privatisation is not co-incidental. It reflects neoliberals' deep suspicion of, if not downright antipathy to, the public sector as inefficient and self-serving, altogether untrustworthy, and its strong preference for the private sector, driven so it is believed to ever-greater efficiency and innovation by the profit motive and business methods.

In the remainder of this chapter, we consider the evidence on the consequences of marketisation, and its attendant condition of privatisation, including the question of how far ECEC markets succeed in achieving their aspirations – and to the extent they do not, why not. We do not, at this stage, question those aspirations, or indeed the supposed virtues of the marketplace in which neoliberalism believes; that is a subject for the final chapter. But first, we outline the global spread of markets and marketisation in early childhood education and care, and in particular in the 'childcare' sector, for it is here, more so than in 'early education', that markets and their logic are most widely and deeply embedded.

The global presence of markets and marketisation

Markets in early childhood education, and particularly in 'childcare' services, are most often associated with the Anglophone world, that group of English-speaking countries that shares certain beliefs and attitudes about the welfare state, encapsulated by the term 'liberal welfare regime'. Such regimes, it has been argued, are characterised by flat-rate, means-tested benefits, a belief in private responsibility for 'care', and an emphasis on private provision and market solutions (Esping-Andersen, 1990). We have already shown how one of these countries, England, has placed markets at the heart of government policy on both childcare and early childhood education, but the same is true of other Anglophone countries, for whom marketisation has become an article of faith.

In neighbouring Ireland, '[t]he dominant model of childcare … is a market one, with expensive fees, variable quality and a regulatory system which focuses on health and safety issues and not children's development' (Society of St Vincent de Paul, 2016, p. 1). A report by An Oifig Buiséid Pharlaiminteach (the Parliamentary Budget Office) (2019), titled 'Childcare in Ireland: An Analysis of Market Dynamics, Public Programmes and Accessibility', examines, *inter alia*, 'The child-care market in Ireland' under the headings of 'demand', 'supply' and 'costs'. Most 'childcare' provision, over 85% by one estimate (Penn, 2014), is in the private, for-profit sector. 'Early education', however, is predominantly provided in primary schools, attended by most 4-year-olds and nearly all 5-year olds; over 90% of these schools are controlled by the Catholic church (O'Kelly, 2018).

On the other side of the world, early childhood education and care in Australia and New Zealand has shifted from the community to

> becoming more commodified and subject to the market than any other form of education, leading to a neo-liberal hegemony … [that] has not only nor-malised the dominance of the market in the provision of such services for children, [but] appears to have limited our capacity to consider/envision the role and positioning of ECEC in society in alternative ways.
>
> *(Press, Woodrow, Logan and Mitchell, 2018, p. 329)*

In Australia, a pivotal moment was the extension in 1991 of public subsidies from community-run, non-profit services to include private, for-profit provision, a move that was followed by a rapid expansion of these providers. Over the last three decades

> a large and sophisticated market in early childhood education and care (ECEC) has emerged […] reforms since the 1980s have underpinned a 'radical mar-ketisation' of the sector […] and by 2017 for-profit companies provided nearly half of all ECEC services […] Government policy has shifted from supply-side finance in the form of operational subsidies and capital grants, to demand side support in the form of direct subsidies to parents.
>
> *(Hill and Wade, 2018, p. 21)*

New Zealand, also, has increased public funding for both not-for-profit and for-profit services, though unlike Australia this has taken the form of direct funding of services. A rapid advance of commercial providers has followed. The result has been that the

> current early childhood education sector [which in New Zealand covers all early childhood services] operates on a market model, albeit funded by a large

public subsidy. Over the past decade, this has led to a small number of corporate and other private players dominating service ownership (teacher-led services including kindergarten) of 54.44% of the sector, and a steady decline in kindergarten, community and other not-for-profit services.

(New Zealand Educational Institute, 2019, np)

Linda Mitchell (2019) writes of how this commodification of early childhood education and care has manifested itself.

Capacity to make profits from early childhood education in New Zealand is well established and advertised. Simply google 'childcare profits' and information about returns for investment in the 'business of childcare' abound. Under the heading 'Booming childcare sector draws investors', the Business section of the national newspaper, the New Zealand Herald, published this: 'Early childhood education is big business in New Zealand and right now it's a seller's market as developers and investors seek to capitalise on the surge in demand for places at childcare centres.' It went on to state that high child participation rates, secure and reliable government funding and population growth 'presents an opportunity for smart property investors' (Business Herald, 4 February, 2017).

(Mitchell, 2019, p. 83)

In the United States, 'a sizeable childcare market has developed. [...] [A]s parents increasingly outsource childcare, it has moved from the private home to the market place [...] [and] today the market provides a significant portion of care (roughly one third) for America's young children' (Harbach, 2015, pp. 659, 662, 668). A similar situation can be found in Canada, which 'for the most part, takes a consumerist approach to child care – substantially relying on a market model' (Friendly, Larsen, Feltham, Grady, Forer and Jones, 2018, p. xi). Jane Beach and Carolyn Ferns argue that 'the child care market shapes every aspect of child care services', including a reliance on private services:

heavy reliance on private (both non-profit and for-profit) licensed services and unregulated arrangements goes hand in hand with a child care market approach because initiating and managing services is a private – not public – responsibility in a market. Parents are left on their own to piece together arrangements with little support

(Beach and Ferns, 2015, p. 58)

But markets in early childhood education are not confined to the English-speaking world. They are spread far more widely. In Continental Europe, there has been a strong policy push for marketisation of 'childcare' (England is unusual in marketising both 'childcare' and 'early education'). As well as England and Ireland, the Netherlands has been at the forefront of this movement. The Dutch Child

Care Act 2005 aimed 'to emphasise parental choice and competition by fostering a private market for childcare. [...] [C]onsumers [were] expected to select the provider that offers best price/quality ratio'; the hope was that 'market forces should therefore increase both internal and external efficiency' (Akgunduz and Plantenga, 2014, pp. 380, 384). Marketisation has led to a big increase in for-profit providers (Penn, 2014), a development less apparent elsewhere in Continental Europe, at least where information is available.

Further afield, the growth of the private-for-profit sector within markets has been extremely rapid, becoming the default option in most low- and middle-income countries (Lloyd and Penn, 2014). 'Childcare' markets are thriving in Asia, with 'early childhood education and teacher education in Asia ... increasingly governed by neoliberal policies, leading to peak activities in privatization, consumerism, standardization and high-stakes testing' (Gupta, 2018, p. 11). Reviewing recent developments in five Asian countries (China, India, Maldives, Singapore and Sri Lanka), Amita Gupta identifies a common theme of neoliberal forces affecting early childhood education and care, marked by increasing private provision with 'centers positioned primarily as businesses and described in market-based language ... transforming them into commodities for consumers' (ibid., pp. 20, 23).

In India, a 2017 report, catchily titled 'India Preschool/Child Care Market By Facility, By Age Group, By Location, Competition Forecast & Opportunities, 2012–2022', predicts a 23% increase in the market by 2022, with 'full day care' services dominating. The research director of the company producing this report adds:

> Preschools & child care market [sic] is booming in India owing to increasing interest among parents for quality early education for their children, as well as due to emerging franchise model to scale up operations among preschool chain owners. Owing to these factors, Indian preschool market is expected to flourish in the coming years. Further, rising income levels and increasingly busy lifestyle, coupled with favorable government initiatives to support child education, are expected to have a significantly positive impact on the country's preschool & child care market over the next five years.
>
> (TechSci Research, 2017, np)

(The above quote is taken from the report's press release, the book's authors being unable and unwilling to pay the $2,500 cost of buying the full report.)

Markets for early childhood education and care are not confined to 'neoliberal' India's emergent middle class, who are abandoning government schools in large numbers (NUEPA, 2016). Arathi Sriprakash and her colleagues have described how such markets have spread throughout the country, including to poor families in rural areas:

> normative discourses of 'school readiness' govern family strategies for early childhood care and education (ECCE). To navigate the demands of a competitive and socially stratified school system, marginalised families saw it as crucial for their

young children to access multiple forms of educational capital: written literacy, discipline, and dominant caste-class codes. In the absence of functioning provision of ECCE by the state, the low-fee and low-quality private market of early childhood education was seen as a key site through which 'school readiness' could be secured … poor families [are] incorporating themselves into a competitive, highly marketized system of low-quality and often developmentally inappropriate early childhood education.

> (Sriprakash, Maithreyi, Kumar, Sinha and Prabha, 2020, p. 331, 332)

Markets and marketisation are also flourishing in other Asian countries. Singapore has 'a private, marketized and even corporatized [ECEC] system', its market described as a 'neoliberal endeavour' (Lim, 2017, pp. 17, 21). Branding of private schools and the emergence of 'niche schools' marketing particular features has become very popular (Gupta, 2018). In China, neoliberalism has led to increasing privatisation of a system that, unlike Singapore, has had a public sector presence. The welfare model of the kindergarten, which was regarded as an outcome of the socialist system, is being changed by neoliberal market reform as Chinese kindergartens have increasingly become self-managed small businesses (Gu, 2006). Between 2001 and 2007, the proportion of early childhood services in the public sector fell from 60% to 40%, while private providers grew from 40% to 60% (Zhou, 2011). Private kindergartens have continued to develop at a faster rate than public ones. By the end of 2013 there were 133,451 private kindergartens, an increase of 8,813 (7.1%) from 2012, accounting for 67.2% of the total number of kindergartens nationwide.

Even the language used to describe some kindergartens is market-based, with an emphasis on marketing brands. One website presents the following description:

> private preschool education institutions in China include Etonkids, Golden Kids International School, Kid Castle, R.Y.B, Golden Cradle, etc, of which Etonkids and Golden Kids International School brand themselves as high-end providers. As far as business model is concerned, Etonkids adopts the model of direct operation, and Golden Kids International School employs a combined model of direct operation and holding venture.

> (Gupta, 2018, p. 17)

In Korea, 'changes in the early 2000s have expanded provision, actively using market forces and market mechanisms' (Chon, 2018, p. 6); legal requirements for private providers were relaxed, overall levels of regulation have remained low and a system of fee subsidy (the childcare benefit card system) was introduced. In both Korea and Japan, more services come from 'market providers' (i.e. private providers) than from public bodies (An, 2013, p. 41). Hong Kong has introduced a voucher system for its private (mostly not-for-profit) kindergartens to make these services for 3- to 6-year-olds more affordable to parents and so increase their ability to participate in this early education marketplace (Yuen and Lam, 2017); vouchers provide another form of demand-side subsidy that was first advocated by Milton Friedman, the godfather of neoliberalism.

As a final example from Asia, early childhood education in Indonesia began to receive greater attention in the 2000s, encouraged by international agencies such as UNESCO and the World Bank, the latter institution having exerted major influence on early childhood education in Asia and beyond through its extensive lending programme. Provision for 3- to 6-year-olds is made in kindergartens, either 'general' or 'Islamic', and nearly all of these are provided privately. According to Vina Adriany, a market operates in which providers strive to attract parent-consumers:

> a growing number of early childhood education institutions follow market-driven pre-school programmes or are operated by international franchises.... Many market-driven school programmes are franchises of global international programmes such as High Scope, Tumble Tots, Beyond Centre and Circle Time (BCCT) and many more.
>
> *(Adriany, 2019, p. 81)*

Early childhood as big business

Under neoliberalism, with its drive for privatisation and marketisation, early childhood education and care, and especially 'childcare', has become big business and on a global scale. Markets have opened up and expanded, where parent-consumers and provider-businesses trade in the commodities of 'child care' and 'education', with the child reduced to being the passive object of these transactions. But marketisation has gone further. There is now a trade in services themselves, in which private nurseries or schools are bought and sold in the marketplace: these institutions have themselves become tradable commodities.

For example, Bright Horizons is a large company running over 300 nurseries in the UK and Ireland and over 1,000 worldwide; its US parent company has a market capitalisation of more than $4.5 billion. It wants to get bigger. In the UK, the company is 'looking to expand our existing portfolio', by developing purpose-built nurseries, converting existing buildings into nurseries, or acquiring individual nurseries or nursery groups – but not anywhere; 'target locations' for expansion must be 'affluent residential areas'. Recent acquisitions include 'kidsunlimited Day Nurseries' (65 nurseries, 2013), Active Learning (nine nurseries, 2015), Asquith Nurseries with Asquith Nannies (94 nurseries, 2016), Zoom Nurseries (five nurseries, 2018) and Yellow Dot Nurseries (12 nurseries, 2018) (Bright Horizons, 2019).

Such large-scale companies increasingly trade across national borders seeking out business opportunities in new countries – they have become multi-national. Christie and Co., whose business is buying and selling businesses, ranging from pubs and hotels to childcare and education, excitedly report in their 'Business Outlook 2018' that

At the start of 2017, we saw [in England] the first major inbound investment in M&A [merger and acquisition] activity from an overseas provider for almost two decades when Magic Nurseries, with 16 children's day nurseries, was sold to Les Petits Chaperons Rouges, a leading private nursery chain in France. The Magic portfolio, comprising a largely freehold estate with 1,076 places, was sold amid much competitive tension from a large, and wide-ranging pool of prospective buyers. The successful purchasers swiftly went on to acquire a further 20 nurseries in September and now have more than 3,000 places – ranking them as a top 10 UK provider – a position secured in less than 12 months following their initial UK entry acquisition.

(Christie and Co., 2018, np)

In early 2019, another French company moved into the UK nursery market. La Maison Bleue, one of the three largest nursery groups in France, as well as the largest in Switzerland and second largest in Luxembourg, bought the Old Station Nursery company and its nine nurseries in England, to add to its existing tally of 300 nurseries. La Maison Bleue is 'backed by investors TowerBrook [a private equity company] and Bpifrance [an investment bank] with a strong ambition to become a leading player in Europe' (Nursery World, 2019a, np). Such corporate investors have identified early childhood education and care as a profitable field.

Cross-border M&A has also gone in the other direction. Busy Bees, the largest nursery group in the UK with over 31,000 places in 2018 and majority-owned by the Ontario Teachers' Pension Plan, bought its first overseas nurseries in 2015 when it purchased 60 centres in Singapore and Malaysia from Knowledge Universal. In 2017 as well as buying Treetops Nurseries in the UK, with its 61 nurseries, it also acquired 78 BrightPath nurseries, run by Canada's only publicly-traded childcare chain. At the start of 2018, Busy Bees announced it was expanding into China:

The nursery group, which already has a 200-place setting in the country, will open a further five settings in China this year, followed by another 27 by 2023, in partnership with its Chinese stakeholder – Oriental Cambridge Education Group (OCEG).

The 'international pre-schools' will be based in locations including Beijing, Shanghai, Nanjing and Xiamen. The setting in Shanghai will provide 230 places for children from three months to six years old. The deal is expected to generate almost £75 million over five years in projected income for Busy Bees and OCEG.

(Nursery World, 2018a, np)

A few months later, Busy Bees had expanded further, this time into Australia, buying Foundation Early Learning, a group with 30 nurseries, whose shareholders included private equity funds. In early 2019, Busy Bees was on the move again, this time buying Giraffe Childcare in the Republic of Ireland, with its 21 nurseries in the greater Dublin area, and bringing the company's nursery tally in the UK and Ireland to 375, with 35,000 children (Nursery World, 2019b). The international buying spree continued, with the acquisition in September 2019 of two more companies, 'Educational Playcare' (19 nurseries in Connecticut) and Doremi (7 nurseries in Milan). The group's CEO, a qualified accountant and previously a partner at Deloitte (see page 64) and a Chief Financial Officer for American multinational General Electric, set out the economic rationale for these latest transactions: '[They] allow us to enter two new markets in the United States and Italy, strengthening our global portfolio and bringing further talent into the Busy Bees business' (Morton, 2019a, np). Expansion in the United States has continued, with the acquisition of EduKids and their 15 centres in New York state (Gaunt, 2020).

Such rapid growth requires capital, some of which has been supplied by a deal done in 2017 with Temasek, Singapore's state investment agency:

> In December, Busy Bees signed a new business partnership with Singapore-based company Temasek, in what was thought to be the biggest nursery investment deal of the year. Temasek acquired a strategic minority stake in the UK's largest nursery group from majority shareholder the Ontario Teachers' Pension Plan.
>
> *(Nursery World, 2018b, np)*[1]

Neoliberalism has opened up other business opportunities in the early childhood field, beyond the provision of services. A by-product of the spread of markets and private providers is the proliferation of 'childcare support industries', facilitating the workings of the market and the private for-profit businesses that make up so much of the marketplace. In New Zealand, there are 'special finance companies', such as *Childcare Finance NZ*, tailored to the specific needs of early childhood services and, in particular, the demand from private service providers for bridging loans to meet the delay in bulk funding payments from government. While in the same country,

> the pressure to meet the reporting demands for [receiving public] funding, particularly as centres increase enrolments and services grow more complex in the kinds of services being offered, has led to the development of a range of specialised software packages for childcare providers. Packages such as *Datacom* and *Inforcare* offer cloud computing for the management of services and help keep track of student's attendance, payroll and so on.
>
> *(Gallagher, 2017, p. 7)*

In England, companies sell similar and additional services to nurseries. For example, Kinderley offers 'Kinderley Together', described as 'award winning nursery management software', which promises to 'streamline EYFS [the English early years curriculum] admin', 'improve tracking and support development' and 'enhance positive engagement with parents', as well as 'better financial management and easy invoicing' (https://kinderly.co.uk/eyfs-app-for-nurseries/). While another software product, 'Kinderley Learn', is an online platform for staff training and continuing professional development, which includes 'bite-sized learning for busy practitioners', a learning bite being a 'piece of learning that will take between 2–5 minutes to complete' (https://kinderly.co.uk/cpd-training/).

Offering yet another support service, Morton Michel advertises itself as a 'childcare insurance specialist', and was a sponsor to 'Childcare Expo' 2019. Childcare Expo is held in three English cities annually, and is advertised as 'an inspiring and informative free event tailored for the early years, primary education and childcare sectors … "where early years means business"'. Then there are property agents who specialise in the buying and selling of private day nurseries, Christie and Co., for example, who we just saw welcoming the entry of a French company into the English day nursery market. In December 2019, this company had 90 nurseries and nursery groups for sale on its books, as well as a range of other services in what they refer to as the 'child centric sector', which spans 'ECEC, children's day nurseries, kindergartens, independent schools, private tuition colleges, outward bounds activity centres, specialist childcare, looked after childcare services, family activities and attractions'. Describing themselves as the 'the market leaders and sector "go to" advisors, from conception to exit', Christie and Co.

> continue to see unprecedented prices for quality businesses being achieved across the UK, Europe and Internationally … [and] take great pleasure in assisting UK, European and global ECEC operators and investors with their business planning, mergers, acquisitions and divestment activity, alongside providing a range of consultancy, valuation, investment and landlord and tenant advisory services.
>
> *(Christie and Co., 2019, np)*

In June 2019, the company's managing director of childcare and education reported bullishly that

> [d]uring the first six months of 2019, while deal volumes have stabilised, the premiums achieved for the most desirable businesses have continued to rise. Demand across the market for businesses of all sizes remains incredibly strong, and indeed the primary trend of 2019 thus far is that demand from buyers is exceeding supply.
>
> *(Nursery World, 2019c, np)*

Another English company, LaingBuisson, describes itself as a 'business intelligence provider' offering 'market, policy and strategy insights, data and analysis across health care and social care'. Its services include regular reports on the UK childcare market, the 15th edition of which is quoted from earlier in this chapter (page 63). These market reports are intended for a wide range of readers – including banks, private equity investors, management consultants and business advisors. The latest, 16th report is advertised as 'vital reading for anyone involved in this highly competitive sector of the UK economy, be they providers, investors or advisors to the sector', the hardback copy selling for £895 (LaingBuisson, 2020).

Similar organisations offer 'intelligence' about the market in other countries and regions. EducationInvestor Global advertises itself as the 'definitive source of financial and market intelligence for the world's growing education markets … [providing] independent and authoritative insight for investors, lenders, advisors and education firms operating across the education sector'. It does this both through publications (the company is part of 'Investor Publishing') and conferences. An example of the latter, focused on the South-East Asia region, was advertised online under the heading 'ASEAN's thriving childcare market: a golden opportunity':

> 2018 saw a flurry of market activity across the [East Asian] early years market, as investors looked to capitalise on the unprecedented increases in demand for early years businesses. Underpinned by a lack of quality day nursery portfolio platforms, the market saw premium multiples being paid for those operatives scaling quality businesses in this fragmented sector.… The Building Generation Next conference is brought to you by EducationInvestor Global.
>
> *(EducationInvestor Global, 2019a, np)*

Another conference, for the Middle East and North Africa, held in September 2019, promised to 'shine a light on areas in which investors are finding scalable investment opportunities in sub-sectors including early years, K12 [Kindergarten to grade 12 in US schools], higher education, and vocational and skills training', and offered a session on early years – 'Establishing a niche nursery proposition in the Middle East' – advertised as follows:

> As in most geographies, early years in the Middle East is a fragmented market in which even the largest players hold relatively small shares, thus paving a long runway for consolidation. Meanwhile, K12 operators continue to see value in bolting nursery offerings onto schools, which in turn function as a student pipeline. But what kinds of offerings are prospective investors interested in? How can nursery operators reach scale across multiple jurisdictions? This panel session will bring together early years operators and investors who will explore market nuances, ask crucial questions around commercial structures, and consider the optimum strategies for growth in this complex market.
>
> *(EducationInvestor Global, 2019b, np)*

Another company in the 'intelligence' business is New York-based TechSci Research, whose report on the market in India is quoted from above (page 68), and which describes itself as

> a leading global market research firm publishing premium market research reports. Serving 700 global clients with more than 600 premium market

research studies, TechSci Research is serving clients across 11 different industrial verticals. TechSci Research specializes in research based consulting assignments in high growth and emerging markets, leading technologies and niche applications. Our workforce of more than 100 fulltime Analysts and Consultants employing innovative research solutions and tracking global and country specific high growth markets helps TechSci clients to lead rather than follow market trends.

While IBISWorld (which 'provides expertly researched business information and market research on thousands of industries') produces 'Day Care – Canada Market Research Report' (cost US$750), and estimates the 'market size' in that country as $9 billion revenue, with good future prospects for the 'Day Care industry in Canada [which] is in the growth stage of its life cycle', driven by the rise in women's employment (IBISWorld, 2019).

From a parent buying a place in a local nursery to corporations expanding globally by buying local nurseries, the market has taken a firm hold of early childhood education and care. We turn now to consider some of the consequences.

Markets and their consequences

One very clear consequence of a market system open to the entry of private providers is the potential for a rapid increase in provision, more rapid and at less cost to public finances than expansion by the public sector – providing the returns are attractive enough to private investment. Especially for countries that have paid too little attention to early childhood provision in the past and have come to realise that such provision is urgently needed, 'low cost' expansion via private providers entering a market can seem a godsend. It is not surprising, therefore, that as Eva Lloyd comments, 'Rapid early childhood service expansion aimed at promoting economic wellbeing almost always relies on increased participation of the private-for-profit sector' (Lloyd, 2019, p. 92).

Rapid expansion by the private sector is often triggered or accelerated by policy initiatives, including new subsidy schemes for parents, so-called 'demand subsidies' (as opposed to 'supply subsidies' where public funding goes directly to services) that give increased purchasing power to consumers entering the marketplace, for example through tax credits or vouchers. Thus in the Netherlands, legislation in 2005 that included a new system of parental subsidies led to immediate increases in private provision; the 'privatisation process can be credited for leading to a market capable of responding to sharp increases in demand' (Akgunduz and Plantenga, 2014, p. 382). Similarly, in England a new system of parental subsidies, introduced in 1999, was used to 'encourage a market of private, voluntary and independent providers.... England experienced a 70% increase in private, for-profit childcare between 2002 and 2010' (Lloyd, 2010). In Korea, active government support for marketisation and privatisation, including a new system for subsidising parents, led to the number of young children in private for-profit childcare services increasing by 78% between 2003 and 2016, compared to 10% for those in non-profit private services and 12% for those in public sector services (Chon, 2018, p. 7). While IBISWorld (2019), in its 2018 report on the Canadian 'day care market', notes that 'the Canadian government has recently approved large increases in subsidies for child care' and cites the '[a]bility to take advantage of government subsidies and other grants' as one of the most important 'Success Factors' for the 'Day care Industry'.

The prospect of accessing public funding is an irresistible lure for private businesses. One of the most striking examples is Australia. In that country, a new funding system that extended parental subsidies to those using for-profit private services, when previously such subsidies had been limited to users of non-profit services, led to the 'demand-driven model of the 1990s [which] attracted for-profit companies into the ECEC sector and delivered a rapid increase in the number of ECEC places available' (Hill, 2018, pp. 24, 25). A related consequence has been the concentration of private service ownership by 'publicly listed commercial companies and Australian real estate investment trusts' (ibid., p. 27), the latter described as providing 'access to assets that may be otherwise out of reach for individual investors, such as large-scale commercial properties' (ASX, nd).

This corporatisation of 'childcare' reached its apotheosis with the rise and spectacular fall of ABC Learning, an Australian company providing 'childcare' centres that grew to the extent that its owner topped Australia's Young Rich List in 2006, with personal wealth of AUS$260 million. The company was not confined to Australia, becoming the world's largest listed childcare provider 'following the acquisition in 2005 of the Learning Care Group, the third largest childcare company in the US, with 460 centres attended by approximately 69,000 children … and franchises in Indonesia, the Philippines and Hong Kong' (Sumsion, 2012, p. 211). By 2007, ABC Learning operated more than 2,300 centres over five countries (including the Busy Bees nursery group in the UK, whose own recent international dealings were described above) and was by far Australia's largest childcare provider, accounting for 20% of childcare places.

But the next year, the company imploded, going 'into voluntary receivership and its highly questionable accounting practices that grossly overinflated its value were exposed' (ibid.). The Australian government was left, metaphorically and literally, holding the baby, compelled to find ways and money to keep the bankrupted company's centres running, until 'eventually, the centres were sold to a consortium of not-for-profit charities, bringing an end to a radical experiment in corporate childcare provision' (ibid.). This sorry story provides a particularly spectacular example of how marketisation and privatisation may expose children, parents and governments to new forms of business risk. But there are many other, less dramatic instances; for example, between April 2018 and March 2019, more than 550 'childcare providers' (covering nurseries and childminders) closed for business in England each month (Morton, 2019b).

On the plus-side, therefore, markets can produce lots of places quickly, basically by bringing in private investment for whom one incentive is the prospect of public subsidies. On the other hand, places can also disappear with little notice leaving children and parents stranded. What about the other claimed benefits of market-isation and privatisation? The results of innovation are hard to assess, given a lack of research into the subject. Moreover, this cited benefit of markets begs the question: what innovation should be valued and what should be questioned? In other words, innovation by and of itself is not an unqualified good. It may meet a need or demand, but the results may prove to be deleterious to children or adults.

Which leaves us with choice, quality and costs, and on all three counts, markets turn out to be problematic. Markets are not, of course, intended to produce conditions of equal choice and quality; the price mechanism means that, in any society with unequal distribution of resources, some 'consumers', those with more resources, will have more choice and access to a wider range and better quality of services than others. The market should ensure that those with less resources have access to some products, but necessarily fewer choices and probably of lower quality than those with more resources. Markets respond to (and reproduce) inequality, they do not contest it.

So it is in 'childcare' markets. Services are not equally accessible to all parents. They are more accessible for higher income parents than others, both because they have more purchasing power and can travel further afield, and because providers flock to the areas such parents live in. There tend to be more private 'childcare' services in some locations than others – what Bright Horizons, in its search for nurseries to acquire, calls 'affluent residential areas'; such companies are not in the business of providing for low-income families living in poor neighbourhoods. Similar disparities affect other groups, Penn (2019b, p. 4) noting that 'private providers tend to be less accessible for children with disabilities or any kind of special need which involves extra expenditure.'

Not just more accessible for some, but also better. Differences in quality, too, are inherent in market provision, indeed it is through such differences that markets are supposed to promote efficiency. As Deborah Brennan and her colleagues conclude in their article on 'The marketisation of care', 'markets almost inevitably therefore lead to increasing inequality in the quality of care' (Brennan et al., 2012, p. 380).

Instances of inequalities in both distribution and quality of services are reported from a number of countries. In England, areas of deprivation have fewer private nurseries and of lower quality (Gambaro, Stewart and Waldfogel, 2014; Melhuish and Gardiner, 2017; SMF, 2017). For example, a study of 3- and 4-year-olds found that while

> Government-maintained schools located in disadvantaged areas and serving disadvantaged children offered quality for three- and four-year-olds that was comparable (and in some cases higher) than schools serving the more advantaged.... Within the private, voluntary and independent (PVI) sector, quality for three- and four-year-olds was lower in settings located in deprived areas; with more disadvantaged user-bases; and attended by individual children from disadvantaged backgrounds.
>
> *(Mathers and Smee, 2014, p. 3)*

The Social Mobility Commission was blunt in its assessment of the situation, also highlighting the inequality associated with the 'PVI' sector:

> The childcare market in England is failing to deliver enough high-quality early years provision, particularly in the most deprived areas. Poorer children, who stand to gain the most from high-quality childcare, are the least likely to receive it.... With the exception of the very least deprived decile, the number of early years settings increases as areas become more advantaged. At the same time, the number of inadequate and requires improvement settings [as rated by Ofsted, the national inspection agency] falls by one-third from the most deprived decile to the least.... [T]he way that the childcare market is functioning has created a situation whereby children in deprived areas are twice as likely to be in childcare provision that is not good enough, compared with the most prosperous areas. Furthermore, structural and financial restrictions constrain the ability of PVI settings, particularly those located in deprived areas, to improve.
>
> *(Social Mobility Commission, 2016, pp. 26, 27, 35)*

Reviewing New Zealand's experience of 'childcare markets' between 2006 and 2016, Gallagher concludes that markets pose 'a problem in terms of equity of provision, as private providers tend to locate in wealthier communities where the participation rates and overall fees can be higher ... [so that such] cherry-picking of locations has produced a highly patchy landscape of provision' (Gallagher, 2017, p. 16). To which the New Zealand Educational Institute (2019) adds that the failings of the market model in early childhood include 'over-supply of services in some areas, but a lack of quality of provision in others'. In Australia, although the demand side funding model and reliance on private for-profit providers 'has dramatically increased the total number of ECEC places [...] ECEC is still in short supply in many locations and parents continue to report major problems with access and affordability'; furthermore, there is 'evidence that the marketized funding model is failing many vulnerable children' (Hill and Wade, 2018, pp. 22, 34).

It's the same story in the Netherlands, where as a consequence of the government introducing a fully demand subsidy funding system in the 2005 Child Care Act (see pages 67 and 75), the provision of child care

> shifted towards wealthy urbanised areas where there is high purchasing power and a high demand for child care. This shift came at the detriment of poorer rural areas from which child care facilities withdrew their activities. On the one hand, this finding suggests that there is a more efficient interplay between supply and demand in the Dutch market for child care. On the other hand, however, this finding seems to substantiate concerns that existed prior to the introduction of the Act that the new financing system might cause child care providers to focus on high-income and more urban markets.
>
> *(Noailly and Visser, 2009, p. 495)*

In Canada, Beach and Ferns (2015) find that 'poor and inequitable access is a hallmark of marketized child care. We may see many child care services opening in a neighbourhood where they would be profitable, but no spaces at all in another neighbourhood despite a great need' (p. 58). While in the United States

> [q]uality of care is the central concern. [...] The overall quality provided in today's market is low. [...] [T]here is too little high-quality care in each type of childcare arrangement and the problem appears to be intensifying. ... [P]oor care is even more characteristic for infants and toddlers than pre-schoolers.
>
> *(Harbach, 2015, pp. 670, 671)*

There is also consistent evidence, from Canada (Cleveland et al., 2008), New Zealand (Mitchell, 2012), the UK (Mathers, Sylva and Joshi, 2007) and the US (Sosinsky, 2012) that it matters who provides early childhood services. As Lloyd and Penn (2014, p. 390) conclude, 'within childcare markets the quality of private-for-profit providers tends to be worse than that of public and not-for-profit services'. Helen Penn, arguing that the financial priorities of nurseries run as private businesses ultimately override the interests of children and families, has recently been even more critical:

> No doubt there are good private nurseries with conscientious owners and inspired leaders who provide a considerate, loving and imaginative service for young children and their families. But in general, a privatized system means that they will always be the exception rather than the rule ... in a demoralizing situation where pay, prospects and job conditions are poor, parents struggle to afford the fees, and vulnerable children receive little, if any, extra support.
>
> *(Penn, 2019a, p. 108)*

Beach and Ferns, drawing on Canadian experience, agree:

> Research has borne out child care advocates' claims that for-profit child care is less likely to provide high quality care than are public or non-profit auspices. But understanding the market's influence on quality goes beyond this to consider the way that the market limits quality and confines our thinking about the possibilities of quality. In a child care market we may see some excellent examples of individual programs, but individual solutions and competition dominate at the expense of improving programs overall.
>
> *(Beach and Ferns, 2015, p. 58)*

If quality is not driven up in childcare markets, when viewed overall, there is no evidence that costs are generally driven down, while in some cases costs rise more than for other goods and services. In Australia, in particular, the modern marketized childcare sector has been marked by rapid price inflation [...] the gross cost of childcare rose by almost 10% per annum between 2003 and 2013, more than three times the average annual increase of the CPI [consumer prices index]. [...] [There have been] large increases in household expend on childcare. [...] However, the impact was not uniform, with households in the bottom two-thirds of the income distribution facing a much higher share of income spent on childcare than households in the top third.

(Hill and Wade 2018, pp. 29, 30, 31)

England shows a similar picture of increases in childcare costs exceeding general inflation. Between 2008 and 2016, childcare costs rose four times faster than pay, with the difference greatest in London where these costs rose 7.4 times faster than pay (Trades Union Congress, 2017). A government report focused on older pre-school children comes to a similar conclusion:

Formal childcare prices to parents have outstripped inflation over the past decade [2005–2015]. The average market price paid for nursery provision for children aged over two has risen by 69% in the last ten years. During this time period, Consumer Price Inflation (CPI) has been only 28%.

(Department for Education (England), 2015, p. 8)

While in the United States, 'many families struggle to afford ever-rising child-care costs [...] low income families are especially vulnerable to the vicissitudes of the childcare market because of limitations on what they can afford' (Harbach, 2015, p. 672).

There is one other reason why, as Penn concludes, '[i]t is becoming more obvious that the private market is highly problematic' (Penn, 2019b, p. 5): the question of accountability, with control of companies providing early childhood services residing with the owners or shareholders.

In a large nursery chain, which owns several hundred nurseries, major decisions may be made at the head-office level, which is distant from the daily work of the nursery, or might even be located in another country. It is notable that although childcare work is heavily gendered – over 95% of childcare employees are women – at senior-management level most childcare companies are run by men, predominantly from a finance or business background. The model of cooperative childcare and democratic decision-making in which staff have a role, and local authorities have oversight and act as co-ordinators and support networks, a model put forward by many childcare advocates, is very far from the reality of most childcare businesses.

(ibid., p. 6)

Put bluntly, marketisation and privatisation in early childhood services are inimical to values of democracy, cooperation and solidarity.

Why don't markets work better?

There are substantial gaps in our knowledge. Despite the growth and extent of markets (and accompanying privatisation) in today's early childhood education and care, relatively little funding has been put into researching how they work and with what consequences, or indeed contrasting them with other ways of organising early childhood services. Even governments that have wholeheartedly espoused marketisation have not thought it necessary to commission studies of this key part of their early childhood policy; their commitment to markets has owed more to belief and a neoliberal sensibility than to systematic analysis, evaluation or, indeed, democratic deliberation of alternatives. Any conclusions about markets and how they work must therefore be tentative and provisional, based on fragmented evidence. But with this major proviso in mind, we can say that the picture available to us does not suggest that markets in ECEC, and in particular those providing so-called 'childcare services', are a roaring success, even in their own terms; overall, they do not seem to deliver their supposed benefits and manifest considerable problems.

Several reasons have been put forward for this apparent market failure. We will consider four here. First, using markets to drive down prices is easier said than done. Early childhood education and care is highly labour-intensive and labour is by far the largest cost item (accounting for 77% of costs in a 2018 study of childcare settings in England (Paull and Xu, 2019)); new technologies cannot readily replace early childhood workers. But in most countries, these same early childhood workers, at least in 'childcare' services, are poorly paid and certainly do not enjoy lavish additional employment conditions. The situation in England is typical, with the childcare workforce in 2018 earning on average £8.20 an hour, only just above the legal minimum wage of £7.83 (from April 2018), and £5 below the average hourly pay for all women workers. So low were earnings, that nearly half (44.5%) of childcare workers claimed means-tested state benefits or tax credits (Bonetti, 2019).

Low pay, so typical of 'childcare workers' not just in England but in other countries too, is matched by low levels of qualification, compared with teachers and, indeed, all women workers. As an OECD study of early childhood policies in 20 countries concludes '[f]igures from various countries reveal a wide pay gap between child care staff and teachers, with child care staff in most countries being poorly trained and paid around minimum wage levels' (OECD, 2006, p. 15). For example, in England, in 2018, 25.1% of childcare workers held a degree as their highest qualification level (Level 6 or higher), compared with 92.8% of teachers and 37.1%% of all female workers; the proportions with a qualification at 'A' level GCE or below (Levels 1–4) was 56.3%, 3.2% and 48.6% respectively (Bonetti, 2019, Figure 20).

An English-government report from 2015 nevertheless argues that savings are possible in staffing costs:

> [Childcare] providers typically use more staff than government regulations require. They report, in part, that this is a quality measure, and that 'slack' is

needed to enable them to cover peaks and troughs in demand. Where providers are operating with 'slack' in the system, they incur higher costs. Parental
demand does not appear to be a factor in encouraging this common practice.
There is evidence that higher quality can be achieved by providers operating
close to or at statutory ratio. Graduate led settings such as school nurseries
operate at high ratio and in general have a reputation for high quality. Our
analysis shows that a 'typical' provider in a private setting could save around
15% of its unit delivery costs by staffing within the statutory requirements.
Similarly, there are potential savings by changing the mix of staff used, within
the limits of regulation. Potentially big savings are available using more variable staffing models to recognise peaks and troughs in occupancy. Increasing
overall rates of occupancy improves efficiency for the same reasons – spreading
costs over a higher number of funded or paid for places.

(Department for Education (England), 2015, p. 9)

Let us accept for the moment that so-called 'slack' in staffing of childcare services is
not justified, and that savings can be made by cutting current staffing levels without
effecting the standard of work. Such savings would, however, be immediately
wiped out if staff were (a) better qualified and (b) better paid; the example given of
'school nurseries' (actually nursery classes) 'operating at high ratio' and with a
'reputation for high quality' is based on each setting including a graduate teacher,
working alongside a non-graduate assistant, and this teacher is paid well above the
level of 'childcare' workers, as indeed is the assistant. If childcare nurseries had a
similar ratio of 50% graduate workers, costs would be far higher even with lower
numbers of staff. Additional improvements to existing poor working conditions
(e.g. adequate pension provisions, available to graduate teachers in schools but not
to most childcare staff; some 'non-contact' time apart from children for workers to
devote to professional development, preparation etc.; and access to good professional development opportunities) would further erode any savings made by having
fewer staff. In short, proposed savings from cutting staffing depend on the continuation of low-level qualifications and inadequate and exploitive pay and conditions among an almost entirely female 'childcare' workforce.

Other savings are proposed in the English government report, but the details
skated over. What exactly would 'changing the mix of staff used' or 'variable
staffing models' entail, not least for the workers involved? While presumably most
childcare businesses would like to increase occupancy rates, rather than keeping
them low on purpose.

Significant containment or reduction of overall costs to reduce prices is, therefore,
an elusive goal, at least if any semblance of quality is to be maintained. It can only be
achieved by bearing down on staffing costs, by worsening adult:child ratios or by
blocking improvements in levels of qualification or to employment conditions, both
likely to be at odds with quality improvement; or by further impoverishing an
already low paid workforce through reducing levels of pay, which is likely to lead to
increasing problems of recruitment and retention, as well as undermining attempts to

improve levels of qualification (already low relative to school teachers). Where this has been tried, in Korea, the results have unsurprisingly not proved encouraging. Due to the marketisation of childcare services in that country, the treatment of

> workers, many of whom have a low income, part-time work, low welfare benefits, and short (1-year) working contracts has been poor (Baek, 2011; Yoon, 2013). In particular workers in private facilities tend to experience more difficulties compared with those in public-based facilities (Baek, 2011, Yoon 2013). Owners in the private sector tend to meet their goals by reducing their personnel expenses, since following government guidelines regarding expenses is not compulsory (Baek, 2011). Therefore, many workers in their twenties and thirties are likely to leave the market altogether, increasing the turnover rate for social care workers.
>
> *(Chon, 2018, p. 8)*

A second reason for market failure concerns demand-side funding, subsidising parents rather than services, the favoured means in marketised systems for injecting public money into early childhood provision. The principle is to empower parents as consumers, and hence improve the workings of the market, by increasing purchasing power especially among those with lower incomes. But this form of public funding has a number of potential drawbacks, that may undermine equality of access and improvements in quality. Some of these were identified by a major cross-national study of early childhood policies in 20 higher income countries, conducted by the Organisation for Economic Cooperation and Development (OECD):

- *Demand-side funding is, in general, under-funding*, and the burden of costs in market-led systems falls essentially on parents, who, in the market economies pay fees ranging from 35% to 100% of the costs of child care, unless they belong to low-income groups. Families with modest resources, who are not eligible for public funding, are often unable to pay such a proportion. As a result, their children can be excluded from participation in early childhood services (Fuller et al., 2005).
- When public funding to the child care system takes the form of subsidies paid directly to parents, *the steering capacity of governments services is considerably weaker than in funding-to-services systems*. Tax rebates and parent subsidies do not support system co-ordination or universal provision or even necessarily, improve in-service training and salaries for staff. When parental vouchers are used to support informal and unlicensed child care as well as licensed providers, the result can be a diffuse network of small-scale organisations and individuals offering an array of child care services (Fuller et al., 2005). Negative practices tend to appear, *e.g.* the growth of unregulated services; the selling of services on appearance and the practice of offering 'slot' services to parents, which undermine all notion of continuity

of relationship for young children, of programming or of developmental progress. [...]

• *Parent subsidies can be problematic in that they may not be used efficiently on behalf of children:* In sum, it [sic] given directly to parents, [the subsidy] may not be passed on fully to providers. On the other hand, parents with low educational levels and unemployed parents have difficulties in claiming what is due to them (United Kingdom Inland Revenue, Analysis and Research, Child and Working Tax Credits, 2004). From a planning perspective, demand side subsidies can also be problematic, as financial flows in a parent subsidy system depend not on the number of eligible children (which can be foreseen) but on how many parents claim tax credit.

(OECD, 2006, p. 116; original emphasis)

A third reason put forward for market failure concerns the behaviour of (in market speak) 'consumers', that is the parents who are buyers of early childcare education and care. Take the key task in such transactions of being an informed consumer. This is hard enough at the best of times, because

[c]onsumers do not usually have easy access to all of the information they would need to judge effectively the value of what is on offer. Reliable and comparable information about the relative quality of different products, even those from the same supplier, often is not available or is manipulated by sellers. Moreover, most consumers would probably not have the background information or time necessary to make use of that information were it available.

(Hammersley, 2013, p. 25)

But the problem is even more acute when it comes to complex services such as early childhood education and care, about which potential purchasers may know little and have no first-hand experience. Writing of the Netherlands, Plantenga observes that 'quality in particular can only be judged to a certain extent by parents' (2012, p. 70), since it is children and not parents who actually attend services. Or, as Sosinsky puts it, 'parents are the purchasers, and not the recipients of childcare and are not in the best position to judge its quality' (2012, p. 142). But making informed judgements is made even harder because

many parents have never purchased childcare before, and by the time they learn what they need to know, their children are old enough so that the parents may never purchase childcare again.... [Furthermore, working parents have] little time to seek out and evaluate childcare, even if they knew entirely what they are looking for.

(Cleveland and Krashinsky 2004, p. 39)

Experience in the Netherlands confirms that

information is a real problem. The consumers [assumed to be parents] do not know every supplier and quite often receive information through informal networks. Furthermore the consumer is only partly able to check the quality of services.... As a form of self-regulation, the sector has adopted a quality agreement with rules about a pedagogical plan, child–staff ratios, group size and accommodation. Parents, though, seem to value different aspects of quality, for example active play, the provision of different activities and short journeys. As a result, parents may overestimate a service's quality.

(*Marangos and Plantenga 2006, p. 19*)

The same is reported from Germany, where a comparison has been made of perceptions of quality between parents and staff across 734 early childhood centres. Both groups were asked to rate a range of quality measures, the result being considerable differences between parents and workers – 'information asymmetries' as the authors put it, who conclude that 'information is not readily available to parents, an issue that should be addressed by policy-makers' (Camehl, Schober and Speiss, 2017, p. 2).

This problem of 'information asymmetries' is symptomatic of a deeper problem with markets in early childhood education and care, and a fourth possible reason contributing to the failure of markets to work well: markets require the adoption of new identities or subjectivities by parents and workers (or at least those who manage services), that of buyers and sellers. As such, both must adopt the mantle of *homo economicus*, both seeking to maximise their own advantage in the exchange process – in which, as already noted, the child has no active role, being merely the object whose care or education is a commodity that needs to be bought. This issue of subjectivities is explored further in the next chapter; for the moment, we will focus on how readily parents and workers assume the identities required by market theory.

Parents, it seems, not only lack the necessary information to be effective buyers, to drive a hard bargain and to get the best value for their money. They are also reluctant to deploy the effective buyer's strongest card – to move their business elsewhere if dissatisfied: for '[a] typical feature of the childcare market is that parents rarely switch once they have opted for a certain childcare provider' (Plantenga, 2012, p. 70). The author of the last comment explains this in the market language of 'high switching costs', including parents' concerns for the adverse effects of 'switching' on children – in other words, young children may be very upset by being moved from one place to another. A similar point, though put in less economistic terms, is made by Gallagher:

There is an emotional 'stickyness' to childcare provisioning, based on the intersubjective and caring relationships which build between parent(s), child and carer (Boyer et al., 2012), which means that changing services is often a last resort, rather than an active strategy in the market. For all these reasons, the very idea of a parent–consumer and the agency they are understood to now have, as imagined in policy, is fundamentally flawed.

(*Gallagher, 2017, p. 21*)

The 2015 report on 'childcare markets and provider costs', published by the English Department for Education and already referred to in this chapter, also notes that '[p]arents tend not to switch providers frequently', but sees this as indicating 'parental satisfaction with provision', despite adding that the authors 'recognise the high costs to switching'. This positive interpretation put on 'low switching' contributes to an 'overall assessment ... that the [childcare] market appears to function reasonably effectively' (Department for Education (England), 2015, p. 7). No attempt, however, is made by the authors of this report to go further into the relationship between low switching and parental satisfaction, nor to engage with the literature that discusses other possible interpretations of why parents may not switch providers frequently.

This failure, or reluctance, to assume their allotted market role, is not confined to parents. It is found, too, among, workers in early childhood services. Two studies by Jayne Osgood involving (female) English practitioners found that they emphasised caring, collaboration and community, values that were perceived to be at odds with, and at risk from, government reforms that emphasised competitive entrepreneurialism and favoured rationality, commercialism and measurability.

> [T]he ethic of care and approaches to management that female managers tend to adopt can be regarded as oppositional discourses to the masculine managerialism ... embedded in government policy designed to promote entrepreneurialism [...] They were resistant to viewing children as financial commodities, but this became inevitable when seeking to make a profit
>
> *(Osgood, 2004, pp. 13, 16)*

This offers an example of how markets and market thinking are not able to 'express and promote many values important to [education], such as mutually shared caring concern' (Held, 2002, p. 32). Of course, over time and under the persistent influence of a dominant neoliberal discourse, identities and values may change; parents and workers may become more entrepreneurial, less 'sticky', less caring, more willing to be good market players, to assume the role of the calculating *homo economicus*. Which begs the question, at the heart of this book: is this what we want for ourselves, our services, our society? Do we really want a neoliberal world populated by *homo economicus*? What values and what ethics really matter to us?

Such fundamental issues – of identity, ethics and values – have led some to argue that the 'childcare' market (indeed, all markets in so-called care services) does not, and cannot, function as markets are meant to do (Ball and Vincent, 2006; Sumsion, 2006; Plantenga, 2012). Choice and competition in these markets are inherently defective, for the actors don't seem to know their roles properly nor want to know them. The problematic situation is summed up by economist Gillian Paull

> Childcare is not a typical good or service. Its inherent nature contains a number of characteristics which create problems in the functioning of the market and means that the market outcomes may not meet parents' preferences at minimum cost.... [T]hese problems fall into five main categories. First, parents may not make the

best choices.... Second, there is considerable variation in the quality of care.... Third, competitive pressures to provide what parents want may be reduced by parental reluctance to express dissatisfaction or to switch between providers.... Fourth, competitive pressures may also be reduced by high entrance costs for new providers.... Fifth, it may be difficult for providers to obtain a highly qualified workforce.... The first two problems affect the ability of parents to make the best choices or express their preferences over childcare options; while the last three reduce competitive pressures for providers to produce the best mixture of type and quality, to produce at minimum cost.

(Paull, 2012, pp. 229–231)

Assuming (and it is an assumption, not a given) that markets are with us for the foreseeable future, what might be done? The ardent marketeer may hope that over time, through prolonged exposure and expectation, parents and workers will better assume their prescribed roles of calculating buyers and sellers, each becoming the ideal neoliberal subject, the mythic *homo economicus*. Though as we have just discussed, this raises major political and ethical questions.

At a more prosaic level, government may intervene to attempt to overcome some of the failures of the ECEC market. Paull sets out three key reasons for government to become so involved in childcare markets: 'to address inherent problems in childcare provision (market failures); to influence parental childcare choices to incorporate social benefits and costs and to reduce inequities in childcare outcomes; or to use childcare to mitigate other inequities' (ibid., p. 237). Harbach develops these broader social rationales by introducing the concept of 'childcare spillovers':

Benefits of high-quality childcare spill over to society at large. Yet families consider only private, internal benefits in determining willingness to pay. The result is market failure ... demand for quality childcare is inefficiently low from a societal perspective, leading to an underallocation of quality childcare in the market.

(Harbach, 2015, p. 684)

The OECD comparative study of early childhood policies picks up on this issue of the wider social value of early childhood education, citing the conclusion of two economists (Cleveland and Krashinsky, 2003) that because of this early childhood services are not appropriate for unconstrained marketisation.

For [the economists], ECEC is a public good, delivering externalities beyond the benefit of immediate, personal consumption. Important national goals are achieved through early education and care, in particular, a significant contribution to the health, development and learning of a nation's children. If this is the case, it is appropriate for governments to intervene in the field, through funding and quality control, particularly if the benefits gained by society are greater than the costs incurred.

(OECD, 2006, p. 117)

What forms might government intervention take, both to improve the workings of markets and to recognise that ECEC is more than simply a private commodity? A number of options are possible, including funding (i.e. subsidising costs, either by direct payment to services or payments to parents); quality control (e.g. stronger regulation of services through setting standards and enforcing them through inspection); support for staff training; provision of information on quality and other facets of services; and encouraging not-for-profit providers.

Countries with marketised early childhood education and care usually do have some form of government intervention, but this varies from the minimal (e.g. Korea, the United States) to the more interventionist (e.g. England, Netherlands). The degree of public intervention called for seems to depend on the broader goals of public policy. Thus, the author of a cross-national review concluded that variable quality and inequitable access would persist unless strong regulations were enforced, including planning controls for entry to and exit from local markets (Penn, 2014). In short, more equality requires more regulation.

But there is a dilemma. If a significant degree of government intervention is needed to mitigate market failure, then the result is to undermine the logic and the workings of the ideal marketplace – the transaction between calculating, self-interested buyers and sellers. Taking account of the best interests of the child (a key principle in the United Nations Convention on the Rights of the Child), of wider social concerns, of the rest of society, takes us a long way from the individual buyer-seller relationship at the heart of the market. Subsidising costs dilutes the market's goal of efficient allocation of resources. Regulation, especially if relatively stringent, is at odds with the principle of calculation and choice, and may hinder innovation.

The conclusion seems clear. If one is concerned with issues of equity, if one is concerned with the best interests and rights of the young child (who without purchasing power is not a protagonist in the childcare market, indeed cannot really act with agency in any market), if one is concerned to improve quality and the conditions of a too-often devalued workforce – then the market by itself will simply not do. At the least, a strongly managed market is called for, what some have referred to as a 'social market', which has been defined as a mixed economy of provision, including private not-for-profit and for-profit childcare businesses, possibly operating alongside public provision, which allows for choice and innovation 'while maintaining a sense of national and community responsibility for services' (OECD, 2006, p. 119). But that, as we shall return to in Chapter 6, is just one way of organising and developing early childhood services. There are alternatives!

For the moment, though, the market retains its sacrosanct position, subject to increasing questioning, but still preserved by neoliberalism's hegemony. This shibboleth, as already suggested, has implications for the assumed subjectivity of parent and worker in ECEC, representing neoliberalism's image of the ideal consumer and seller. We now turn to explore this area of images further. What images does neoliberalism have of the child, the parent, the early childhood centre and the early childhood worker? What is, in short, neoliberalism's imaginary?

Note

1 These examples of the trade in early childhood centres are just a few taken at random from the news section of *Nursery World*, a long-established UK magazine for the early years sector, which has similar news stories in most of its issues.

4

NEOLIBERALISM AND ITS IMAGINARY

Neoliberalism, as Tronto puts it, 'creates its own vision of society and of human living within such a society' (Tronto, 2017, p. 29). That vision consists of beliefs about how society should be organised and function and of how people should relate and behave in such a society – 'of human living'. As discussed in the previous chapter, the market and market transactions are at the centre of this belief system, supported by certain valued behaviours: competition, calculation and the exercise of individual choice. This neoliberal vision is also based on beliefs about individuals and institutions, about who and what they are. In the words of Cristina Vintimilla, '[w]e are called to think about neoliberalism, not only as a state's economic orientation, but as particular modes of subjectivity, and how one becomes (or may resist becoming) a neoliberal subject, especially through the project of education (Vintimilla, 2014, p. 80). Neoliberalism, in short, values and calls for 'particular modes of subjectivity' – expressed in a set of images about how subjects should be under neoliberalism. Put another way, these images are social constructions, constituted by the dominant discourse of neoliberalism, inscribed with its beliefs, conceptions and visions; they are neoliberalism's imaginary.

These images are normative, representing the identity or subjectivity that neo-liberal beliefs ascribe to people, but also to institutions; according to these beliefs, this is who people and what institutions, such as early childhood centres, should be. But they are also productive, in that neoliberalism seeks to produce or create people and institutions in its own image – a process that Foucault terms sub-jectification, the formation or production of subjectivity through power relations, dominant discourses and regimes of truth. As Brown says, also referring to Fou-cault, neoliberalism 'is a form of political reason and governing that reaches from the state to the soul' (Brown, 2015a), that is it reaches into our innermost being, attempting to mould our hopes, desires and fears, our very sense of who we are.

To achieve this, neoliberalism relies on its position as a dominant discourse or regime of truth, insisting there is only one way to think, speak and be, that any other way of being, of thinking of the self, any other image is aberrant, not normal. But subjectification is not just a matter of governing, of applying external forces and incentives, of a mixture of persuasion and coercion as to how to be and to exist. It only works in the long term if individuals come to own the identities ascribed by neoliberalism to themselves, to other people and to institutions, if the individual governs her or himself by making neoliberalism's desires and norms their own desires and norms, adopting neoliberalism's normative images as their normative images – or as Bronwyn Davies and Peter Bansel put it, if 'subjects will take themselves up as the newly appropriate and appropriated subjects of the new social order' (2007, p. 248).

The subject then is 'governed by others and at the same time [is the] governor of him/herself' (Ball and Olmedo, 2013, p. 87). This process of self government is what Foucault terms 'governmentality'. 'Governmentality'

> refers to the way in which people and populations come to be governed or managed not through external coercion, but by more subtle and more effective practices. These practices work directly *on* us, steering us towards desired behaviour. But they also work *through* us, acting on our innermost selves, reaching to the innermost qualities of being human: our spirit, motivations, wishes, desires, beliefs, dispositions, aspirations and attitudes. So though we are directly governed, the most important effect is that *we govern ourselves* – conduct of our own conduct – in ways that conform to the dominant regime
>
> (Dahlberg and Moss, 2005, pp. 18–19; emphasis added)

To take an example we develop below, neoliberalism's image of the parent is (*inter alia*) as a consumer, seeking to purchase a commodity – 'childcare' or 'education' – in a competitive market place through the exercise of individual choice and economic calculation. The problem for neoliberalism is that parents may initially be reluctant to conform to this image, disinclined to assume this identity; they may simply think of themselves as local citizens or residents who want their child to go to a good local centre, perhaps provided by the local council, along with other children from the neighbourhood – a public service for the community. But over time, neoliberalism creates conditions that encourage and expect consumer behaviour from parents. A market is created, parents can choose from a variety of centres spread over a larger area, private providers move in, public services are cut back or treated as quasi-businesses, information on competing providers is made available to enable parents to be better informed consumers, parents (not centres) are subsidised, a language of choice and consumerism is increasingly heard around early childhood services. Faced by these conditions, parents begin to adapt their behaviour, to adopt the role of consumer, perhaps reluctantly initially, but then with increasing diligence and belief. The next stage is for parents to embody this consumer subjectivity, to actually begin thinking of themselves as consumers who must shop around in search of the best buy, to envisage early childhood centres as businesses offering commodities for sale, to see the idea of a market of competitive centres as a perfectly natural state and an inevitability – indeed, they are no longer able to envisage an alternative, for example as members of a local community using the same good local public centre as everyone else in that community. In this way, neoliberalism's normative image of the parent as consumer has become internalised, this identity or subjectivity has been assumed; the parent now governs her or himself, striving to live up to the norm of being an informed, calculating and self-interested consumer.

Similar processes of subjectification, the assumption of an identity under the pervasive influence of a dominant discourse, are not confined to parents. For instance, Lynn Fendler has coined the term 'developmentality' to describe how educators (or children) can come to understand themselves in terms of developmental norms: '[developmentality focuses] on the self-governing effects of developmental discourse in curriculum debates. Developmentality, like governmentality, describes a current pattern of power in which *the self disciplines the self*' (2001, p. 120; emphasis added). Developmentality thus becomes a 'mode of subjectification', the identity of both educator and child inscribed by developmental norms and the importance of their attainment; the former becomes a calculator, the latter a subject of calculation.

An important factor in neoliberal success is, therefore, for people to embody a neoliberal subjectivity for themselves and to take for granted, as normal and self-evident, neoliberalism's images of others and of institutions like early childhood centres. While a major threat to the neoliberal project is if people reject neoliberal images; if, for example, they ignore or refuse their own neoliberal subjectivity, insisting on cooperating with and caring for others in a collective response to common needs and shared interests, rather than constantly competing in the untrammelled pursuit of their own self-interest. Given what is at stake, 'subjectivity is the key site of neoliberal government', meaning 'the production of particular sorts of "free" ethical subjects – striving, enterprising, competitive, choosing, responsible' (Ball, 2016, p. 1134); it is where, ultimately, the neoliberal project will stand or fall. So, neoliberalism works remorselessly to produce subjects, including through the project of education, to convert the normative 'you should be' into the actual 'this is who I am', a desired state in which people internalise neoliberalism's images, accepting them as natural, normal and desirable, a state of willing consent not grudging acceptance.

Subjectivity, our image of ourselves and others, is then not only a 'key site of neoliberal government', but also potentially a site of resistance to such government; as we urged in Chapter 1, we must avoid the trap of falling into despair and hopelessness and reject the inevitability of neoliberalism and its imaginary. We shall return to this crucial issue in the final chapter, to the need to understand the power wielded by neoliberalism without at the same time losing heart. For the moment, we will offer a sliver of hope before embarking on this chapter's exploration of neoliberalism's imaginary and its productive effects.

Neoliberalism may be insistent about how subjects should be, complying with its images: but it is possible to refuse this subjectivity, through what Ball refers to as a 'politics of refusal', and thus begin a 'process of struggle against mundane, quotidian neoliberalisations, that creates the possibility of thinking about education and ourselves differently' (Ball and Olmedo, 2013, p. 85), and by so doing begin to take an active role in one's own self-definition. This requires self-questioning, asking 'what kind of self, what kind of subject have we become, and how might we be otherwise?' (Ball, 2016, p. 5). This is a questioning of personal identity that involves the care of the self: 'a continuous process of introspection, which is at the same time attuned to a critique of the world outside.... [This is] the art of voluntary inservitude, of reflective indocility' (ibid., p. 8). Amidst the neoliberal onslaught of subjectification, we can hold on to the question: how might we be otherwise? We will develop this theme and strategy, resisting neoliberalism through a politics of refusal and care of the self, in Chapter 6.

Of particular relevance to this book are neoliberalism's images – or social constructions – related to early childhood: of young children, of their parents, of early childhood centres and of early childhood workers. In this chapter, we explore these images, the neoliberal imaginary for early childhood education and care. But first, developing what we wrote in Chapter 1, we consider neoliberalism's more generic image of people, of human beings, or at least of *adult* human beings, and the way it constructs that image through viewing the world through one particular perspective: the economic lens.

The economic lens

We have argued in Chapter 1 that 'economisation' is a defining feature of neoliberalism, involving, as we said, 'the conversion of non-economic domains, activities and subjects into economic ones and the insertion of economic rationality into every nook and cranny of life'. In other words, everything is seen and understood in economic terms, and 'economy becomes an entire way of life, a common sense in which every action – crime, marriage, higher education and so on – can be charted according to a calculus of maximum output for minimum expenditure ... [and] can be seen as an investment' (Read, 2009, p. 31). This extends to neoliberalism's images, which being constructed by the way neoliberalism sees and understands the world means taking shape through an economic lens, a lens

> through which everything is 'economized' and in a very specific way: human beings become market actors and nothing but, every field of activity is seen as a market, and every entity (whether public or private, whether person, business, or state) is governed as a firm [...] Above all, it casts people as human capital who must constantly tend to their own present and future value.
>
> (Brown, 2015a, np)

We have already met, in Chapter 1, neoliberalism's generic image of the human being – or rather, as we shall explain later in this chapter, of the *adult* human being. This is *homo economicus,* a human being who thinks, relates and acts in exclusively economic terms, exercising an obsessive instrumentalism 'in which every action –

crime, marriage, higher education and so on – can be charted according to a calculus of maximum output for minimum expenditure'. This is a subject who is responsibilised, meaning that ideas of collective or social responsibility for well-being and risk-sharing are eroded, to be displaced by the assumption of private responsibility for managing not only a wide array of consumer decisions (including which nursery or school to choose) but also for most of life's ups and downs. This citizen who identifies themselves fully with neoliberalism

> makes no claims for protection against capitalism's suddenly burst bubbles, job-shedding recessions, credit crunches and housing market collapses, its appetite for outsourcing or newfound discovery of pleasure and profit in betting against itself or betting on catastrophe. This citizen also accepts inequalities as basic to capitalism's health [...] This citizen releases state, law, and economy from responsibility for and responsiveness to its own condition and predicaments, and is ready to sacrifice to the cause of economic growth and fiscal constraints when called to do so.
>
> *(Brown, 2015b, pp. 218, 219)*

In this neoliberal imaginary, all individuals 'take on (and desire to take on) responsibility for their own well-being. The "social" and the economic are constituted, in this discourse, as binary opposites, with the economic in the ascendant and the social representing all that good economics is not' (Davies and Bansel, 2007, pp. 251–252).

The neoliberal image of the human being is also as autonomous and free: not bound by the constraints of dependency and inter-dependency; not emmeshed in webs of mutuality and collective support; enabled to make individual choices across all aspects of her or his life, from choosing which toilet paper to buy to choosing which nursery or school to send her or his children to. Free, in fact, to choose anything – except, that is, to choose *not* to assume the freedom of individualised choice and responsibility, to choose *not* to be the neoliberal subject. Free, in rhetoric and on paper, yet managed, controlled and governed to assume a very particular subjectivity.

This responsible, autonomous and free subject must also be, as Tronto puts it, 'self-mastering' (Tronto, 2017, p. 29) – self-centred, self-contained, self-regulating, self-disciplined, self-possessed and self-interested, a utility maximiser who is for ever calculating and seeking the best value from life's endless transactions; constantly competitive, choosing and striving; and inscribed with the market as human nature – a 'market actor', a competitor 'guided above all other impulses by the urge to get ahead of our fellows' (Monbiot, 2017, p. 30). *Homo economicus* is in a constant state of calculation and transacting, of buying and selling. As a buyer, she or he is a consumer or customer. As a vendor, *homo economicus* is seeking to sell commodities, products that can be bought and sold – including herself or himself.

For in a competitive world, the ideal neoliberal subject is an entrepreneur of the self, determined and enterprising, for ever working on themselves and making choices to further their own interests and those of their family by improving their market position, increasing the price they can command. This is particularly evident in the neoliberal labour market, whose precarious forms of employment reinforce the need for such entrepreneurial subjectification.

> The contemporary trend away from long term labor contracts, towards temporary and part-time labor, is not only an effective economic strategy, freeing corporations from contracts and the expensive commitments of health care and other benefits, it is an effective strategy of subjectification as well. It encourages workers to see themselves not as 'workers' in a political sense, who have something to gain through solidarity and collective organization, but as 'companies of one.' They become individuals for whom every action, from taking courses on a new computer software application to having their teeth whitened, can be considered an investment in human capital.
>
> (Read, 2009, p. 30)

The subject who is an entrepreneur of the self, a company of one, must pay constant attention to maintaining and enhancing their human capital. Human capital, a concept that has already cropped up in previous chapters, is central to neoliberalism's economic image of the human subject. In Brown's words at the start of this section, neoliberalism, above all, 'casts people as human capital who must constantly tend to their own present and future value' and for whom every action 'can be considered an investment in human capital'. Human capital is at the heart of the entrepreneurial self, with 'each individual [having] to become an entrepreneur of him/herself, to become "human capital"' (Lazzarato, 2009, 120), and with 'individuals now deemed responsible for their own "self-capitalising" over their lifetimes' (Lingard, 2009, p. 18). As entrepreneurs of the self, 'self-capitalising over their lifetimes', neoliberal woman and man are perfect expressions of *homo economicus*, rational economic beings in constant pursuit of self-interest in a competitive world. In short, human capital theory encourages and makes possible 'a "new type of individual", an individual formed within the logic of competition – a calculating, solipsistic, instrumentally driven, "enterprise man"' (Ball 2013b, p. 132).

So in the neoliberal imagination, *homo economicus* is a consumer, a market actor, an entrepreneur, and a quantum of human capital, constantly seeking to make themselves more marketable through enhancing their capabilities in order to become more efficient, more productive and more responsive to the constantly changing demands of the market. Which calls for a quality particularly valued in the neoliberal subject: flexibility, being ready, willing and able to respond to the unceasing shifts of the market. As Fendler (2013, p. 119) puts it, 'current social circumstances call for "flexible" and "fluid" ways of being ... flexibility is vaunted as the cutting-edge solution to the challenges of productivity in a fast-moving global economy'. Not just flexible, but with a 'positive, willing attitude', ready with solutions to any challenge, compliant and unquestioning. Subjectification with a smile!

The image of the young child

Loris Malaguzzi, one of the greatest educationalists of the 20th century and a leading figure in the creation and evolution of the world famous early childhood education in the Italian city of Reggio Emilia, was very clear about the importance of the image of the child, since this image was productive in so many ways, pedagogically, culturally, socially, politically. He was also very clear about the importance of being explicit about the choice of image, a choice that should be a democratic political choice from an array of alternative images: 'A declaration [about the image of the child] is not only a necessary act of clarity and correctness, it is the necessary premise for any pedagogical theory, and any pedagogical project' (cited in Cagliari, Castagnetti, Giudici, Rinaldi, Vecchi and Moss, 2016, p. 368). His declaration, his political choice, shared by the educators in Reggio Emilia, was very clear and very bold:

> There are rich children and poor children. We [in Reggio Emilia] say all children are rich, there are no poor children. All children whatever their culture, whatever their lives are rich, better equipped, more talented, stronger and more intelligent than we can suppose.
>
> *(ibid., p. 397)*

This 'rich' child is born with a hundred languages, is a protagonist and an active citizen of society: such children are 'not bottles to be filled' but 'active in constructing the self and knowledge through social interactions and inter-dependencies … not bearers of needs, but bearers of rights' (ibid., p. 369). Such children are constantly causing wonder and surprise by doing what is totally unexpected, beyond what the adults around them could have imagined, and demand 'rich' educators, able to recognise, value and respond to this vivid image of the child.

Declarations about the image of the child are not to be found in neoliberalism. In this respect, of course, neoliberalism does not stand alone; policy-makers or researchers in the early childhood field have rarely made such explicit statements. This silence reflects the positivism that inscribes neoliberalism, a paradigm that does not subscribe to the social constructionist perspective with its recognition of images or social constructions and their significance, including how they are productive of pedagogical theory and pedagogical projects. Rather, in positivism, there is only an objectively true child, revealed through the workings of science and the application of objective scientists. In this absence of declarations, therefore, we must infer what is the image of the child (or indeed of the parent, the early childhood centre and the worker in that centre) in neoliberalism, since the absence of a declaration – a statement of image – does not mean that neoliberalism does not have an image. It is there, just not recognised or declared; the image is implicit and unstated but nevertheless present and productive.

That neoliberal image seems to speak of a child who is lacking, as Tronto has pointed out:

There is a further problem [with neoliberalism's image of the ideal subject]: not all people can be self-mastering. The idea that 'everyone' is free in a free market society ignores the realities of dependency and domination.... [A]ny 'free market' excludes some people, those who are deemed incapable of 'choosing' and are reduced to the status of 'learning'. Children are among those who are, historically, not ready to choose.

(Tronto, 2017, p. 34)

The child is not capable of self-mastery and not ready to choose, is in a deficient state of dependency and domination. In short, incapable of functioning as *homo economicus* and lacking that essential quality of human capital, so not ready yet to join the fray of life as a market actor and as an entrepreneur of the self. This is the young child as a *tabula rasa* or empty vessel, starting life with little or nothing, setting out on a process of being filled with prescribed and transmitted knowledge, social skills and dispositions (e.g. rational choice, individual responsibility, flexibility and self-regulation (Bradbury, 2013)). Early childhood, indeed all childhood, is thus reduced to the status of becoming, to being a transition stage *en route* to an ultimate destination of achieved adulthood by which time she or he will have assumed the requisite identity: a self-mastering, self-interested and responsibilised subject; an informed and calculating consumer; and a 'resilient, compliant, skilled worker able to grow the nation's wealth' (Stuart, 2011, p. 109).

To achieve this destiny, the child has become 'an object of governmental scrutiny because the "science" of ECE demonstrates that "[l]earning abilities, emotional and social skills develop together" (Shonkoff, 2010)' (ibid.). This calls for investment, especially through education and training, to acquire the human capital that will be so crucial to personal success and national survival. And now, so it is claimed, research shows that such investment should start young, when it will secure the best returns. Such research focuses on

the best time in students' life trajectory for efficacy of investment (e.g. Bils & Klenow, 2000; Garces, Thomas, & Currie, 2002; Steuerle, 1996). Investment in adolescents paid poor returns (Duncan, Ludwig, & Magnuson, 2007a; Nores, Belfield, Barnett, & Schweinhart, 2005); a more effective investment was to target funding towards preschool children's education. Economic estimates are that returns to the state may be $8 for every $1 invested at preschool level (Duncan, Ludwig, & Magnuson, 2007b, p. 143). Thus early intervention spending makes good economic sense, as 'early investment produces the greatest return in human capital' (Heckman, N.D., p. 3).

(Stuart, 2011, pp. 93–94)

Indeed, the young child *is* an investment. Putting money into this investment, and the earlier the better, will produce subsequent human capital and give a great rate of return in the future. But for the moment, the neoliberal image of the young child, in stark contrast to Malaguzzi's 'rich' child, emerges as a 'poor' child, a not-yet adult, waiting in the ante-chamber of life where she or he can be prepared or readied through 'early intervention' using effective ('evidence-based') technical practices – or 'human technologies', a concept we will explain and illustrate in the next chapter – that will secure predetermined and standardised outcomes deemed indicative of the gradual acquisition of human capital and eventual emergence as a market actor. The investment required is long-term, as children are investments in the future, with rewards coming through in later life.

This image of the child is a bleak one, as Natasha Lennard writes in her review of John Harris's 2018 book 'Kids these days: Human Capital and the Making of Millenials', in which he argues that the millennial generation, reaching adulthood in the early 21st century, can be understood as the result of contemporary capitalism converting young people into 'human capital'. Being viewed as human capital, she argues,

> reduces people to no more than potential earners, with their value determined by their imagined future capacity to make money based on their current skillset and social position. It's a way of reconfiguring young life into market terms. And it has informed every stage of the millennial generation's development: schools organized by competitive standardized testing; résumé-building extracurriculars for the wealthy; zero-tolerance policies and the constant threat of prison for poor kids; monitoring and control of childhood behavior; prescription drugs, and little free time to play, all justified by the myth that turning yourself into better human capital guarantees a better future. [...]
>
> Turning a generation into human capital provides capitalists with a steady supply of workers.
>
> *(Lennard, 2018, np)*

Not just a supply of workers, then, but a supply of the right kind of workers.

But there are two other images of the young child that run through neoliberal discourse. The first is suggested by Stuart when she writes of the child 'constructed as 'saviour' of both the state, her community and her 'dysfunctional family'' (Stuart, 2011, p. 110). This is the child as redemptive agent, capable of delivering the world from the failures of today's adults and of ensuring national survival and success through the prospect of abundant human capital – a source of future hope, but all dependent on early intervention with effective technologies. This image is not a new one, with origins in the 19th century institutionalisation of childhood and the emergence of accompanying 'psy-sciences'. As Amos Hatch explains

> [t]his emerging reliance on science and technology, coupled with a romantic view of the purity and perfectability of the child, led to the perception that children are appropriate vehicles for solving problems in society. The notion was that if we can somehow intervene in the lives of children, then poverty, racism, crime, drug abuse and any number of social ills can be erased. Children became instruments of society's need to improve itself, and childhood became

a time during which social problems were either solved or determined to be unsolvable.

(Hatch, 1995, pp. 118–119)

The redemptive narrative has been recast under neoliberalism to include new sciences and technologies and new aspirations. But it continues to offload the responsibilities of today's adults on to younger generations, holding out the prospect that investment and intervention in early childhood will absolve adults from the need to take difficult decisions and decisive action here and now.

The second emerges from growth in the collection and analysis of data from and about children, the process of what has been termed 'datafication' that we discuss in the next chapter. As Takayama and Lingard (2019, p. 464) put it, such datafication 'necessitates the acceptance of a highly reductive, decontexutualised pedagogic logic, where children are seen more as data than human beings'. The image, in short, of the young child as a collection of numbers, the task of education being to steer these numbers in a certain direction.

The image of parents

In a neoliberal world, in which everything is marketable and marketised, early childhood education and care is, as we shall discuss below, imagined as an industry in which businesses compete for customers in the market place. Who then is the customer and consumer seeking the commodity offered by these businesses, and calculating the best buy taking account of need, preference and available money? In this scenario, the young child herself obviously cannot be, since as we have seen she is not yet capable of assuming the role of *homo economicus*, not least because she has no money of her own and is unready to be a market actor. The only possibility is the 'parent', who is imagined in this purchaser role: thus, '[r]econstructing ECEC as a business proposition ... refocuses the status of the family using the service to that of consumer, instead of citizen and member of a community' (Press et al., 2018, p. 334).

More specifically, the 'parent-as-consumer' is in practice usually the mother, who is assumed to be primarily responsible for making a choice of early childhood provision, both because of a lingering view that young children are primarily women's responsibility; and because of a parallel assumption, widely held, that 'childcare' is needed not because both parents (where, of course, both are living together) are in the labour market, but because the mother has decided to go to work, the father's employment being a taken-for-granted assumption. In this way too, in most cases it is the mother who is assumed to have all or most contact with the provision, once chosen, and to deal with any consumer problems arising along the way.

While this image of parent-as-consumer is often again implicit, not spelt out, on occasion it is made explicit. An example is a 2017 article in 'Which?', the magazine of the Consumer's Association, an independent, non-profit organisation in the UK that in its own words has been 'championing the cause for consumers since 1957, asking probing questions of businesses and manufacturers, and pursuing the answers that put you in the driving seat' (www.which.co.uk/about-which/who-we-are). The article, titled 'Choosing a childcare provider: Understanding the journey', discusses results from 'a representative survey of 3,600 UK adults in May 2017, asking consumers about their experiences of a range of public services including childcare'. It argues that '[c]hoosing formal childcare is one of the first big decisions a parent will make for their child', and that '[c]hildcare is a market where there is a lot of choice but consumers can find it a difficult market to navigate'. Here we see the juxtaposition of 'choosing' and 'consumer' alongside the image of early childhood provision as 'childcare' (https://consumerinsight.which.co.uk/articles/choosing-a-childcare-provider).

But there is another image of the parent in neoliberalism: the parent as a quantum or stock of achieved human capital. Having accumulated human capital through education and other experience, the adult entering the labour market needs to ensure this asset can be effectively put to use, in her or his own and the nation's interest. For parents of younger children this will mean access to 'childcare', as a way of delegating caring responsibilities through purchasing services in the market place. Without such access, not only will existing 'human capital' be unused, it may well waste away since '[t]he stock of human capital in the economy depends not only on initial education and training, but also on work experience via on-the-job training and learning by doing' (Joshi and Davies, 1993, p. 50); a parent's time away from the job, to care for a child, is a wasted opportunity to further increase 'human capital'. The conclusion, from a human capital perspective, is clear:

> Better childcare could enable the economy to utilise and conserve the stock of human capital embodied in women who become parents.... Childcare is an investment in human capital.... Particularly if daycare continues while children are at primary school, the earnings gained represent conservation of this human capital. For the woman of middle-level skills, whom we have considered, about 20% – 30% of the earnings gained arose from wage conservation. For the increasing number of women with higher skill levels, there is more to conserve.
>
> *(ibid., pp. 51, 59)*

Once again, the term 'parent' can distract from the reality that the image here is gendered, it is of the mother, because, as just noted, the father's employment and the application of his human capital is often taken as read. The onus, therefore, is on the mother to make the arrangements needed for her to deploy, conserve and augment her human capital by remaining in the labour market. Such assumptions may be gradually changing, but for the moment it seems safe to say that the image of the parent under neoliberalism remains, first and foremost, an image of the mother.

The early childhood centre

Early childhood education and care can be provided in a wide range of settings. For the purposes of this discussion, we will focus on settings that might be described as centre-based or 'early childhood centres' – nurseries, creches, kindergartens, preschools and schools, and exclude those that are in private homes, whether childminders/family day carers or nannies. The primary image of such centres under neoliberalism is, once again, economised. The centre is constructed as a business competing to sell a commodity ('childcare', education) in a marketplace to private consumers, and as such is part of an industry consisting of similar businesses populating the same market. As Woodrow and Press put it, drawing on experience in Australia, 'the Neoliberal ethos appears to be generating new discourses in the way that childcare is perceived, transforming it into a commodity for (women's) private benefit rather than as a public good' (2018, p. 537).

Some of these 'businesses' will not be privately run, but may be provided and managed by public bodies, albeit still operating in the market and perhaps, too, expected to behave as a business. But many others will be private, and many will be for-profit businesses. As such, they can and will be bought and sold, just like any other private business. Here is just one example of many, chosen at random:

> Redwoods Dowling Kerr is delighted to announce the sale of Attenborough Day Nursery in Beeston, Nottingham. The owners of Attenborough Day Nursery, Mr and Mrs Bentley contacted the specialist childcare team at Redwoods Dowling Kerr as they wished to discuss the sale of their business. Mr and Mrs Bentley made the decision to sell their nursery due to pursuing other business interests. As the UK's leading broker in the childcare market, Redwoods Dowling Kerr quickly generated interest for the Nottingham nursery. Mr and Mrs Bentley were looking for a buyer who had a genuine interest in maintaining the nurseries [sic] success. Mr and Mrs Bentley wanted to find someone with an existing presence within the childcare sector, who would build upon the solid foundations, ensuring the continued growth of the nursery. The successful offer was accepted by Ms Warburton who has experience within the childcare industry and currently has two other well established, successful businesses. Ms Warburton was initially attracted to Attenborough Day Nursery because of its popular location within Nottingham, as well as its on-going successful reputation. The business provides an excellent opportunity for Ms Warburton to develop and expand her ever growing portfolio of nurseries.
>
> *(Business Buyers, 2018, np)*

Such sales often use the services of a specialist 'broker in the childcare market', their owners treating them as any other private asset. The broker from whose website the example above is taken describes itself as 'the UK's leading healthcare and childcare broker', and offers bespoke services aimed at clients who are looking to expand and grow their business; new entrants looking to acquire a business; and those looking to sell to realise maximum value for their investment. Our experienced team are market leaders, working with clients to realise and achieve their goals. Our approach ensures that we research the global business community to find the right buyer or acquisition target for our clients.

(https://redwoodsdk.com/)

But as Human Capital Theory has intruded further and deeper into early childhood education and care, a second image of the early childhood centre has aligned itself with neoliberalism's preoccupation with the formation of human capital. The centre's image has evolved from a business supplying 'childcare', to a business also actively engaged in the early formation of human capital, responding to the argument that such formation should start early in life, so imagining the early childhood centre as a 'site of efficient investment' (Stuart, 2011, p. 206).

As such the early childcare centre is further imagined as a factory or processing plant, applying effective 'human technologies' to produce standardised and predetermined outcomes for young children, outcomes expressed in terms of developmental or learning goals, and embodying the acquisition of competencies and skills that represent the initial building blocks of human capital and ensure the young child is ready or prepared for the next stage of human capital formation – compulsory primary schooling.

It is striking how far the language of 'school readiness' has permeated early childhood education and care in recent years in many countries, producing an image of the early childhood centre as a foundation stone or launch pad for compulsory schooling. Back in 2006, an important report from the Organisation for Economic Cooperation and Development, *Starting Strong II*, concluded that a 'discourse about readiness for school is increasingly heard' (OECD, 2006, p. 219), in particular in English-speaking countries, but noting its wider spread, being 'carried by American (English-language) research to all countries.... [where it holds] out the promise to education ministries of children entering primary school prepared to read and write' (ibid., p. 63). The early childhood curriculum for England, the Early Years Foundation Stage, is typical in its emphasis on this readying or preparatory role: '[The EYFS] promotes teaching and learning to ensure children's "school readiness" and gives children the broad range of knowledge and skills that provide the right foundation for good future progress through school and life' (Department for Education (England), 2017a, p. 5).

The language of readying young children through early intervention can go well beyond preparation for primary school, to later stages of education and, ultimately, the workforce. Take, for example, The Council for a Strong America, a bipartisan, non-profit organisation that 'engages law enforcement, military, business, faith and sports leaders who promote evidence-based policies and programs that enable kids to be healthy, well-educated and prepared for productive lives' (www.strongnation.

org/about/our-organization/mission-vision). One of the Council's five constituent organisations is 'ReadyNation', a body consisting of '[b]usiness executives building a skilled workforce by promoting solutions that prepare children to succeed in education, work, and life'; it has '[o]ver 2,300 business leaders to promote: Early childhood education to prepare kids for success in school, the workforce, and life' (www. strongnation.org/readynation/about-us).

One of these business leaders is P. Scott Ozanus, Deputy Chairman at KPMG (a multinational professional services network, and one of the Big Four global accounting organizations) and a member of the ReadyNation CEO Task Force on Early Childhood. In a 2017 blog titled 'Early childhood as the foundation for tomorrow's workforce', he explains his interest in early childhood.

> Why is a company that employs over 189,000 people around the world, and hires about 40,000 people every year, concerned with early childhood?
>
> It's because all over the globe, countries and companies face a common challenge: How best to strengthen their economy and workforce, while also taking societal concerns into consideration. Early childhood is key to a productive current workforce as well as nations' future success....We want children to have access to programs that can put them on the path to academic, career, and life success. We want them to have the characteristics businesses value most, such as the ability to communicate well or collaborate effectively. ... [Professor James] Heckman says the return on investment in early childhood is even higher than the stock market from World War II through 2008.
>
> *(Ozanus, 2017, np)*

This discourse of readying, implying a deficient, unready subject who needs to be acted upon is not confined to nation states or businesses. It is the language, too, of international organisations. For instance, the second part of the fourth goal of the United Nations' Sustainable Development Goals is, by 2030, to 'ensure that all girls and boys have access to quality early childhood development, care and pre-primary education so that they are ready for primary education' (https://sustainabledevelopment.un.org/sdg4).

The image of the early childhood centre as a factory or processing plant, investment in which will produce outcomes that will ready children for the future, is positively and optimistically portrayed by proponents of human capital, many drawing (like P. Scott Ozanos) on the work and claims of James Heckman, another winner of the Nobel Prize in Economics.

> Heckman's arguments now suggest that improved social skills learned at ECE are traits that will make for efficient and effective future workers. Social rather than academic skills are essential workers' traits, Heckman suggests. Early targeted investments build the attitudes and dispositions required by compliant workers in the twenty-first century (Heckman, 2000b, 2008; Heckman & Masterov, 2006).... Thus early intervention spending makes good economic

sense, as 'early investment produces the greatest return in human capital' (Heckman, N.D., p. 3).

(Stuart, 2011, p. 94)

The so-called 'Heckman curve' (Figure 4.1) offers a vivid representation of this conclusion that early years 'programmes represent the best rate of return on investment in human capital', since the 'earlier the investment, the greater the return' (cf. https://heckmanequation.org/resource/the-heckman-curve/). The following quotation, from a blog by the Institute for New Economic Thinking, an American think tank, headed 'Heckman Study: Investment in Early Childhood Education Yields Substantial Gains for the Economy', gives a flavour of the ardent enthusiasm and unquestioned belief among those who adopt this factory image of the early childhood centre, as well as the economistic language that accompanies the image:

A groundbreaking study published has found that high-quality birth-to-five programs for disadvantaged children can deliver a 13% per child, per year return on investment through better outcomes in education, health, social

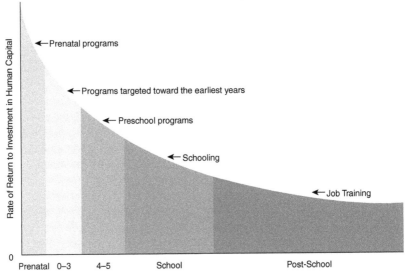

FIGURE 4.1 The Heckman curve

behaviors and employment — which reduce long-term taxpayer costs and equip country's workforce for a competitive future. Nobel economics laureate and Institute for New Economic Thinking Advisory Board member Professor James Heckman and colleagues from the University of Chicago and the University of Southern California's Schaeffer Center have released their findings in a Human Capital and Economic Opportunity working group paper titled The Lifecycle Benefits of an Influential Early Childhood Program.

Heckman and his colleagues believe their findings underscore the need for increased access to comprehensive, high-quality child care and preschool options for disadvantaged children and families. 'High-quality early childhood programs can boost the upward mobility of two generations by freeing working parents to build their careers and increase wages over time while their child develops a broad range of foundational skills that lead to lifelong success,' noted Heckman. 'The data speaks for itself. Investing in the continuum of learning from birth to age 5 not only impacts each child, but it also strengthens our country's workforce today and prepares future generations to be competitive in the global economy tomorrow'.

(Institute for New Economic Thinking, 2016, np)

For Heckman and others, the early childhood centre as factory for the production of human capital is of particular effectiveness for 'disadvantaged children and families'; rates of return on investment are highest for this group. As such, it is a means of engineering equality – or at least equality of opportunity. This belief that early childhood education and care can level the playing field, a popular expression in such circles, has become common wisdom in recent years, including among influential international organisations, such as the World Bank and UNESCO, whose Director General, opening a World Conference on Early Childhood Care and Education in 2010, asserted that:

[Early childhood programmes] increase education attainment and productivity, resulting in higher earnings and social mobility. No matter what internationally agreed goal you take, it is the poorest and marginalized groups that are deprived of education, health care and other basic human entitlements required to live in dignity. Early childhood care and education is a starting point for levelling the playing field. It is the greatest of equalizers.

(UNESCO, 2010b, pp. 3–4)

By ensuring equality of opportunity, the early childhood centre, applying 'high-quality child care and preschool options', ensures that (in the words of a former President of the World Bank) 'a person's life achievements are determined primarily by his or her talents and efforts, rather than by pre-determined circumstances such as race, gender, social or family background' (Wolfowitz, 2006, p. xi) (for a fuller and critical discussion of the widely accepted view that early childhood education and care can ensure equality of opportunity, see Morobito, Vandenbroeck and Roose, 2013).

FIGURE 4.2 The early childhood centre as factory

But not all see this economistic image of the early childhood centre in the same roseate light. Some find the extravagant claims unconvincing, even incredible, as we shall discuss below. Others find the technical and instrumental image itself troubling, a perspective expressed in the work of Francesco Tonucci or Frato, an educational researcher and satirical cartoonist. Figure 4.2 is an example of his work, his own image of the early childhood centre as processing plant or factory, a disturbing image of the violence to children he associates with human technologies and standardised outcomes.

Early childhood worker

The image of the 'poor' child, a reproducer of knowledge, values and identity, and yet to be realised human capital; the image of the parent as consumer and realised human capital seeking to achieve and maintain the best returns on that capital; the image of the early childhood centre as business and as factory or processing plant, a site for investing in the efficient achievement of certain outcomes, the first stage in the development of human capital and readying the child for the next stage, compulsory primary schooling. Given these images, what consequent images can we infer for those working with children in early childhood centres? Who is the early childhood worker in the neoliberal imaginary?

First, especially for those in more senior, even ownership, roles, the image of the early childhood worker is an entrepreneur, a businesswoman or businessman and a manager, needing to ensure the success of their business; this is as important as any pedagogical identity. This image has been central to the English government, with its strong commitment to marketisation and privatisation of early childhood provision. A 2003 research report for the government, titled 'Developing the Business

Skills of Childcare Professionals: An Evaluation of the Business Support Programmes' noted that

> the business skills that professionals hold have been identified as a key factor hampering the sustainability and longevity of much provision (DfES, 2001). The Department [for Education and Skills, DfES] believe that if childcare provision is to meet strategic targets, and therefore the needs of parents and local communities, then the ability of providers to financially manage their setting effectively, is key. As a result, in April 2001, the DfES gave funding to all local authorities to appoint a Business Support Officer, in order for business support activities to take place in all areas, with the intention of improving the business skills providers hold.
>
> *(Osgood, 2003, p. 12)*

This attention to business skills, for the early childhood worker as businesswoman or businessman and manager, has continued. For example, a 2011 research report, funded again by the English government, and titled 'Improving business skills in the early years and childcare sector', reported that 'on average just over half of providers (58%) [in the four early years sectors] have accessed business skills training', and concluded that

> [t]here is clearly a need and a demand for more business skills training across the whole of the early years sector. Confidence in business skills is fairly low, understanding about business skills is variable and only around half of the research sample has ever accessed training.
>
> *(Office for Public Management, 2011, pp. 1, 4)*

While a 2017 government policy paper titled 'Supporting early years providers to run sustainable businesses', concludes that, following a new policy of providing 30 hours free 'childcare' for 3- and 4-year-olds with employed parents, it is 'more important than ever that providers have good business skills and respond to the needs of parents' (Department for Education (England), 2017b). Among the various government offers of business support is guidance on 'Business insights from successful early years providers', and the commissioning of a consortium, 'Childcare works', who will 'work closely with local authorities and providers to make sure they have the tools and knowledge to create and maintain sustainable business models', including 'training providers in business remodelling, business planning and working flexibly and sustainably'.

One of the most important business skills for the early childhood entrepreneur is marketing, including market research, as this website funded by the English government reminds its readers:

> Marketing is critical to all types of business. Early years and childcare providers are a unique type of business organisation as you are marketing yourselves to

parents and carers to offer to look after and educate their children. This means that you need to think carefully about what messages you want to give to both parents and children about your provision, and what you can offer.... One of the easiest ways to begin a successful marketing strategy is to start with the customer. Ultimately, your customers determine whether you stay in business or not, so it's important to put yourself in their position and find out what their wants and needs are, and what they think about you. Although it's important to put the customer at the heart of your market research, you will also need to think about the market that you operate in more broadly.

(*Foundation Years, nd*)

But what of the remainder of the early childhood workforce, the 'childcare' workers or teachers working directly with children? In the past, especially when 'childcare' was less in policy favour in many countries, indeed was viewed as unimportant or undesirable for very young children except in special and pressing circumstances, the image was often of the worker as substitute mother, offering a second best to maternal care, or the worker as nurse, focused on hygiene and physical safety – the term commonly used in the United Kingdom was 'nursery nurse'. The image was, as Vintimilla puts it, 'first and foremost as care providers and protectors', deploying 'traditional female virtues' (2014, pp. 84, 85) – and indeed the image of the early childhood worker was (and still is) of a woman.

Today, as early childhood provision has become a policy priority, not only to enable maternal employment but to promote readiness for school and human capital, the worker's image has shifted: to that of a 'competent technician' (Osgood, 2009), trained in a range of discrete and measurable competencies, whose primary task is to deliver, and document delivery of, prescribed outcomes through the transmission and re-production of pre-set knowledge and values, carefully following a script spelt out by pedagogical programmes or guidelines, for example contained in detailed curricula. This is the early childhood worker as purveyor of 'prophetic pedagogy', where all learning is determined in advance, a concept we discuss in the next chapter.

Megan Gibson and her colleagues offer a variant, the image of the early childhood worker as 'investment broker' or 'economic custodian', whose role is to ensure the investment made in young children does not go to waste (Gibson, McArdle and Hatcher, 2015, p. 323). In constituting this image, they draw on an analysis of a key policy document, issued in 2007 by the federal government in Australia, 'New Directions for Early Childhood Education', in which 'early childhood was repositioned as a key player in the country's economy', essential for the nation's prosperity, so necessitating investment. In this new discourse,

The child in an early learning programme is produced as a commodity that will provide economic benefits in the future.... Where children are 'economic commodities', their teachers are constituted as 'economic custodians'. They are now called upon to nurture the child as economic commodity, although more importantly to ensure the investment is warranted – and pays off…. Under the discursive conditions produced in New Directions, teachers are now charged with 'growing' investments, not flowers in the garden (Kindergartens). They must look after 'economic units' … [having] the responsibility to increase the value of children as economic units and aid them to develop into productive units that are now part of the broader economy and country. The intersections of these discourses – economics/investment/developing child – produce a new type of childhood and produce [early childhood] teachers in new and particular ways.

(Gibson et al., 2015, p. 328)

This 'competent technician' or 'economic custodian' is subject to 'the fallacy of certainties' and the 'anxiousness to pursue outcomes' (Fortunati, 2006, 38), symptomatic of a neoliberal culture of performativity in which 'what is valued has increasingly become compliant employees who have the skills and knowledge to perform the job required without asking questions' (Simms, 2017, p. 1) – a compliance enforced by increasing surveillance. We shall look in more detail in the next chapter at this culture and at how the early childhood worker, tasked with pursuing outcomes to ensure investment pays off, is increasingly brought under managerial control.

Consequences of neoliberal imagery

The dominance of neoliberal images discussed so far has served to marginalise or obscure other possible images. Brown cites '*homo politicus*' as one example of an image effaced, an image of the democratic citizen.

Until recently, human beings in the West have always been figured as more than *homo oeconomicus*. There have always been other dimensions of us imagined and cultivated in political, cultural, religious, or familial life. One of these figurations, which we might call *homo politicus*, featured prominently in ancient Athens, Roman republicanism, and even early liberalism. But it has also appeared in modern democratic upheavals ranging from the French Revolution to the civil rights movement. *Homo politicus* is inconstant in form and content, just as *homo oeconomicus* is, and certainly liberal democracy features an anemic version compared to, say, Aristotle's account of humans as realizing our distinctively human capacities through sharing rule in the polis. But it is only with the neoliberal revolution that *homo politicus* is finally vanquished as a fundamental feature of being human and of democracy.

(Brown, 2015a, np)

Tronto offers another image erased, '*homo carens*' (caring people), which was 'part of the solidarity of working-class parties in the first half of the 20th century that emerged to create systems of social security, income support, 'social rights' and health care throughout Northern Europe' and which 're-emerged to challenge colonial, sexist and racist worlds in the 1960s' (Tronto, 2017, p. 36). These are just two of a variety of rich images available to express the complexity, diversity and potentiality of human beings. The same is true if we look more specifically at images of the young child, the parent, the early childhood centre and the early childhood worker.

In place of this richness, neoliberalism offers a simple, one-dimensional and impoverished economic image of adult humanity: *homo economicus,* a competitive entrepreneur, constantly seeking personal advantage and building the value of her or his personal brand. Jeremy Gilbert argues that this is not only a 'poor' image, but also sits uncomfortably with what people want:

> [T]his is a notion that would have seemed strange and repugnant to most people in most cultures at most points of history before the 1980s. Most people still don't want to be subject to neoliberal norms. They want to make friends because making friends is nice, not just because an extensive network of contacts will give them a competitive advantage in the job market.... Teachers want to teach and students want to learn because teaching and learning are fundamental to any ful-filled human existence, and not just so that corporations that students will work for can make more money.
>
> *(Gilbert, 2020, p. 65)*

Similarly, 'poor' images are evoked for the child, the parent, the early childhood centre and its worker, images that displace a variety of alternative possible images that are complex, multi-dimensional and rich. For example, images of the 'rich' child as a protagonist, citizen and active co-constructor of knowledge, values and identity from the moment of birth; images of the parent as a citizen, member of a community and competent to participate in the democratic life of early childhood centres 'because they have and develop their own experience, points of view, interpretation and ideas' (Cagliari, Barozzi and Giudici, 2004, p. 30); and images of the early childhood centre as a 'social good or a collective public service' (Penn, 2018), as a public space, and as a place of encounter for citizens of all ages, a public resource capable of a wide range of projects, and a site of democratic experi-mentation; and the image of the early childhood worker as a democratic profes-sional capable of experimentation and research, reflection and judgement and able to enjoy 'the pleasure of amazement and wonder'. Instead, the business model infused with new public management paralyses, distrusts and demoralises workers and leads to an 'inevitable' de-professionalisation as their capacity to make locally based autonomous judgments is removed (Connell, 2013, p. 108).

Under neoliberalism, it has been argued, professionalism presents as a problem to overcome rather than as a resource (Ball, 2017). The problem lies in a concept of professionalism that emphasises not only autonomous judgements, requiring trust in such judgements, but also critical thinking and analysis of power. Overcoming that problem requires asserting control over the early childhood worker through managerial technologies, including New Public Management's emphasis on performance, a process that can be described, as above, as de-professionalisation – or else described as a particular neoliberal understanding of professionalism, narrow and instrumental, viewing it as something that is 'measurable, manageable and standardisable', about performing to achieve prescribed criteria and requiring a 'neo-liberal "regulatory gaze" that controls these emerging professionals' (Dunn, 2010, pp. 52, 50).

Another consequence of the neoliberal image of the child, parent and early childhood centre is the vulnerable position in which it leaves the child, reduced essentially to a passive object – to be cared for, to be acted upon, to be a source of future human capital and profit, and whose interests are secondary to those of the parent-consumer and the business-provider. As Sirene Lim says of the highly marketised system in Singapore,

> As businesses, ECCE centres do not necessarily focus on the best interests of young children because such services are created to meet the needs of adults, and as such, a privatised ECEC sector cannot always provide optimal conditions for the care and education of young citizens within diverse and socially stratified societies. A marketized care and education system thrives on competition while promising consumer choice (Brennan et al., 2012). This market competition *foregrounds adults' needs and desires because they are the fee-paying consumers and not their children.*
>
> *(Lim, 2017, pp. 21–22; emphasis added)*

The potential vulnerability of the 'poor' child of neoliberalism, who has no standing in the market and is caught between fee-paying consumers and provider-businesses, is recognised by the United Nations Committee on the Rights of the Child in its General Comment No 16 on 'State obligations regarding the impact of the business sector on children's rights'. This is insistent that

> States must ensure that all legislation, policies and programmes that deal with business issues are not intentionally or unintentionally discriminatory towards children in their content or implementation; for instance, those that address access to employment for parents or caregivers, or access to goods and services for children with disabilities.
>
> *(United Nations Committee on the Rights of the Child, 2013, p. 5)*

There is a further problem, it seems to us, in the neoliberal image of the child as 'human capital': it is reductive and demeaning, degrading the child to an economic object, to be weighed in the balance and perhaps found wanting. Indeed, as we noted in Chapter 1, the term 'human capital' was originally 'considered too debasing to be used publicly', that is before neoliberalism took hold and made it more acceptable to think and talk about human beings in economic terms as 'capital', to be placed alongside other forms of capital. Perhaps we should be less accepting again. For once we begin to talk about people in such economistic terms, to adopt such calculating imagery, to value them in terms of the return they represent on investment, then we risk losing sight of their intrinsic value, their rich and varied potential, their humanity.

The image of the early childhood centre as factory, actively working on the passive child to produce predetermined outcomes, is a cause for concern on three further counts. First, because *it lets neoliberalism off the hook*. What do we mean? As we have seen, it is argued that ECEC provides a sure-fire means of ensuring 'equality of opportunity', by enabling all children to start life on a 'level playing field'. As a senior World Bank official puts it:

> Much more important than inequality of outcomes among adults is inequality of opportunity among children.... The idea of giving people equal opportunity early in life, whatever their socioeconomic background, is embraced across the political spectrum – as a matter of fairness for the left and as a matter of personal effort for the right.
>
> *(Giugale, 2009, p. xvii)*

As this quotation suggests, 'equality of opportunity' is a far safer ambition than 'equality of outcome'; everyone can sign up to it, not least because early childhood education and care seems to offer an uncontroversial technical solution to its achievement, and one that conveniently contributes to a depoliticisation and individualisation of inequality. For if everyone is granted equality of opportunity through access to early childhood education and care, future inequality of outcome can only be due to subsequent individual failings and inadequacies, since in the World Bank's words 'a person's life achievements are determined primarily by his or her talents and efforts'. Providing early childhood education and care, therefore, absolves neoliberalism from any responsibility for inequality and negates the need for more radical political measures, such as strong redistributive policies.

This seems to us highly problematic. First, because inequality of outcomes among adults should be considered as of equal importance to inequality of opportunity among children, both being undesirable. Indeed they should both be considered inexorably intertwined, both being the product of unjust societies and both feeding off each other: for 'the whole idea of accepting inequalities of outcome, whether as desirable or simply as inevitable, and focusing instead on equalising opportunities, neglects the obvious point that parents' outcomes are children's starting-points' (Swift, 2020). Indeed, parents' outcomes have a major influence throughout children's childhoods, with parents in higher status and higher income occupations doing whatever it takes – moving house to be near a 'good' school, paying for private tutors, arranging educationally enriching experiences and so on – to ensure their children's success and to protect them from falling down the social ladder. Thus, inequality of outcome – expressed in parental class and education – is fundamental to children's success at school and beyond (Bukodi and Goldthorpe, 2018), and ensuring genuine equality of opportunity would have to go far, far beyond young children attending early childhood services that deliver predetermined outcomes. In short, the model of providing a level playing field in early childhood, after which everything is down to individual talents and efforts, seems naïve and unrealistic in equal measure, serving mainly to legitimise and excuse neoliberalism's harsh effects.

Second, because it must be questioned whether early childhood education and care has the near miraculous effects claimed for it – and in addition to enhancing education and employment, these claims extend to many other areas, including the improvement of health and the reduction of criminality and a wide range of other unwelcome social behaviours. As the Australian Labor Party claimed in a document issued just before winning the 2007 election, in which it proposed the modest goal of universal early childhood education for 4-year-olds:

> Investing more in human capital formation and investing it earlier leads to increased educational attainment and labour force participation, with higher levels of productivity. It also helps tackle disadvantage, dependency on welfare, our hospitals and our criminal justice system. Australia will face a new set of economic and social challenges in coming decades, and it will need a work-force with higher productivity and participation. Early childhood learning and care are a major part of meeting this challenge.
>
> *(Rudd and Macklin, 2007, p. 3)*

Such extravagant claims are based on various research studies and in particular a small number of what have been termed 'iconic studies', which James Heckman and others draw on heavily. These studies, often local and often from the United States, have been criticised – though mention is rarely made of this. But even if we do accept, without question, the results of such local studies, there is no evidence that 'quality' early childhood education and care has, by itself, made any difference at a *national* level.

Take, for instance, the United States, the main source of extravagant claims for early childhood education and care. It is difficult to discern here any impact on child or adult outcomes *for the country as a whole* after many years of early childhood intervention programmes and research, including Head Start, a major national programme started in 1965, targeted at low income preschool children and their families, and covering not only early education but also health, social services and parental involvement. Despite being one of the richest nations on earth, child poverty and child mortality in the United States remain high (OECD, 2017), and the country ranks 26 for child well-being from among 29 advanced economies (UNICEF, 2013). Social mobility has declined sharply since 1980 (Davis and Muzumder, 2017). While levels of imprisonment are by far the highest of OECD member states (Statista, 2019), and drug addiction is rampant, with 130 Americans dying each day from overdosing on opioids and the cost of prescription opioid misuse running at over $78 billion a year (National Institute of Drug Abuse, 2019); Case and Deaton (2020) have written about 'deaths of despair' among working-class white men from drug overdose, alcoholism and suicide, which have risen dramatically over the past 20 years, and now claim hundreds of thousands of American lives each year. While despite all the talk of enhancing human capital, workers' earnings have stagnated for decades, so that 'today's real average wage (that is, the wage after accounting for inflation) has about the same purchasing power it did 40 years ago – and what wage gains there have been have mostly flowed to the highest-paid tier of workers' (Desilver, 2018).

Maybe such failure is because any modest positive effects of early childhood education and care have been more than cancelled out by the multiple and massive adverse effects of neoliberalism – the decline in the number of good jobs offering a secure income and career progression and the rise of insecure and low paid employment, the erosion of trade unions and collective bargaining, the weakening of the welfare state, and increased inequality. For inequality 'seems to make countries socially dysfunctional across a wide range of outcomes' (Wilkinson and Pickett, 2009, p. 174). As we documented in Chapter 1 (see page 15), over recent years the United States has experienced high and growing inequality, leading to what Nobel-prize winning economist Paul Krugman terms the 'Great Divergence' to describe the widening gap between the economic elite and the great majority of citizens. Moreover, in a highly competitive society, the Matthew principle – to he who hath shall be given – operates with minimum constraint, so that

> when it comes to widening opportunities, what matters isn't people's absolute level of education, which has indeed become less tightly linked to their class origins, but their educational qualifications relative to others. Education is, in large part, a positional good: what counts is one's place in the distribution. Measured that way – the way that employers and parents tend to see it – there has been no change in the association between children's origins and their educational qualifications. *Educational expansion has had no impact on more advantaged parents' capacity to secure for their children a higher place in the queue.*
>
> (Swift, 2020; emphasis added)

All this points to an obvious, but often overlooked, conclusion: that achieving a better society is a complex and extremely demanding process, for which no (early) educational short-cut is available, requiring instead serious and sustained political commitment to social justice and the implementation of wide-ranging policies. Certainly, early childhood education and care has its part to play – but as a part of something much bigger. This argument has been strongly made by Edward Zigler, one of the founders of the Head Start Project in the United States, when reflecting on its 40th anniversary:

> There is no magical permanent cure for the problems associated with poverty [...] Expecting the achievement gap to be eliminated [through early intervention like Head Start], however, is relying too much on the fairy godmother. Poor children simply have too much of an environmental handicap to be competitive with age-mates from homes characterized by good incomes and a multitude of advantages.
>
> Are we sure there is no magic potion that will push poor children into the ranks of the middle class? Only if the potion contains health care, childcare,

good housing, sufficient income for every family, child rearing environments free of drugs and violence, support for parents in all their roles, and equal education for all students in school. Without these necessities, only magic will make that happen.

(Zigler, 2003, p. 12)

Naomi Eisenstadt, who led the English government's ambitious early intervention programme Sure Start for its first seven years, reflecting on 'what I have learnt and what I have achieved', comes to a rather similar conclusion, writing that the most important lesson for her

is the need to address inequality as well as poverty and low attainment.... We set out with Sure Start to improve the educational, social and emotional development of young children living in poverty so as to reduce the chances of growing up to be poor as adults. We have probably achieved the first part of that aim, but have been less successful in the second part [...] I believe that without significant redistribution of wealth across social classes, where you are born and who your parents are will remain a significant determinant of life chances [...] The expectation that early years services, however wonderful, could affect overall inequality was unrealistic. This shift will come from wider social reforms.

(Eisenstadt, 2011, pp. 160–161)

Our second cause for concern about the early childhood centre imagined as a factory is *its premise about present purpose and future prospects*. The assumption is that the centre-as-factory is presently preparing the child for a future in a competitive, capitalist economy, committed to consumption and growth, and holding out the promise of rich rewards for successful preparation. This is business as usual, the present leading inevitably to a future of more of the same, a future in which some will succeed and prosper, while others will not. For most, though, things can only get better.

But they won't and they can't. Faced by multiple, inter-connected environmental crises and facing looming catastrophe for humanity (and many other species),

education cannot be merely about preparing the next generation for their future anymore, simply presuming their future will be an improvement compared to the life of those before them. Facing ecological facts, however, it is sadly not exaggerated to say we are living in extreme times, in which preparing the children for their future means to prepare them for the possibility of not having a future. If we want to prevent this very real possibility, education needs to include the present generation *assuming responsibility* for the consequences of their collective actions by solving as much of the crisis as possible in their own lifetime [...] [W]hat we [the present generation] *can* do is: change ourselves and fix as much as we can in our lifetime. We made our bed, now it's time to lie in it. 'I don't want your hope ... I want you to panic … And then I want you to act … I want you to act as if the house was on fire, because it is' (Thunberg, 2019).

(Su and Su, 2019, np; original emphasis)

Viewed in this light, the whole readying discourse, and the early childhood centre's role in that discourse, is not only a means of shifting responsibility for the future from today's adults to today's children, but it culpably ignores the question of what that future will be. If there is any readying to be done, it is not in the interests of producing flexible, compliant workers for an ever more competitive and consumption-driven market economy; rather it is to 'acquire the knowledge, skills, and dispositions necessary for living in such a way that one minimizes the harm one does to human and non-human others' ability to live well in the world now and in the future' (Ruitenberg, 2018, p. 113). And shouldn't we, today's adults, urgently seek to acquire for ourselves such knowledge, skills and dispositions, focusing on the here and now? Do we not have a responsibility to do so? Facing ecological facts in extreme times thus seems to signal the death knell for neoliberalism and for its images.

The third cause for concern about the image of the early childhood centre as factory actively working on the passive child is that this image contributes to *strong governing of both young children and early childhood workers*. Such governing, the argument goes, is called for to ensure effective performance: that children achieve the outcomes prescribed for them and that workers ensure that their charges do so, and that therefore together they deliver the high return on investment expected by early intervention. This strong governing is also necessitated because the worker-as-technician is viewed as a self-interested and essentially untrustworthy individual whose performance must be monitored, managed and moulded through techniques of management, which will ensure conformity and passivity. This neoliberal image, in turn, conflicts with an alternative image of the educator-as-professional,

> who has traditionally [not] wanted to have the terms of their practice and conduct dictated by anyone else but their peers, or determined by groups or structural levers outside of their control. [Such] professionalism is systematically at odds with neoliberalism, for neoliberals see the professions as self-interested groups who indulge in rent-seeking behaviour. In neoliberalism the patterning of power is established on contract, which in turn is premised upon a need for compliance, monitoring and accountability organized in a management line and established through a purchase contract based upon measurable outputs
>
> *(Olssen and Peters, 2005, p. 325)*

The strongly governed environment of the neoliberal early childhood centre, rooted in the scepticism of public choice theory and fuelled by the principles of new public management to pursue the aims of human capital theory, is the subject of our next chapter, where we also introduce the concept and practice of human technologies as a means of effectively managing performance, both of children and early childhood workers.

5

NEOLIBERALISM AND GOVERNANCE

The relationship between neoliberalism and the state is complex and ambivalent. On the one hand, neoliberals are suspicious and distrustful of the state; in particular, they dislike the idea of state or public provision of services and the interference with the market that this often brings with it; such services, they believe, are also likely to be less efficient and innovative. They are sceptical, too, of the claims made by public sector workers to be 'public servants', guided by professional values and judgements, regarding them as no different to anyone else, self-serving in pursuit of their own interests. Yet they do not discount the state and its role entirely; as we said in Chapter 1, '[t]oday's neoliberals seek to redefine the role of the State, not to destroy it; that role is reconfigured, away from being a provider of services and a guarantor of citizen rights, to being an enabler of markets and guarantor of other conditions needed for a neoliberal society'. They expect the state to contribute to the formation of the neoliberal subject and the creation of 'human capital', both necessary conditions for an efficient market economy based on competition, choice and calculation.

The state for its part has a strong interest in fulfilling these roles efficiently, if the nation it represents is to survive and succeed in an increasingly competitive global market (see Chapter 2) or, as some see it, an increasingly competitive

> global education race [that] now pits countries, regions, and school systems against one another, with the popular media and politicians using the data from international testing programs to announce winners and losers. Fear of falling behind haunts policy-makers and shapes educational priorities around the world.
> (Sellar, Thompson, and Rutkowski, 2017, p. 3)

To be a winner is essential, the perils of falling behind the field and becoming a loser to be avoided at all costs.

A Minister responsible for early childhood education in England expressed this sentiment in a speech to coincide with the publication of a government policy paper in 2013:

> The 21st century will belong to those countries that win the global race for jobs and economic advantage. In order for every adult to fulfil their potential, they need to be properly equipped with essential skills from the very beginning of their lives.
>
> *(Truss, 2013, np)*

A year later, the same Minister, in a speech titled 'The global education race', offered a further blunt warning: 'nations with highly educated populations are going to dominate economically. Highly skilled people will improve their country's future prosperity and success. Likewise, nations that fail to get the best out of their citizens will experience relative decline' (Truss, 2014, np).

Education, then, is the key to the survival and success of the nation state – and the earlier it starts the better. But how is that state to ensure that education delivers? For applying neoliberal principles, the supply or delivery of education is in the hands of autonomous businesses competing for the custom of individual consumers in an educational marketplace. Yet faced by this welter of competing providers, the state somehow needs to impose control to forge certain common and necessary outcomes. How can it do this?

Public funding has a part to play, it being recognised that the education market will fail without substantial public investment; through such funding, the state has leverage. But that by itself will not ensure the required outcomes, that bundle of knowledge, information and skills that add up to maximising human capital. For that to happen, the players in the education market must be governed, left neither to follow their own inclinations nor the vagaries of that market; they must follow a formula that readies the student for each successive stage of the education system, until they are finally ready for transiting from the education market into the labour market, replete with human capital, a flexible and compliant worker, *homo economicus* incarnate. What is needed is governance.

Governance encompasses the processes and means of governing or managing an organisation or system, and in this chapter we will examine the governance of early childhood education and care services by the neoliberal state. We will argue that it does this in three main ways. First, by the application of New Public Management principles, introduced in Chapter 1, in particular an emphasis on output control by the setting of explicit standards and measurement of performance. Second, by making performance visible and public through the publication of inspection reports and other information, so stimulating the forces of competition. Third, by means of governmentality, that process of governing the self or self disciplining that we explained in the previous chapter, a process by which all participants involved in the education system come to embody and espouse the behaviours and outcomes desired by the state, accepting them as normal and necessary, whether these be, for example, developmental stages or learning goals or some notion of 'readiness'.

In looking in more detail at this governance of ECEC by the neoliberal state, we shall be identifying an array or assemblage of what have been termed 'human technologies'. When hearing the term 'technology', it is understandable to think of machines and gadgets; but the concept of technology can be extended to processes and methods of working applied by people, for example government, to people with the aim of better controlling or governing them. In the words of the sociologist Nikolas Rose, human technologies are

> technologies of government ... imbued with aspirations for the shaping of conduct in the hope of producing certain desired effects and averting certain undesired events.... [W]ithin these assemblages, *it is human capacities that are to be understood and acted upon by technical means* ... [including] forms of practical knowledge, with modes of perception, practices of calculation, vocabularies, types of authority, forms of judgement, architectural forms, human capacities, non-human objects and devices, inscription techniques and so forth, traversed and transacted by aspirations to achieve certain outcomes in terms of the conduct of the governed.
>
> *(Rose, 1999, p. 52; emphasis added)*

What we have done in this chapter is to look at neoliberal governance of ECEC by focusing on the case of one country: England. We acknowledge that England is probably the most fully developed and extreme example of such governance today, because of its unique combination of the strong neoliberal dispositions of successive national governments going back to the 1980s, exemplified by the 1988 Education Reform Act (see Chapter 2), together with the centralised power of these governments. For England is, in the words of a senior civil servant, 'almost the most centralised developed country in the world' (White, 2015, np); bodies that might elsewhere contest or mitigate the application of neoliberal governance by the state (states or provinces in federal systems of government, local government, trades unions, universities) do not exist or have much reduced power in England, especially following their sustained undermining by central government since the 1980s. Having said that, readers in other countries may well recognise some of the features of neoliberal governance apparent in the English case; they are unlikely, however, to be so comprehensively and forcefully developed and applied.

One other distinctive feature of ECEC in England should be noted, for it affects the coverage of this case. By international standards, English children enter primary school at an early age; compulsory school age is 5, but the great majority of children in England start the first (reception) class of this stage of education when they are only 4 years of age. We have therefore extended our case study of governance in England up to the age of 6 years, when most children in Europe are just beginning primary schooling, while their peers in England are already into their second year.

Neoliberal governance of education is, however, no longer confined to the nation state. A 'global education race', with nations competing in a global market, is increasingly subject to global forms of governance. We shall show how a new, global form of governance of ECEC is beginning to emerge, delivered by the OECD, a powerful international organisation we have already met in Chapter 2. This new development is part of a wider project of creating and imposing a world-wide system of uniform outcomes and standardised performance measures for the whole of education.

Neoliberal governance has certain intended consequences in mind, in particular that a market of disparate and competing providers should produce certain uniform and prescribed outcomes. But it has other, unintended consequences, consequences that, in our view, are often highly adverse to both children and adults involved in early childhood education and care. We conclude the chapter by considering some of these consequences.

Neoliberal governance in action: the case of England

Standards and performance

A tsunami of data

In Chapter 1 we described the rise of New Public Management, neoliberalism's way of governance, and its main principles. These included explicit standards of performance and greater emphasis on output control; as part of the introduction of New Public Management, 'performance measurement was introduced in the 1980s in public organizations together with a faith in result-driven management' (Bjørnholt and Larsen, 2014, p. 400). In Chapter 2 we examined the application of this agenda to compulsory education since the 1980s through an analysis of the Global Education Reform Movement (GERM), with its emphasis on standards and testing. The result has been the production of vast amounts of data, with education described, assessed and governed by numbers, becoming an exemplar of how '[n]umbers have achieved an unmistakable political power within technologies of government ... [and become] crucial techniques for modern government ... indispensable to the complex technologies through which government is exercised' (Rose, 1999, pp. 197, 198).

Compulsory education was the first sector in England to feel the impact of these New Public Management principles, starting with the introduction of a prescriptive national curriculum in 1988, setting out what children should be taught to ensure each pupil is given the same standard of education, followed by a nationwide testing regime – Standardised Assessment Tests (SATs) for 7-year-olds (1990), 11-year-olds (1994) and 14-year-olds (1997), though this last assessment was subsequently dropped. Early Childhood Education and Care was initially omitted from this emergent system of standard setting and performance measurement, a reflection of the low priority it still had for government in the 1980s and early 1990s. This changed in 1997, when a

Labour Party government under Tony Blair came to power, and made ECEC a national priority. Alongside policies to expand provision of services and increase funding, with a strong emphasis on marketisation and private provision as the vehicles for delivery, the government introduced a matrix of governance measures. Early years, like compulsory education, became an 'auditable commodity' (Ball, 2003, p. 225) through the measurement of standards and assessment of performance.

The preceding Conservative government, at the end of its period in office, had begun to recognise the need for early education with prescribed standards, and published in 1996 *Nursery Education: Desirable Outcomes for Children's Learning on Entering Compulsory Education* (School Curriculum and Assessment Authority, 1996), a document that summarised the goals for learning to be achieved by English children by the time they entered compulsory education. But the big push for 'outcome control' came after 1997. 'Desirable Outcomes' was replaced, in 2000, by *Curriculum Guidance for the Foundation Stage* (Qualifications and Curriculum Authority/Department for Education and Employment (England), 2000), defining the 'foundation stage' as a distinct phase of education for children aged 3- to 5-years-old and setting out six areas of learning – personal, social and emotional development; communication, language and literacy; mathematical development; knowledge and understanding of the world; physical development; creative development. Each area came with a set of related 'early learning goals', explicit standards of performance.

This was, in turn replaced, in 2008, by the *Early Years Foundation Stage* (EYFS) (Department for Children, Schools and Families (England), 2008). The EYFS incorporated curriculum and standards for services for children from birth until the end of the first year in primary school, a document encompassing the whole of ECEC. In two volumes – a statutory framework and practice guidance – running to 160 pages, the EYFS set out 69 Early Learning Goals (ELGs), a set of outcomes for each of the 'six areas of learning and development'.

Standard-setting was followed by performance measurement. The *Early Years Foundation Stage Profile* (EYFSP) (Qualifications and Curriculum Authority, 2008) was also introduced in 2008, to measure children's performance in obtaining the specified ELGs at the end of their Reception year (i.e. the first year in primary school), usually at age 5 years. Its main aim, according to government, was 'to provide a reliable, valid and accurate assessment of individual children at the end of the EYFS' (Department for Education (England), 2013, p. 7). The profiling of each child, made by teachers mostly on the basis of observations, involved assessing children on 13 scales, each divided into nine 'points', with the procedure specified in detail in a handbook running to 90 pages.

The EYFSP was revised and somewhat simplified in 2013 (Standards and Testing Agency, 2013), the accompanying handbook reduced to 62 pages. This followed the production of a revised EYFS in 2012 (Department for Education (England), 2012), in which the Early Learning Goals were reduced from 69 to 17 – though with some sleight of hand, since the new learning goals now include a number of 'sub goals', similar in type to the 'goals' in the 2008 EYFS. For example, Early Learning Goal 9 for 'Reading' has three components,

> Children read and understand simple sentences. They use phonic knowledge to decode regular words and read them aloud accurately. They also read some common irregular words. They demonstrate an understanding when talking with others about what they have read.
>
> *(ibid., p. 8)*

The revised goals place more emphasis on literacy and numeracy, while the stated intention of the revised EYFS is to promote 'teaching and learning to ensure children's "school readiness" … [giving] children the broad range of knowledge and skills that provide the right foundation for good future progress through school and life' (Department for Education (England), 2017a, p. 5). Such changes place an intensified performativity and 'school readiness' demand on young children (Lee, 2020).

Under the revised EYFSP system, children are still assessed by reception class teachers, on the basis of observations and 'best fit' judgements against prescribed criteria, but now for the 17 ELGs, with each child rated on a 3-point scale for each goal: 1 (Emerging), 2 (Expected) or 3 (Exceeding). The child is then judged whether to have acquired sufficient ELG 'passes' to be awarded an overall 'Good Level of Development' (GLD). If a child has achieved their GLD then they are deemed to be 'school ready'; if not, then they are not school ready. To be assessed as 'school ready', a child has to achieve at least a score of 2 in all areas of learning, the hardest to achieve being early literacy and numeracy, where the criteria for success have become much more demanding. Local Authorities use a system of inspection and moderation to mark the accuracy of teachers' judgements.

While the EYFSP has been evolving, two further assessments have been added to the expanding grid of performance measurement. In 2011 the English government introduced the *Phonics Screening Check* (PSC) for 6-year-old children, intended to raise early years literacy standards and promote the teaching of 'systematic synthetic phonics' (Department for Education (England), 2012, p. 5). The PSC is a standardised pass/fail test in which children decode a mixture of 20 real words and 20 pseudo-words or 'nonsense' words, and it must be re-taken by those pupils who 'fail' to score an arbitrary mark of 32. It is a 'high stakes test' as government requires schools' PSC pass rates to increase annually, with their results posted on the web for public accountability and comparison (Flewitt and Roberts-Holmes, 2015).

These measures of performance are all statutory, required by government of primary schools and of providers of early years services, or at least those who receive public funding. There are, however, further measurements that are non-statutory, though widely applied through *Development Matters in the Early Years Foundation Stage* (DM), which is described as 'non-statutory guidance material [that] supports practitioners in implementing the statutory requirements of the EYFS' (Early Education, 2012, p. 1). This 47-page document, produced in 2012 and covering children from birth to 5 years, takes the form of 'development statements' that are presented as indicative of what might be expected, and observed, of children at different ages if they are on track to meet each of the Early Years Foundation Stage's 17 Early Learning Goals. For example, for the first ELG, 'making relationships', evidence that a child from birth to 11 months is learning includes observing the following 'development statements':

- Enjoys the company of others and seeks contact with others from birth.
- Gazes at faces and copies facial movements. e.g. sticking out tongue, opening mouth and widening eyes.
- Responds when talked to, for example, moves arms and legs, changes facial expression, moves body and makes mouth movements.
- Recognises and is most responsive to main carer's voice: face brightens, activity increases when familiar carer appears.
- Responds to what carer is paying attention to, e.g. following their gaze.
- Likes cuddles and being held: calms, snuggles in, smiles, gazes at carer's face or strokes carer's skin.

Similar lists 'for observing what a child is learning' are given for children aged 8–20 months, 16–26 months, 22–36 months, 30–50 months and 40–60+ months, and for each age range for the remaining 16 ELGs.

The document is at pains to emphasise flexibility and to recognise variation in children's 'development':

> Children develop at their own rates, and in their own ways. The development statements and their order should not be taken as necessary steps for individual children. They should not be used as checklists. The age/stage bands overlap because these are not fixed age boundaries but suggest a typical range of development.
>
> *(ibid., p. 6)*

Yet what DM adds up to is a vast and detailed matrix of performance measures, literally hundreds of 'developmental statements', that define how a normal child should be and that direct the attention and observations of practitioners to whether or not children measure up.

Yet another system of performance measurement was added in 2015: the *Progress or Integrated Health Check*. This is a 'progression measure' of health and education for children between the ages of two to three-years-old. It brought together two existing reviews, combining the Early Years Foundation Stage progress check at age two from education with the Healthy Child Programme Review at age two to two-and-a-half from public health. A child's progress is measured across a range of areas including health, social skills, behaviour and well-being, and speech and language skills. Where measured progress across the year has been less than expected interventions and support are put into place to ensure that the child meets the expected standards. The progress measure draws upon the 'complementary skills and experiences of health and early education practitioners and parents' perspectives' and is designed to 'facilitate earlier identification of any developmental needs and the offer of appropriate support or interventions' (Blades, Greene, Wallace et al., 2014, p. 22).

So, over the last 20 years, the English state has created a 'delivery chain' of standards (Ball, 2012) for children from birth to 6-years-old, and accompanying performance measures, a national system of performance management that strongly governs early years education and care. It prepares and readies the young child for the test-based culture of compulsory schooling, with its 'high-stakes' SATs at age 7 and 11. Figure 5.1 illustrates component of the intense governance of English education from birth to 11 years, a constant regime of standards and measurement, by which the neoliberal-infused state has sought to manage, from a distance and in great detail, both children and the practitioners who work with them.

What is also striking is the restlessness of this neoliberal governance, constantly changing, adding and (on occasion) removing, forever seeking better measurement and better control, forever pursuing improved surveillance. In the case of ECEC in England, more change is in the offing, in the form of yet another performance measure, a national standardised test to be applied to 4-year-olds in the first (reception) class of primary school: *Reception Baseline Assessment* (RBA). An initial attempt by the English Department of Education to introduce RBA led to its withdrawal in 2016, in the face of strong opposition from early years professionals (see Chapter 6) and research that cast doubt on the procedure. However, not daunted, government redoubled its efforts with a contract worth nearly £10 million, awarded in 2018, for the National Foundation for Educational Research (NFER) to develop a second RBA, a standardised, prescribed and scripted computer-based test for full national implementation in the 2020–2021 academic year.

The RBA will test 4-year-olds on two areas of learning: mathematics (covering 'early calculation', 'mathematical language' and 'early understanding of shape'); and literacy, communications and language or LCL (covering 'early vocabulary', 'phonological awareness', 'early reading' and 'early comprehension'). It uses an online

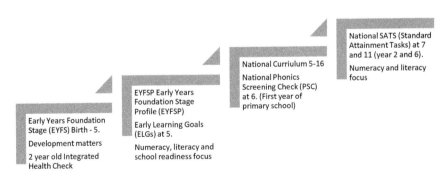

Early Years Foundation Stage (EYFS) Birth - 5.
Development matters
2 year old Integrated Health Check

EYFSP Early Years Foundation Stage Profile (EYFSP)
Early Learning Goals (ELGs) at 5.
Numeracy, literacy and school readiness focus

National Curriulum 5-16
National Phonics Screening Check (PSC) at 6. (First year of primary school)

National SATS (Standard Attainment Tasks) at 7 and 11 (year 2 and 6).
Numeracy and literacy focus

FIGURE 5.1 The English regime of standards and measurement for children from birth to 11-years-old

scoring system 'to maximise the manageability of the administrative tasks, enabling quick, easy and automated recording' (Department for Education (England), 2019a, p. 5) and to produce an aggregated score for maths and LCL. The purpose of this digital test is, in the words of the DfE, to 'provide an on-entry assessment of pupil attainment to be used as a starting point from which a cohort-level progress measure to the end of key stage 2 (KS2) [that is, at 11 years old] can be created' (DfE 2019b, 4). Children's scores on the assessment will not be made available to schools, but 'will be recorded in the national pupil database'[1] (ibid., p. 9) and through this database, schools' progress across seven years of schooling, from age 4 to 11 will be measured and judged by government. RBA, therefore, will be a key tool of management, and hence holding schools to account for progress during primary schooling deemed inadequate; or in the official language again, 'to support the accountability framework and help assess school effectiveness' (Department for Education (England), 2014, p. 1).

This latest version, too, has met with widespread opposition (Goldstein, Moss, Sammons, Sinnott and Stobart, 2018; Roberts-Holmes, Lee, Sousa and Jones, 2020), the joint general secretary of England's largest teaching union complaining that 'the government persists in spending millions on assessment systems for which there is no evidence of value, when teachers and parents are crying out for serious investment in early years education' (Bousted, cited in Russell, 2020).

At the same time that it has been striving to introduce a RBA, the English government has signed up to yet another form of performance assessment, this time an attempt by the Organisation for Economic Cooperation and Development (OECD) to add to its growing armoury of ILSAs – 'international large-scale assessments'[2] – with a new standardised testing regime aimed at 5-year-olds (who in most countries, unlike in England, are still in ECEC services). The *International Early Learning and Well-being Study* (IELS) aims to measure and compare performance in participating countries for early learning 'domains' that include emerging literacy, emerging numeracy, self-regulation, empathy and trust; OECD has stated that IELS will produce 'internationally comparable data that will enable countries to compare the relative strengths and areas for development in their own ECEC (early childhood education and care) systems with those in other jurisdictions' (OECD, 2015, p. 103).

The first round of assessments took place in autumn 2018, with results published in March 2020 (see the IELS website at www.oecd.org/education/school/early-learning-and-child-well-being-study/). However, only three countries signed up to participate in this initial exercise: Estonia, United States – and England. Despite much criticism, the English Department for Education has again persisted with a new testing regime, echoing the OECD's rationale by stating that the IELS 'will enable the (English) department to robustly compare our policies and performance to other countries ... and will facilitate our assessment and development of early years policy' (Department for Education (England), 2017c, p. 1).

As discussed in Chapter Two, the spread of international testing regimes gives international organisations such as the OECD immense power, handing to them the ability to define, develop and measure universal education standards across countries, assessing national performance against these standards, and offering advice on what countries should do to improve their performance. In this way OECD has become education arbiter, judge and counsellor rolled into one. What is in it, then, for the English government? The opportunity to add to its battery of performance measures and so to govern even more strongly the market in ECEC services over which it presides. If the RBA enables within country comparison of schools and other early years settings, the IELS offers a complementary process enabling the English government to 'benchmark' national performance against its international competitors in the global race for economic success and survival.

Where to and what for

Where does this tsunami of data generated across England wash up and for what purposes is it intended? The final destination in most cases is the central government, in London, and the National Pupil Database (see footnote 1). It is used, for example, to compile national comparative datasets of local authority EYFSP results (Department for Education (England), 2019) (see Figure 5.2 for an example of a table produced by central government from EYFSP data).

In the case of the EYFSP, local authorities first collate all results from schools in their area before passing this data on to central government. Local authorities may also use this data to act as agents of central government in governing schools and practitioners, with pressure on local authorities to improve results year by year, pressure then passed on to schools. As this comment from a 2015 study shows, such pressure can take extreme forms verging on bullying.

We 'name and shame' by showing all the school names. Some schools didn't have any children at 'working above the expected level' so you say 'well your

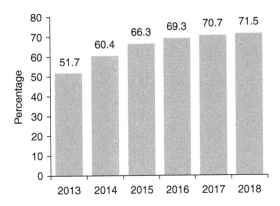

FIGURE 5.2 Percentage of children achieving a good level of development in England, 2013 to 2019 on EYFSP

Source: Department for Education (England), 2019, p. 1

statistical neighbour has this percentage so how come you haven't?' And they think 'I'd better go back and have another look at that'.... It does challenge them and that's why we do it.

(Local Authority Advisor cited in Roberts-Holmes, 2015)

Whether at central or local government level, a major purpose of gathering all this information is to better control, regulate and govern, in a situation where government has contracted out delivery of services to markets and private providers. Of course, as Foucault has described and discussed, the state's use of statistics and data has a long history in regulating and governing populations going back to the 19th century or earlier. But more recently there has been a step change in this process: at the beginning of the 21st century, the digitalisation of numbers and its associated 'data deluge' (Kitchin 2014, p. xv) has enabled a greatly enlarged scope and accelerated pace of data collection and analysis called 'datafication' (Lingard, 2009). Datafication in the early years and beyond operates as an increasingly powerful and ubiquitous managerial technology, strongly governing schools and families (Bradbury and Roberts-Holmes, 2018, p. 38).

Datafication and the digitalisation of data has enabled an escalation in the use and comparability of standardised assessment and intensified the numerical measurements of child and service performance – and hence the more effective management of that performance, and the creation of a climate of 'performativity', a concept we intro-duced in Chapter 2 when discussing compulsory education. Ball defines performativity as 'a technology, a culture and a mode of regulation that employs judgements, com-parisons and displays as means of incentive, control, attrition and change based on rewards and sanctions' (2003, p. 216). Performativity demands the regular publication of statistical databases, numerical audits, comparable results and other visualised performance indicators. Digitalisation has enabled these 'existing techniques of accountability, performativity and human capital development to be reworked, reinforced, and reproduced as well as accelerated to high velocity, scaled up to voluminous capacity and expanded in scope to encompass a wider variety of inputs' (Williamson, 2017, p. 95). The generation of a multiplicity of comparable datasets and visualised performance tables leads to a hyper-governance of education because it has become easier and faster to identify 'best practices' and 'what works' (and at the same time 'underperforming' schools). For David Beer (2018, np),

[t]he core idea is that data enable people to get ahead of the game and that these analytics provide them with an edge on their competitors. Here we see the model of the market and notions of hyper-competitiveness solidifying – alongside these we are told that we need to constantly be picking up the pace.

Early years visualised performance indicators steer and govern early years education in the direction of *calculable pedagogies* that produce required results. Measurements of performance are passed to senior management who organise Pupil Progress Meetings that 'require teachers to share evidence of pupils' progress with members of the leadership team and be accountable for progress' (DfE, 2010, p. 45). A study of three English early childhood settings reports on this phenomenon, with the teachers describing:

> [h]ow they were increasingly subjected to the demands of data production.... For the early years teachers in this study, the focus of assessment data was the concept of constant progress through the Early Years Foundation Stage; everyone must be tracked to ensure they are moving forwards. This requires ever more detailed data, to show the incremental progress of the children.

As the head of a nursery school said:

> Where do you stop with it because there is so much of it! Health data, education data, family support data and well-being data and to be perfectly honest I just can't cope with that much detail all the time! So I have put people in place who can manage that data.
>
> (Roberts-Holmes and Bradbury, 2016, p. 605)

Datafication enables a ubiquitous and all-seeing 'dataveillance', which permits stronger management of performance. As we shall see shortly, it not only enables stronger external management, by government and its agencies; it also leads to stronger internalised management or governmentality, where the self manages the self. But there is a third function. Data, and especially comparable data, is seen as an essential tool of and condition for the informed consumer, that self-interested and calculating ideal subject of neoliberalism, able to work the market to best effect by weighing up the pros and cons, costs and benefits of competing products, supplied by data. The tsunami of data on ECEC has been intended to serve this purpose too.

The English Government in 2010 stated that it wished to publish the EYFSP results by school in order to 'help people make informed choices' (Ward, 2010, np). Although so far neither EYFSP nor GLD data are publicly available at school level, the possible shape of things to come can be seen in the public availability of SATS scores for 11-year-olds on the English Department for Education's 'Find and Compare Schools in England' website (www.gov.uk/school-performance-tables). Here, parents can search for specific schools by name and postcode, then have the option of creating and saving 'a comparison list' of schools, as if shopping on Amazon.com or using a comparison website. The site visually displays the chosen comparison schools' SATs data using a crude traffic light colour scheme providing a 'very public technology of performance' (Ball, Maguire, Braun, Perryman and Hoskins, 2012, p. 514) intended to help parents with their decision making.

The screen shot of two nearby schools (Figure 5.3) shows how much progress pupils have made in reading, writing and maths between the end of key stage 1 (7 years) and the end of key stage 2 (11 years), based on SATs results. Each individual school's data is compared to pupils across England and colour coded. In the above comparison list the first school's reading performance is labelled as 'above national

Progress score in reading, writing and maths

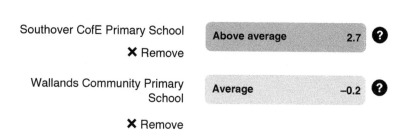

Reading

Southover CofE Primary School
✖ Remove

| Above average | 2.7 ❓ |

Wallands Community Primary School
✖ Remove

| Average | –0.2 ❓ |

FIGURE 5.3 Progress score in reading, writing and maths for two neighbouring schools
Source: www.gov.uk/school-performance-tables

average' and colour coded as green symbolising its winning position in the reading race. However, this school's writing and maths are noted as slightly below the national 'Average' and colour coded as yellow, signifying could do better. The second primary school displays writing and maths data 'well below national average' performance and so is displayed in red highlighting its 'failure'.

A further visualised display on the same page (Figure 5.4) graphically demonstrates the two school's performance relative to national 'expected standards', in which again the second school comes out worst. But because these displays – 'data

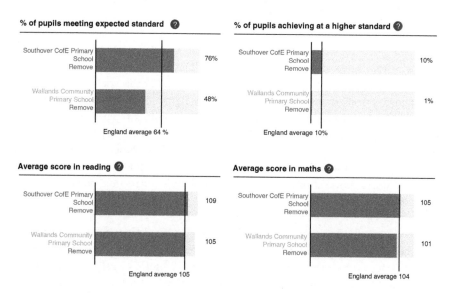

FIGURE 5.4 Performance of two schools relative to national 'expected standards'
Source: www.gov.uk/school-performance-tables

dashboards' – contain no contextual information, it is not apparent that this 'below average' school includes a high number of children with special educational needs in a dedicated Unit.

If and when the English government installs its latest performance measure, Reception Baseline Assessment, further graphics may well be added to each school's data dashboards, purporting to show pupil progress from school entry to the end of key stage 1 (7 years), yet more data for the savvy consumer to factor into their calculation of which school to choose.

Inspection made public

Ofsted (Office for Standards in Education) is a non-ministerial department of the English government established in 1992 to inspect and regulate schools and colleges (Steele, 2000). Since then its scope has increased substantially, to include all residential and other care services for children and young people, and all non-school-based ECEC services, including nurseries, playgroups and childminders. It is a huge and powerful managerial tool. The agency works closely with government to further policy aims, such as a focus on literacy and numeracy. In 2013, it 'toughened up' inspections noting that early years settings must have an 'extremely sharp focus' on communication and language if they were to be granted the coveted and marketable 'outstanding' label (Ofsted, 2013, p. 9). More recently, Ofsted has stated that 'the teaching of reading, including systematic synthetic phonics, is the core purpose of the Reception Year' (Ofsted, 2017, p. 7), in preparation for the Year 1 Phonics Screening Check, and praises early years settings that have based their literacy and maths upon Year 1 primary school National Curriculum expectations.

Following inspection, Ofsted grades schools and other ECEC settings on a four-point numerical scale: 1 ('Outstanding'), 2 ('Good'), 3 ('Requires Improvement'), 4 ('Inadequate'). A separate grade is provided for the Early Years Foundation Stage in primary schools, that is for children up to 5-years-old, but this grade 'contributes to the judgement about the overall effectiveness of the school'. In arriving at its grades, Ofsted uses a mixture of curriculum observations, interviews with staff and pupils, and parents' feedback – and comparison with national performance data (Ofsted, 2019b). In a study of 20 reception class teachers, Roberts-Holmes (2015, p. 306) reported the effects of this data-based requirement upon primary school teachers and a Local Authority Advisor, and how increasing datafication has become bound up with inspection.

> We're totally data driven. If the data is good Ofsted leave us alone but if the data is poor they drill right down into everything. We'll be punished if we have poor data, so obviously it's a huge huge pressure to get the data looking good. Ofsted take the data from Year 6 and work back and see where they were in Year 2 and Reception. So it has really influenced thinking.
>
> *(Deputy Head)*

It's all based on data. Ofsted are saying that if the teaching is good the data should be good and if there's bad teaching there is bad data. So the data is driving the pedagogy.

(Local authority Early Years Advisor)

We have constant meetings looking at the data. It has become very clinical and children have just become numbers.... In this game, you gotta play the game. If you're being judged on a score – teach to it – you're a fool if you don't. You must teach to the test – that's the agenda.

(Reception Teacher)

Being labelled as 'Requires Improvement' or 'Inadequate' can potentially have dire consequences for a school or other early childhood setting, threatening jobs or the setting's very existence. The prospect of inspection failure, therefore, is meant to spur management into greater efforts to identify failings and improve performance, and hence govern themselves more strongly. No school or other early years setting can be content but instead has to be constantly self-reforming, self-improving and ever vigilant in showing progress. To obtain the required standards, schools subject themselves to a wide array of efficiency 'reforms' which are 'all assembled and infused with the aim of the government of capacities and habits' (Rose, 1999, p. 53).

You have to track children all the time and I have to add everyone's data at the end of each term to the school tracker. Have they performed appropriately and if not why not and what interventions are going to have to go in? Nobody's allowed to fall behind. The tracking begins from Nursery in the [EYFS] Prime Areas and right through to year 6. If you are exceeding at the end of Reception you have to show that you are exceeding at the end of KS1 and if not then we are not doing our job.

(Deputy Head, cited in Roberts-Holmes and Bradbury, 2016, p. 604)

But Ofsted as a neoliberal form of governance, like datafication, is not confined to assessing performance, praising the compliant and punishing the errant. It also works through other means. Inspection per se is not a neoliberal tool, having been deployed for centuries as a direct form of bureaucratic or autocratic control; what turns inspection into a neoliberal form of governance is making its results publicly available to inform consumers and hence bring market discipline to bear on providers. Its inspection reports of individual settings – whether of nurseries or schools – are available to the public online, including on the 'Find and Compare Schools in England' website. The consumer, therefore, is expected to check out not only data dashboards, but the latest inspections of the options they are considering, taking these into account in their final choice.

Ofsted (2019) has recently set out its plans to overhaul the inspection system in response to a variety of criticism, including de-contextualised data-led judgements, increases in teachers' administrative workloads, and a narrowing of the curriculum to a performance-led focus on numeracy and literacy. Under its new Education Inspection Framework, Ofsted will adopt a more nuanced and 'rebalanced inspection', which allows headteachers to analyse and explain school's internal data, including their own judgements and proposed actions; the aim is to enable inspectors to judge how this data has been achieved and to what extent they are the result of broad and rich learning or simply 'gaming' and 'off-rolling' (Ofsted, 2019). The role of inspection, it is claimed, 'is to *complement*, rather than intensify, the focus on performance data and measures' (Ofsted, 2019, emphasis added).

Ofsted insist that 'data should not be "king"' (Ofsted, 2019, p. 1), yet it still plays a central role in the revised inspection system. Not only will schools have to show how they are working with data, but within the new Inspection Framework, '[i]nspectors will use published, national performance data as a *starting* point in inspection' (ibid.; emphasis added). The inspection regime will also retain key features of the previous system. Ofsted can still inspect without providing notice or warning to schools, and it will retain its harsh four-point judgement scale, which threatens to undermine its intended reforms.

> The danger to Ofsted is that all the advances in the draft framework will be set at naught if it persists with these grades, because teachers will see the progressive language as a sham, hiding an iron fist behind all the gentle talk of taking 'a rounded view of the quality of education'.
>
> *(Coffield, 2019, np)*

Ofsted and its inspections will continue to play a pivotal role, not only in the operation of a competitive market in schools and other early childhood services, but also in their centralised governance.

Governmentality

Neoliberal governance, we have argued, works in several ways. By increasing the data available, it enhances the power of management, including in this case central government. By increasing the data that is public, it not only constructs parents as informed consumers but enables them to 'apply a market pressure upon schools' (Jones, 2016, p. 143). But it also works through its effects on those who provide services, in this case early childhood education and care, whether teachers, childcare workers or others. These effects are both blatant and insidious, but either way the end result is the same: workers govern themselves to the ends required by the powers-that-be.

As we described in the last chapter, through the workings of governmentality what is originally imposed externally by management can become embodied by those who are managed, so that they end up 'owning' the values, assumptions and goals of management – in effect, they end up managing or governing themselves. What began as a possibly contested external imposition becomes internalised and self-evident. This process can easily occur with the performance standards so central to neoliberal governance. 'Developmental statements' or 'learning goals' or other required outcomes become taken for granted, treated as normal, their achievement part of professional identity as early years workers come to embody the demands of management; more and more they come to govern themselves to these ends. 'Playing the Ofsted data game' had become a central and pressing concern for the early years teachers in Roberts-Holmes' (2015) study, so that increasingly their pedagogy was framed by the necessity to produce the correct performance measurement data, rather than by their own values and principles.

Similarly, Bradbury (2013) noted how the EYFS Profile scores were produced, managed and changed to be 'acceptable' to the local authority. Data itself had come to partly represent the teachers' pedagogical focus and to be a means by which to measure their competence and ability; the constant collection, production and delivery of data had turned into 'an enacted fantasy' in which 'their investment in the fabrication is immense' (ibid., p. 633). Within early years settings, workers end up hyper-governing themselves as 'centres of calculation' and 'calculating selves', ensuring that everything is quantified and accounted for. This self-governance positions them as 'data entry clerks' who both capture data but who are also captured by the data they collect.

The authors of the 'developmental statements' in 'Development Matters' may not want these statements to be used as a checklist. Yet it is difficult to see how they will not become so in many cases, as practitioners are judged, and are expected to judge themselves, in terms of their ability to perform, to deliver prescribed outputs, to achieve required standards. That is how such human technologies work.

Consequences of neoliberal governance

Performance

In 2013, 51.7% of children achieved the EYFS Profile 'Good Level of Development' rating, but by 2016 this had jumped to 69.3% and to 71.8% in 2019. Given the power of the human technologies available to and deployed by neoliberal governance and the sustained application of such technologies focused on prescribed performance standards, it would be surprising if there was little or no registered change in outcome.

However, there continues to be lower attainment for boys than for girls, particularly for summer-born boys, and for children from disadvantaged socio-economic backgrounds. For example, in 2019 the percentage achieving at least the expected level in all ELGs varied from 63.1% in Middlesbrough, a city with high levels of deprivation, to 80.6% in the wealthy London suburb of Richmond upon Thames; while the attainment gap between all children and the lowest-attaining 20% of children varies from 22.1 percentage points in Richmond upon Thames to 45.5 percentage points in far less affluent Middlesbrough (Department for Education (England), 2019b, pp. 1, 10).

Recent analysis by the Educational Policy Institute of early years attainment since 2013 suggests that very little progress has been made in closing the gap between advantaged and disadvantaged children. A regime of constant standards and measurement, they conclude, has meant that 'inequalities have stopped reducing and have started to widen' so that 'the gap will never close without systematic change' (Hutchinson, Reader and Akhal, 2020, pp. 11, 8). This bears out the general conclusion by Pasi Sahlberg and William Doyle that '[s]ome fifteen years of standardized testing-based education reform has succeeded in eliminating play in school, but it has failed in its chief objective – closing the infamous achievement gaps between affluent and low-income pupils' (2019, p. 167). (The Covid-19 pandemic has greatly exacerbated educational inequalities with the National Foundation for Education Research stating that by September 2020 'the gap between disadvantaged pupils and their peers had increased by 46%' (Sharp et al., 2020, p. 1) in primary and secondary schools in England. This widening gap is likely to be replicated in the early years.)

The validity of some standardised measurements has come in for critical scrutiny. The claim by the English government that a Reception Baseline Assessment test can be a good predictor of children's future attainment – and that schools can therefore be held accountable if predictions are not realised – has been questioned. Jones (2018) notes that 'socioeconomic background is a much stronger influence on progress than any school effect' (https://neu.org.uk/assessment/baseline-test-nobody-wants). While an expert panel from the British Educational Research Association stated that the proposed introduction of Reception Baseline Assessment in 2020–2021 would be 'flawed, unjustified and wholly unfit for purpose … [and] would be detrimental to children, parents, teachers and the wider education system in England' (Goldstein et al., 2018, p. 5). This conclusion was based upon evidence that as a progress measure across seven years, RBA would provide low levels of reliability leading to highly unreliable value-added calculations, unfit for holding schools to account, and that the whole project is an untried experiment that cannot be properly evaluated until at least 2027 (when the first RBA tested cohort reach 11 years). The English Department for Education has said that Reception class teachers, who will undertake the assessment, will receive simple narrative results for each child after the test, leading the panel to state that

> some children – particularly the summer-born, those with English as an additional language and those with special educational needs – could be unnecessarily labelled as low-ability at the very beginning of their education, with the risk that premature judgements about their abilities may then become 'self-fulfilling'.
>
> *(ibid., p. 8)*

Children's complex realities remain 'a source of unmeasured bias' in the RBA, so that the RBA is likely not only to disadvantage children unfairly, but also to 'systematically favour schools serving fewer disadvantaged pupils, and penalise schools serving higher numbers of disadvantaged children' (ibid., p. 18).

A more general criticism of the value of standardised assessments comes from the great Italian educator, Loris Malaguzzi. He considered what he called 'American' or 'Anglo-Saxon testology' to be a highly reductive and distorting process 'where it is enough to do some tests on an individual and immediately the individual has been defined and measured in some way', the result being 'a ridiculous simplification of knowledge, and a robbing of meaning from individual histories' (cited in Cagliari et al., 2016, pp. 331, 378). In other words, with its narrow focus on test items, on whether children can do items a, b and c, standardised testing totally fails to provide a rich and nuanced understanding of what each child actually can do. Simplification and robbing of meaning reach new levels in the proposed RBA assessment, where children are reduced to numbers then stored in a central database and used to determine the performance of schools.

This line of argument has been developed in a statement about the IELS from Reconceptualising Early Childhood Education, a movement starting in the United States in the 1980s, whose members 'share a concern about privileging particular sets of beliefs or forms of knowledge (or "grand narratives" that typically reflect western or Eurocentric values), which can create power for certain groups of people and oppress others' (RECE, nd).

> Instead of careful, culturally and contextually appropriate consideration of the achievements of early childhood systems in diverse countries, and of systemic evaluation of the actual outcomes for children, families and society, IELS appears to adopt a strategy that favours largely decontextualised comparison and measurement of narrowly defined predetermined outcomes.
>
> It is our concern that such an approach will not provide necessary or meaningful information for decision makers and early childhood leaders in participating countries and beyond. What it will do is draw early childhood education firmly into a global framework of standardised assessment across all tiers of the education system, from early childhood to higher education.
>
> *(Urban and Swadener, 2016, p. 4)*

Standardised assessment is, in short, a measure of conformity to an externally-derived and decontextualised norm applied in the interests of managing performance. It is a form of mapping that tells us little about the individual children who are subjected to it: 'all we know is how far this or that child conforms to certain norms inscribed on the map we use.... The maps, the classifications and the ready-made categories end up replacing the richness of children's lived lives and the inescapable complexity of concrete experience' (Dahlberg, Moss and Pence, 2013, p. 39).

Pedagogy and play

The growing emphasis, in England and elsewhere, on early childhood education and care preparing young children for primary school has been termed 'schoolification', an expressive term for the demands of primary education 'taking over early childhood institutions in a colonising manner' (OECD, 2006, p. 62). This process is becoming apparent in many countries, and spreading the symptoms of GERM into ECEC. Combined with human technologies to further this aim, schoolification has brought the threat of calculable pedagogy leeching into the early years, narrowing the education on offer as a focus on literacy and numeracy leads 'to neglect of other important areas of early learning and development' (ibid., p. 42).

These features – a narrowing education and inappropriate pedagogy – are apparent in England. The proposed RBA, undertaken during the first six weeks 'settling in' period in reception class, focuses on early numeracy and literacy, and strategically aligns education for 4-year-olds with later stages of primary education: as one teacher put it 'the message is that you need to be putting more weight on your English and maths than the rest of it and that's what's measurable' (cited in Roberts-Holmes et al., 2020). Similarly, the standardisation of early literacy and the need for 6-year-olds to perform well in the Phonics Screening Check has cascaded into the early years where children as young as 3-years-old are prepared and trained in phonics (Bradbury and Roberts-Holmes, 2017).

Schoolification is, however, particularly apparent for 4-year-olds, who find themselves in reception class in primary school: from the moment they 'enter the reception class, the pressure is on for them to learn to read, write and do formal written maths. In many schools, children are identified as "behind" with reading before they would even have started school in many other countries' (Whitbread, 2014). A reception class teacher describes how since 2010

> we have seen the curriculum narrowed and impoverished by an over-focus on literacy and numeracy at the expense of a broad and balanced curriculum. The teaching of numeracy and literacy has become overly prescriptive and formal as a result of this, ignoring the ways in which children develop emergently. Instead of focusing on laying the foundations, both for understanding and also for developing a love and enjoyment of reading, writing and maths, we are increasingly pressured to force children to become 'school ready'.
>
> *(personal communication to authors)*

Adverse pedagogical trends stemming from schoolification are reinforced as standards and their management have come to 'stand for, encapsulate or represent the worth, quality or value' (Ball, 2003, p. 217) of early years education. For with a focus on the attainment of managerially-prescribed standards comes what Loris Malaguzzi termed a 'prophetic pedagogy', which

> knows everything beforehand, knows everything that will happen, knows everything, does not have one uncertainty, is absolutely imperturbable ... This is something so coarse, so cowardly, so humiliating of teacher's ingenuity, a complete humiliation for children's ingenuity and potential.
>
> *(cited in Cagliari et al., 2016, p. 422)*

The end result of such pedagogy is that 'pupils of every age are increasingly being required to learn things for which they are not ready, and this leads to shallow learning for the test, rather than in-depth understanding which could form a sound basis for future learning' (Hutchings 2015, p. 5).

This pedagogical turn towards calculation in the service of linear knowledge transmission and predetermined outcomes, driven by standard setting and performance measurement, marks a move towards formal teacher-led instruction, and a move away from a pedagogy of playful learning that welcomes risk-taking, spontaneity and imagination and which has traditionally been associated with the first years of primary schooling in England. Early years education is at high risk of becoming a narrow arid utterly predictable undertaking, devoid of creativity, excitement, wonder and joy. A recent report into the EYFS has highlighted the 'importance of all children experiencing more opportunities for play, language consolidation and extension and opportunities to develop their wider learning dispositions and capacities' (Pascal, Bertram and Rouse, 2019, p. 56) because children's intellectual and emotional 'self regulation' skills are supported through physical, social and pretend play.

One way of enacting a more formal and prophetic pedagogy focused on standards is the introduction into ECEC settings of a particular human technology: 'ability grouping' of young children, from as young as 3-years-old, dividing them up on the basis of predictions of current and future performance for different subjects. This has spread as a calculated strategy to achieve required ELG and PSC outcomes, demonstrating the governing power of performance measures and inspection. In a national survey, ability grouping of children aged between three and five-years-old was found to be most common in Phonics (76%), Maths (62%), Reading (57%) and Literacy (54%), which is not surprising given the performance management focus upon these areas (Bradbury and Roberts-Holmes, 2018). Many early years teachers, such as the ones quoted here, have accepted this technology as necessary given the importance of testing for themselves and their schools:

> Grouping in a data driven world seems to be becoming the norm. This sadly takes away from child led play time as we are forced into writing and reading constantly.
>
> The constant fixation on data results, means that grouping becomes necessary.
>
> They are streamed by ability for phonics because of the phonics test.
>
> *(Bradbury and Roberts-Holmes, 2017, p. 26)*

> Formal learning is now coming down from Year 1 [in primary school], through Reception [class] and into the Nursery class with the three year olds that I teach.... We were explicitly asked by our headteacher to make nursery 'more formal' which means more direct teaching of maths and phonics.
>
> *(Roberts-Holmes, 2014, p. 307)*

In other research, Roberts-Holmes found that early years teachers, with the encouragement of Local Authority advisors, used a particular form of ability grouping known as 'educational triage' to ensure that children achieved the required ELG targets.

> It's about who's going to achieve the GLD [Good Level of Development]. So we say 'they're easily gonna make it, thank you very much'. And we say 'they're never going to make it so go over there and have a nice time' and we look at the middle group. We target these children because they are the ones who may make it. It's the same as Year 6 SATs. So you put all your effort and intervention into those that are just below and it's a very unfair system.
>
> *(London LA Early Years Advisor, cited in Roberts-Holmes, 2015, p. 308)*

'Triage', therefore, involves identifying a particular group of young children who, with dedicated teacher intervention, are predicted to achieve a 'Good Level of Development'. By making it, they raise the average score of the whole class to the required national threshold. However, the consequence of the teacher focusing upon this group is that those children deemed not able to obtain the threshold receive less teacher attention. Similarly, those who are 'easily gonna make it' also receive less teacher attention. Educational triage has more often been associated with older primary and secondary children (Gillborn and Youdell, 2000; Marks, 2012), but has now become an early years performance management strategy, an egregious example of schoolification – with serious consequences for children.

Triage and ability grouping 'frequently leads to inequity and deepening disadvantage' (Hamilton and O'Hara, 2011, p. 714), causing or exacerbating the underachievement of disadvantaged children, children designated as having Special Educational Needs (SEN), and summer-born children, particularly boys, because ability grouping systematically disadvantages such children (Francis et al., 2017). They are more likely to be placed in the 'bottom' group (Gillborn and Youdell, 2000), hence most likely to miss out, while the borderline children, who will have the most impact on attainment data, 'get the extra'. This technology also takes no account of how, in the words of this teacher, '[c]hildren learn and mature at different times. It's wrong to label children into daily ability groups at this age. We all learn in different ways, at different times and have different talents' (cited in Bradbury, 2019, p. 6)

A child's initial placement into an ability group can have long-lasting consequences; the majority of young children placed into particular ability sets or streams will stay in their assigned ability groups throughout their schooling (Dixon, 2002). The UK's Social Mobility Commission (2016b, p. 37) has reported that 'setting can have a profound negative impact on pupils' future social mobility' because disadvantaged children are more likely to be placed in lower sets with less well qualified staff (Dunne et al., 2011; Francis et al., 2017; Hallam and Ireson, 2007). Research from the United States has found that labelling children at school as 'low ability' can have an impact throughout an individual's life (Boaler, 2005). The effects of this technology, therefore, can well outlast school.

In particular, early ability grouping can have a profound impact on expectations that 'create possibilities for who we are and might be' (Ball, 2013, p. 98), forming negative learner identities amongst young children themselves. Judging, labelling and placing young children into more or less fixed ability groups effectively negates, excludes and 'steals' children's confidence, aspirations and their diverse and creative 'one hundred languages'. Hallam, Ireson and Davies (2004, p. 527) showed that primary grouping by ability 'caused pupils' status to be defined *by* their ability'; while Boaler (2013, p. 147) has noted that children 'take a very clear message' from ability grouping practices – 'some children are clever and some are not'. Writing earlier, the same author has described how ability grouping acts as a 'psychological prison' that 'breaks ambition' and 'almost formally labels kids as stupid' Boaler (2005, p. 141).

The following poignant example shows how ability grouping serves to dramatically create and reinforce negative self-fulfilling prophecies. A teacher recalls how a 7-year-old girl's aspiration to be a doctor like her mother was discarded when she was moved down a set.

> She said, 'I used to want to be a doctor like my mum but since I moved to the middle set I've realised that that's not something I can do because I'm not good enough so I'm thinking about what else I might do in the future'.
>
> *(cited in Bradbury and Roberts-Holmes, 2017, p. 41)*

The end result of the system of neoliberal governance, with its emphasis on outcomes and measurement, and the pedagogy it fosters, may well be counterproductive, leading some children to disengage from school. As this primary school head teacher observes:

> Over one-third of Year 6 children failed SATs last year [in England]. That's a group of 11-year-olds being sent to secondary [school] feeling that they haven't achieved.... The system of accountability means children are part of a machine. They're a number, a percentage. Perhaps they'll think that education isn't for them.
>
> *(cited in Ward, 2019a, np)*

Images

In Chapter 4, we discussed the neoliberal image of the young child, in particular as a quantum of human capital. But neoliberal governance of ECEC produces a further image: of the child as an assemblage of data, her history and meaning reduced to a collection of numbers produced by checking, testing, assessment and screening. This datafying of young children is eloquently expressed by the poet Michael Rosen (2018), available from his blog: http://michaelrosenblog.blogspot.com/2018/02/the-data-have-landed.html. Put less succinctly, children come to be 'made up' through data accumulated from the growing matrix of health, social and education assessments so that 'the data produces the learner as much as the learner produces the data' (Williamson, 2016, p. 139). The danger becomes that children's complexities and contextualised lives are reduced, simplified and 'datafied' (Lupton and Williamson 2017, p. 787). Algorithms, with potentially limited pre-determined goals, expectations and pathways become a possibility so that datafied children

> are configured as algorithmic assemblages as the result of these practices, with the possibility that their complexities, potentialities and opportunities may be circumscribed. They are encouraged to view and compare themselves with others using these assemblages from very early in the lifespans.
>
> *(Lupton and Williamson 2017, p. 8)*

Children so configured are, indeed, robbed of meaning.

Children's well-being

Will Davies notes that 'buried within the technocratic toolkits of neoliberal regulators and evaluators is a brutal political philosophy. This condemns most people to the status of failures with only the faint hope of future victories to cling onto … and leads to a depressive-competitive disorder' (Davies, 2015b, p. 179). Within a neoliberal education, performativity's brutal 'depressive-competitive disorder' is considered as 'a necessary and unavoidable evil' (Stedman Jones, 2014, p. 338) because it spurs everyone on to ever-greater effort, efficiency and productivity. But there are major downsides.

Take the example of ability grouping as a means to maximise performance in standardised assessments. This creates insecurities and stress as children are threatened with being labelled 'losers' and of being left behind in the competition; Zeng, Hou and Peng (2016) found that ability grouping can lead to anxiety and panic attacks and children being emotionally 'distraught' at an early age. The daily lived school reality for children labelled as low ability can be brutal, as described by a primary school head teacher:

> These children are pulled out of broad curriculum subjects to try to close the gap. Their experience at school must be horrible – in assembly they've got to do phonics intervention, then a phonics lesson, a literacy lesson, a maths lesson, lunch, reading, extra reading intervention and then speech intervention. What else are they learning about the world? They are six years old, and all their school experience tells them is that they are failures (already) and have to be pulled out constantly to work on things their peers can already do, and miss out on the fun bits of learning.
>
> *(Hutchings, 2015, p. 41)*

The following teacher can even now recall her own experience of ability grouping when she was a young child:

> I remember when I was in Year 1 [5–6-years-old], I was put on the table where the children were struggling and I still remember that, that I was put on

the struggling table. It was horrendous for my self-esteem. I still remember it now

(cited in Bradbury and Roberts-Holmes, 2017, p. 23)

Yet even though she so personally and vehemently disagrees with ability grouping, recalling its detrimental effect on her own well-being as a child, she feels compelled to apply it now in her school to obtain the required performance measurements.

Neoliberal governance's belief in standards and performance measurement have made English children 'some of the most over-assessed in the modern world' (Asthama and Boycott-Owen, 2018, np). Harvey Goldstein has noted the detrimental effects of this school accountability regime on children's well-being:

The problem is at the moment the accountability component dominates everything else and it distorts the curriculum, it distorts learning, it distorts children's behaviour. There is lots of evidence now about the stress that children go under. Assessments should not be doing that to children. Assessments should be encouraging children to learn.

(Goldstein, 2017, p. 16)

Brown and Carr (2018, p. 20) argue that 'the neoliberal educational model itself creates the perfect platform for a mental health crisis in young people'. A recent survey found that 89% of teachers consider that testing and exams were the greatest causal factor of students' poor well-being and mental health (Association for Teachers and Lecturers, 2016, p. 12). In another recent survey of primary school headteachers, eight out of 10 reported an increase in children presenting with mental health issues due to the pressure to perform in primary school SATS, and that over the past two years levels of stress, anxiety and panic attacks in primary children had risen by 78%, fear of academic failure by 76% and depression by 55% (Weale, 2017).

Some research has further indicated a direct link between the pressure to perform in the educational system and the development of suicidal thoughts and behaviour (Sharp, 2013, p. 10; ChildLine, 2014, p. 37). A primary teacher in a survey in 2019 conducted by the New Education Union stated: 'SATs pressure and general expectations are taking their toll on more vulnerable pupils; We have nine-year-olds talking about suicide' (Weale, 2019a, np). Young Minds (2017, p. 20) has estimated that three children in every classroom have a diagnosable mental health problem, and recent research with 10,000 children has shown a quarter of girls (24%) and one in 10 boys (9%) are depressed at age 14 (Patalay and Fitzsimons, 2018). This mental health crisis is most damaging for disadvantaged pupils, pupils with Special Educational Needs and pupils with low attainment (Hutchings 2015, p. 5).

These signs of stress are not confined to older children. Jarvis (2016, p. 15) noted that for many early years children, especially boys, the relentless pressure to perform at such a young age was developmentally inappropriate and 'results in a tsunami of mental health problems'. More recently, the test developers for the RBA have contended that their system of algorithmic routing is supposed 'to prevent [4-year-old] pupils from being presented with too many activities in which they are unlikely to be successful and the possible discomfort that pupils may feel if they are unable to complete an activity' (NFER, 2019, np). However, Reception teachers working with the assessment in its pilot phase often disagreed.

> Some of them [children] were excited and engaged with the assessment but some were intimidated and scared. They knew they were being assessed and many were scared of 'getting it wrong'. They are 4 YEARS OLD! When there have been reports out recently about older children feeling so much stress and anxiety about tests, education and learning I think this is simply embedding it earlier. We are going in the wrong direction here!.
>
> *(teacher cited in Roberts-Holmes et al., 2020)*

Bearing also on children's well-being, the RBA intrudes into classroom life at the sensitive settling in period, when children are just starting primary education, taking at least ten hours for a class of 30 hours, time arguably better spent in building positive relationships with very young children in their early weeks at school. Instead, the relationship between teacher and child is mediated through a screen-based script that minimises meaningful teacher-pupil dialogue and interaction. The Association for Professional Development in Early Years has warned that 'children at the very start of their school experience should not be used in an experiment in an ill-advised accountability system' (TACTYC, 2019, p. 5).

Hyper-accountability, professional identity and early years workers' well-being and mental health

Neoliberal governance takes its toll, too, on the teachers and other workers on the receiving end: it induces fear, anxiety, humiliation and compliance. Stephen Ball has coined the term 'terrors of performativity' (see chapter 2) and argues that the potential threat of a poor Ofsted grading incites these 'terrors' in school workforces so that they become 'whatever it seems necessary to become in order to survive' (Ball, 2003, p. 225). The effect of such human technologies as decontextualised data dashboards and Ofsted inspections is that schools and teachers are humiliated and intimidated into focusing upon improving performance data by whatever means is necessary for survival in the harsh competitive market – a graphic example of what Mirowski (2013, p. 92) calls neoliberalism 'revelling in the public shaming of the failed and the hapless'.

Faced with these terrors, 'the heart of the educational project is gouged out and left empty' (Ball, 2003, p. 225) as teachers are incited to 'fabricate' a narrative of performance. As if in an abusive relationship, teachers and other early childhood practitioners who perform correctly are praised whilst those who do not properly submit to being governed are disciplined, humiliated and terrorised. For example, with its enormous power, a frequent emotion aroused by the prospect of an Ofsted inspection is fear, a fear that comes to dominate daily working lives:

A lot of the paperwork is unnecessary, but we felt we had no choice because we feared inspections by Ofsted.

Ofsted scares us too much!

I feel that the fear of Ofsted makes people in the sector fearful. Every inspector is different so people get told different things about what they should and should not be doing.

(Early years workers, cited in Pre-School Learning Alliance, 2018, p. 6)

'The grip of a culture of fear' (Weale, 2019, np) powerfully governs and produces docile and obedient services and practitioners, who concentrate on demonstrably meeting Ofsted's demands in order to survive and potentially thrive. The toll it takes is evident in these comments from three workers in the early childhood sector in England:

I get frustrated with all the paper work. Some of it is overload and some essential ... but it's an uneven balance in the wrong direction. Ofsted scares us too much!

The overwhelming amount of paper work needed to prove to Ofsted that you are performing correctly is challenging (cited in Pre-School Learning Alliance, 2018, p. 6).

I should be in classrooms supporting colleagues but I spend far too much time looking at assessment data and it is for proving to Ofsted that we are great. I'm an expert at speaking to Ofsted and tell them everything they want to know about data in our school. But actually I would be far more effective if I were in class and the children would benefit more. But I get patted on the head by Ofsted because I really know that data.... The head's job rests on whether the data is good or bad, so this in turn puts masses of pressure all the way down through the school and into the early years.

(Deputy Head teacher, cited in Roberts-Holmes and Bradbury, 2016, p. 606)

These examples of the negative impact of a feared inspection system show how a culture of fear can envelop early childhood educators, even trumping and over-riding professional judgements, values and principles. A similar experience, of feeling torn between what is right professionally and what is required to do to meet managerial demands, is reported by teachers piloting the new standardised test for 4-year-olds in England – Reception Baseline Assessment.

Reception teachers felt conflicted and anxious in attempting to meet the formal school-based testing demands of RBA, and at the same time trying to settle and develop caring relationships through play, dialogue and meaningful activities with the children. This reconfiguring of Reception teachers away from their caring pedagogic values of observing and listening to young children and towards a screen-based scripted standardised test, led to professional unease, frustration and stress. RBA redefines the holistic care and well-being of young children as being attainment in prescribed, narrow, school-based academic goals.

(Roberts-Holmes, 2020, np)

Professional identity is corroded by this performative culture, steering practitioners away from the pedagogical values and principles that may have brought them into the work in the first place or which they learnt during their education. Instead of a feeling of joy and creativity in working with young children, the teacher's subjectivity becomes 'made up' by performance data, and in order to survive the teacher must adopt a compliant pedagogy that prepares children to 'pass' tests: as one teacher plaintively puts it, '[w]orking in early years used to be all about the children. Now it is all about the paperwork and constant changes to legislation' (Ward, 2019, p. 4).

An extreme example of such 'values schizophrenia' (Ball, 2003) is the head teacher referred to above feeling compelled to introduce ability grouping despite having suffered its negative effects as a child herself. All is sacrificed to the cause of performance, and that means jettisoning much that is of great personal and professional importance:

In the performative accountability culture of education in the 21st century, efficiency is seen as 'a good thing' irrespective of the cost to people – intensification, loss of autonomy, monitoring and appraisal, limited participation in decision-making and lack of personal development are not considered.

(Perryman and Calvert, 2019, p. 4)

In this brave new world of datafication, performativity and accountability,

management is altering social connections and power relations to less democratic and caring forms and … radically undermining the professionalism of teachers in the hunt for measures, targets, benchmarks, tests, tables, audits to feed the system in the name of improvement.

(Ball, 2016, p. 1046)

Early years workers are reduced to data technicians performing fixed 'solutions' to demonstrate competence. In England, for example, faced by the digitised and scripted nature of the RBA or the IELS, stripping away the need for any professional judgement, they become 'commodity scanners', scanning children as data objects as if in a supermarket. Working in this way in 'regimes of performativity', 'experience is nothing, productivity is everything' (Ball, 2016, p. 1054); educators

are no longer encouraged to have a rationale for practice, an account of themselves in terms of a relationship to the meaningfulness of *what they do*, but are required to produce measurable and 'improving' outputs and performances, what is important is *what works*.

(Ball and Olmedo, 2013, p. 91)

This generates feelings of devaluation and worthlessness, clearly felt and expressed by these reception class teachers talking about their experience of participating in a pilot for the RBA (cited in Roberts-Holmes et al., 2020, p. 44):

My skills and experience will become invalid; my years of experience must count for a lot and I do not want them to be overridden by a two dimensional format. I value the relationships developed with the children immensely; for me that's a significant aspect of the EYFS teacher.

[The RBA] will just be used as a stick to beat schools with later down the line. Who is this data for?! Another potential attack on teachers and staff when children do not make 'expected' progress.

'Soul destroying' is the word because it is not helping me and I trust my own professional judgement more.

The entire idea is simply ridiculous and could only have been motivated by a fundamental mistrust of Early Years and Primary School teachers.

Teachers wanted a more inclusive and democratic approach to education that involved teachers and Ofsted engaged together in a trusting and dialogic relationship:

It is high time for the government to bring trust back into the equation. Trust teachers to teach and children to learn. Make schools accountable for carrying out ongoing reflection, research and professional dialogue rather than producing decontextualised data. Change the role of Ofsted from 'inspector' to critical friend. Put children, not outcomes first.

(personal communication by reception class teacher to authors)

The hyper-accountability culture has created a pervasive malaise among teachers working with young children, described in a recent research study as a 'discourse of disappointment that hangs over teaching', 'a somewhat bleak picture of teacher well-being within a culture of accountability and performativity', and '"loss of self", causing physical and mental illness, and prompting some to leave the profession' (Perryman and Calvert, 2019, p. 17). Further recent research paints a similar bleak picture, with teachers' mental health

adversely affected by negative school cultures that limit teacher agency and deprofessionalise teachers.... Unfortunately, far too many of these dedicated teachers are working in school cultures that place them under excessive surveillance, where they are undervalued by senior leaders and where they don't feel they belong. Far too many teachers in the early stages of their careers are experiencing mental ill health and burning out and are opting to leave the profession within three to five years.

(Glazzard, 2019, np)

But the toll is not confined to early years teachers working in schools. In a 2018 of the mental health and well-being of 2,039 early years practitioners, mostly working in the 'child care' sector in England, the most commonly cited mental health impacts experienced due to work were fatigue (60%), loss of motivation (58%), anxiety (57%) and insomnia (53%), while a quarter (26%) had experienced depression (Pre-school Learning Alliance, 2018). High workloads, financial pressures from a lack of Government funding, and low pay, were the main sources of stress cited by these early years practitioners. And underpinning this were the demands made upon them by neoliberal governance:

> Many respondents also voiced concerns that paperwork demands are negatively impacting on the amount and/or quality of time they are able to spend with the children in their care. One stated: 'The red tape and paperwork has become over the top, which means the staff spend half their time filling in paperwork, instead of what really matters which is of course the children. This leads to staff taking work home.' Another commented: 'The paperwork and EYFS goals are ridiculous. I do not agree with the way the UK government perceives children as robots reaching milestones at set points in their lives.'
>
> Some also argued that an increasingly paperwork-led approach to assessing child development means that this process has become a tick-box exercise with limited benefits for children's learning.... [As one respondent put it] 'Early years has become about making [children] fit a criteria – no consideration is given to the speed the children learn at the moment.... Everything is now about ticking the right box'.
>
> *(ibid., p. 7)*

Perhaps not surprisingly, early years practitioners are voting with their feet. In the survey quoted above, 25% of respondents were considering leaving the early years sector due to stress or mental health difficulties. While another report in 2018 found a disturbing combination of falling qualification levels across the early years sector combined with high turnover rates that 'have been steadily increasing over the last few years, in line with a similar trend affecting other phases of the education system' (Bonetti, 2018, p. 12).

This chapter, focusing on the case of England, has explored neoliberal governance of early childhood education and care through the management techniques of New Public Management: an expanding and intertwined system of standard setting and performance measures, regular inspection and published outcomes. Through this process young children and practitioners become made known, visible and thus governable and amenable subjects who are prepared and readied for the competitive high performing demands of a test-based culture in compulsory schooling and ultimately of a competitive global economy, where the worker's performance is constantly monitored, appraised and managed. Early years children and practitioners carefully govern their own conduct to ensure regulatory compliance and avoidance of the harsh consequences of failure.

But this relentless hyper-accountable culture leads to detrimental pedagogical practices such as a narrowing of the curriculum, prophetic pedagogy and ability grouping as practitioners attempt to maximise performance. It impoverishes yet further the image of the young child. And it is leading to a range of adverse consequences for both the children and the adults involved in early childhood education and care. In particular, the unintended consequences for both children and teachers include stress and depression brought about by a competitive-depression syndrome of never being good enough and constant status anxiety.

In particular, we have highlighted how children of ever younger age are becoming subject to a hyper-surveillant 'data gaze', which exerts 'pressure on those being observed and becomes a pressure in our own lives to live up to the norms, expectations and searing surveillance that the data gaze brings' (Beer, 2017, p. 127). The data-gaze is endlessly incomplete and restless, seeking 'to expand its reach, increase the data accumulated and further embed data-led thinking into decision making' (Beer, 2019, 127); it is never satisfied and constantly seeks out new spaces for intervention as it pushes the boundaries of economic and performance rationality into the new territory of ECEC. As the data-gaze pushes down deeper it illuminates, colonises and governs the early years through performativity; practitioners become the watched watchers, who *both see* their data-led performances and in turn are *seen by* the overseers monitoring their data-led performances. In this way the data-gaze tightly manages and governs ECEC, this 'data-led watchful politics' (Amoore and De Goede, 2005, p. 230 in Roberts-Holmes, 2019) of 'anticipation, precaution and pre-emption' (Lentzos and Rose, 2009, p. 235) ceaselessly seeking out pupils and teachers who may potentially pose performance threats.

In these developments we can discern the shape of things to come − or rather the shape of things to come if things continue as they are. An increasingly detailed and invasive data gaze on young children (and their families), including not only education but other area such as health, combined with increasingly powerful algorithmic predictions will enable both stronger management and the increasing reach of what has been called 'surveillance capitalism' (Zuboff, 2018). Commercialised state digital governance and the biopolitical management of populations in the era of social media and big data will become ever more possible. Datafied children and teachers become hyper-governable subjects through biopolitical intervention. For example, algorithmic governance may in the future be used to enable automated sorting and classifying of children into groups according to predicted performance (Eubanks, 2019). Or to take another example, in the future personalised and precision data may enable more targeted and focused governing by monitoring and measuring children's emotions and 'helping' the 'underperforming' child make 'better' emotional choices, such as grit and perseverance, that are more compliant to the performative interests of the school or other early childhood centre. Or, a third example, it is possible to envisage real time data-streams that enable mass surveillance of school populations and anticipatory interventions to ensure a predetermined trajectory remains on course.

Such data-streams and dataveillance are prophetic, that is,

[t]hey enable the future to be seen and an imagined future to be part of the present decisions that are taken. They see everything in detail; nothing escapes their sight. Their vision is omnipotent and sharp.... They are the smart thing to be involved with, giving the edge over competitors.... These things, these dreams, are at the heart of the data imaginary.

(Beer, 2019, p. 33)

In this way, as in Malaguzzi's 'prophetic pedagogy', everything will be known beforehand with no room for uncertainty, everything reduced to the pursuit of standardised outcomes and high performance.

Notes

1 'The National Pupil Database (NPD) holds a wide range of information about students who attend schools and colleges in England. The NPD combines the examination results of pupils with information on pupil and school characteristics and is an amalgamation of a number of different datasets, including Key Stage attainment data and Schools Census data (formerly known as PLASC), which are linked using a unique identifier for each pupil. The dataset is made available for research purposes by the Department for Education' (https://beta.ukdataservice.ac.uk/datacatalogue/series/series?id=2000108). This means that personal details are linked to pupils' attainment and exam results over a lifetime school attendance. In October 2018 the database contained over 21 million individual named pupil records.
2 See Chapter 2 for details of other items in the OECD's armoury of international large-scale assessments.

6

RESISTANCE, CRISES AND TRANSFORMATION

> We view neoliberalism as deeply problematic, eminently resistible and eventually replaceable … we think neoliberalism has little or no future and turn to alternatives; for if the neoliberal mantra has been 'there are no alternatives', ours is that 'there are alternatives'
>
> *(Chapter 1)*

Neoliberalism has been immensely influential globally for more than a generation, governing how we understand the world, how we think about ourselves and others and institutions, and how we behave and relate. That influence has been felt far and wide, and in many fields, including early childhood education and care. Yet neoliberalism remains widely unrecognised and little understood: to return to Mirowski's quote from Chapter 1, 'even at this late hour, the world is still full of people who believe neoliberalism doesn't really exist'.

Even if the existence of the subject is broached, people may struggle to see the relevance of neoliberalism to their lives, including to their education and employment. Cristina Vintimilla includes neoliberalism in the early childhood courses she teaches at a Canadian university, and notes it can either provoke 'a tense, awkward moment of silence' or 'become a source of contestation'.

> A colleague asked me once, 'Why should one teach neoliberalism in an early childhood degree?' My students have asked: 'Why should we bother studying this?'; 'Why should we bother with neoliberalism when we have to learn how to teach children?'
>
> *(Vintimilla, 2014, p. 79)*

We hope in the course of this book to have provided some answers to these understandable questions. We have tried to show how neoliberalism contaminates so much of early childhood education and care (as well as all other education), through its beliefs and values, its commitment to markets and private provision, its economistic goals and instrumental rationality, the images it holds of children, parents, centres and workers, and the technologies it adopts and applies to manage performance, assure desired outcomes and achieve a high rate of return on investment. So, it matters very much that all those engaged, in one way or another, with early childhood education and care should understand what neoliberalism is, how it works and to what effects – then decide where they stand, taking a position.

As a dominant discourse or story, neoliberalism's beliefs, values and practices (whether or not individuals associate them with the term 'neoliberalism') have become widely accepted as self-evidently true, inevitable and invincible. In many respects, write Frances Press and her colleagues, 'the influence of neo-liberalism and its effects have assumed the status of the "new normal"' (Press et al., 2018, p. 329). There is, its adherents assert, no alternative to neoliberalism, it is the only show in town.

We disagree. There are alternatives and some of these are preferable to neoliberalism – or so it seems to us, and in thinking this, we are not alone. In this concluding chapter, we discuss why we think that neoliberalism, in general and in particular in the field of ECEC, is (as we wrote in Chapter 1) 'deeply problematic, eminently resistible and eventually replaceable'. By doing so we want to contest what Roberto Unger calls 'the dictatorship of no alternative', and argue for a democratic politics of education, one where neoliberalism cedes its arrogant claims to being the one and only way to go and accepts instead the more modest status of being one story among many that can be told about early childhood education and care.

Neoliberalism: deeply problematic

Neoliberalism as a theory, ideology, movement or narrative is a political choice, not a necessity. By which we mean it is not some immutable law of nature nor a divinely ordained truth, indisputable and inescapable. Rather, it is just one answer to a political question or set of questions – such as, what sort of society and life do we want for ourselves and our children? With what fundamental values and ethics? What is our image of the subject? These questions by definition have no one right answer, only various possible, and often conflicting, answers. So political questions require political choices made between alternatives – and neoliberalism would not be the result of our political choices. We say this for several reasons.

First, because of the political question that lies at the heart of this book: Do we really want to live as neoliberal subjects in a neoliberal society? For us, the answer is clear. Neoliberalism's 'vision of society and of human living within such a society' is deeply unappealing, not least 'the belief that the market should direct the fate of human beings (rather than human beings should direct the economy)' (Davies and Bansel, 2007, p. 253). Equally disagreeable is neoliberalism's 'cynical view of human beings which prioritises individual self-interest and an egocentric ontology' (Venn, 2018, p. 101): the image of the human being as *homo economicus* and as human capital, to the exclusion or sidelining of all other images. If, as was suggested in Chapter 1, the term 'human capital' was initially 'considered too debasing to be used publicly', it is time, we think, to re-discover that distaste for the reduction of human beings to units of economic accounting. Which is not, it should be said, to deny the place or significance of the economic in life, but to put it in perspective, as servant rather than master, which also means holding open what we want and expect from the 'economic'. How can the economy best serve caring, sustainable and flourishing lives and societies?

Similarly unappealing to us is neoliberalism's disdain for the 'public' and public services, its distrust of those who work in these services, its fundamentalist belief in the commodification and marketisation of everything and everyone, and its 'will to govern' as inscribed in new public management. The end result is a shrivelling of the public domain, that space open to all citizens, children and adults, 'where strangers encounter each other as equal partners in the common life of the society, a space for forms of human flourishing which cannot be bought in the market' (Marquand, 2004, p. 27); and also the assumption of a deeply distrustful and transactional view of humanity and life that is simplified and reductive, impoverished and uninspiring, an endless round of contracts, performance and measurement.

It is not just that we find neoliberalism unappealing, showing little recognition of the richness and complexity of life and failing to offer the ingredients of a flourishing and fulfilling existence. Our second reason for rejecting neoliberalism as our political choice is because its consequences for individuals, families, communities and societies are so harmful, as we have discussed in previous chapters. We see the anger, divisions and alienation that have swept so many countries in recent years – not least the UK and the USA, the heartlands of neoliberalism – as in large part the culmination of a 40-year utopian experiment that has proven to be dystopian.

We see, too, how neoliberalism has undermined democracy. Democracy was not in perfect health before the rise of neoliberalism. But it has suffered a marked decline under the current regime. One cause has been the increasing political influence of an economic elite who have been the main winners under neoliberalism. Another has been the 'privatizing [of] a range of state services [that] has undermined the effective capacity of the state to democratically govern the quality and character of many public services' (Wright, 2019, p. 112). These have made governments and their electorates seem increasingly impotent, as too has the behaviour of global corporations whose only loyalty is to shareholders and the bottom line.

Our third reason is that neoliberalism, with its voracious desire for increased consumption and economic growth, is unsustainable in a world facing environmental catastrophe on many fronts, including global heating, climate change, lethal pollution, resource depletion and dwindling bio-diversity, to name but some of the dangers threatening mankind's very existence and the precious environment on which that existence depends. It is no exaggeration to say, as Couze Venn does, that we are at 'a moment when the world seems more fraught with danger than at any time in history' (2018, p. 1), a view endorsed by the Bulletin of the Atomic

Scientists whose Doomsday Clock is now (in 2020) at one hundred seconds to midnight with its prospect of a man-made global catastrophe (https://thebulletin.org/doomsday-clock/current-time/). Our future as a species depends on finding new and respectful ways of relating to the environment, which will require what Naomi Klein (2015) calls 'heavy duty interventions' (such as sweeping bans on polluting activities, large subsidies for green alternatives, and new public works programmes), as well as the renewal of solidarity, care, inter-dependence and democracy, values disdained by and inimical to neoliberalism. The social and political, too, will have to escape the clutches of the economic, asserting human beings' direction of the economy and technology in the interests of all. Co-operation rather than competition must be the order of the day if humankind is to have any hope of defusing the dangers it faces.

Then fourthly, neoliberalism does not in practice function as the perfect machine its advocates claim, whether manifest in the disastrous failure of markets to self-regulate leading up to the 2008 financial crisis or in the imperfect workings of the childcare market. As economist Ha-Joon Chang concludes,

> what we were told by the free-marketeers – or, as they are often called, neo-liberal economists – was at best only partially true and at worst plain wrong … [for] the 'truths' pedalled by free-market ideologues are based on lazy assumptions and blinkered visions.
>
> *(2010, p. xv)*

Chang follows on by demolishing what he terms 23 of the biggest economic myths of our time, starting with the myth of the free market: the free market, he shows, does not exist. In short, neoliberalism is damaged goods, its claims increasingly discredited.

To dislike and have doubts about something is not the same as to expect its decline and fall. But for reasons we shall discuss later, we think it possible, even likely, that neoliberalism is entering into crisis: if not the end, then the beginning of the end may well be nigh. It will, we think, be deposed from its dominant world position. But in the meantime, it retains that position, a predatory economic system still focused on ever increasing commodification, marketisation and privatisation (Venn, 2018), and whose assumptions, images and valuers have wormed their way into individual and societal psyches. For those who share our distaste, how can neoliberalism be resisted here and now?

Neoliberalism: eminently resistible

Neoliberalism's days as a dominant discourse may be numbered, but it remains immensely powerful for the moment. Many are disciples, subscribing to its beliefs and aims; many more, though not signed-up supporters, have nevertheless embodied and are governed by and through neoliberal tenets as well as being inscribed by neoliberal subjectivity. Yet, as we suggested in Chapters 1 and 4, there is no cause to despair, remembering Foucault's words: 'In power relations there is necessarily the possibility of resistance because if there were no possibility of resistance (of violent resistance, flight, deception, strategies capable of reversing the situation), there would be no power relations at all' (Foucault, 1997, p. 292). In this section, we consider resistance in the here and now, mentioning some of the possibilities that already exist for contesting the neoliberal grasp on early childhood education and care, recognising that resistance need not be head on, large-scale or high profile; it may instead take the form of what Rose refers to as 'minor engagements … [which] are cautious, modest, pragmatic, experimental, stuttering, tentative … [and] concerned with the here and now, not with some fantasized future, with small concerns, petty details, the everyday and not the transcendental' (Rose, 1999, p. 280). In short, resistance as 'minor politics'.

Becoming a critical thinker

Resistance here and now, in the face of a hegemonic neoliberalism, may take various forms. A precondition for any form of resistance is the recognition of what must be resisted, and in this respect, as we argued at the start of this book, neoliberalism has been rather effective, hiding in plain view, leaving many people not understanding what it is or how it works; in this way, even after decades of this ideology holding sway, it remains invisible to many people. So resistance requires the constant work of making neoliberalism and its consequences visible, and by doing so enabling individuals and groups to see and think things differently, bearing in mind Foucault's advice that 'as soon as one can no longer think things as one formerly thought them, transformation becomes both very urgent, very difficult, and quite possible' (Foucault, 1988a, p. 155).

Once aware of neoliberalism and its effects, and beginning to think differently, resistance here and now means constantly contesting its beliefs and claims, through the application of critical thinking, so eloquently described by Nikolas Rose:

> [Critical thought is about] introducing a critical attitude towards those things that are given to our present experience as if they were timeless, natural, unquestionable: to stand against the maxims of one's time, against the spirit of one's age, against the current of received wisdom. It is a matter of introducing a kind of awkwardness into the fabric of one's experience, of interrupting the fluency of the narratives that encode that experience and making them stutter. … As Gilles Deleuze puts it, thinking of Nietzsche, things and actions are already interpretations. So to interpret them is to interpret interpretations: in this way it is already to change things, 'to change life', the present – and oneself.
>
> *(Rose, 1999, p. 20)*

Critical thinking is then about asking why we think, talk and act in particular ways; it is about questioning what seems or presents as self-evident and incontestable – 'timeless, natural, unquestionable'; it is about being sceptical towards dominant narratives, 'the maxims of our times', like neoliberalism itself, with their truth claims; and it is about being aware that there are always alternatives, different perspectives, different interpretations, and so we are never dealing with inevitabilities but rather always have choices to make.

When it comes to the subject of this book, it means questioning the assumptions and assertions of neoliberalism, both in general and specifically in early childhood education and care. What is happening here? Why is it happening? Why do we talk this way? To whose benefit? With what effects? Why this and not something else? This is, in the words of Foucault, 'the movement through which the subject gives itself the right to question truth concerning its power effects and to question power about its discourses of truth. Critique is the art of voluntary inservitude, of reflective indocility' (Foucault, 1997, p. 386), of standing 'against the maxims of one's time, against the spirit of one's age, against the current of received wisdom'.

In asking such questions, we are 'interrupting the fluency of the narratives that encode [one's] experience and making them stutter', and by so doing undermining the taken-for-grantedness of those narratives, narratives such as neoliberalism. But we are doing something else too: revealing the politics that underlies policies and practices. Neoliberal apologists would like it to be thought that their advocacy, for example of competitive markets or private provision, is a necessary response to how the world is, the only possible solution to, for example, providing early childhood services – that these are not political choices but 'timeless, natural, unquestionable' verities. But in reality, they are making political choices in response to political questions – because there *are* other possibilities, alternatives in conflict with neoliberalism's choices.

We could choose, for example, to decommodify early childhood education and care, scrapping a system of commodified private services competing in a marketplace, and create instead a system of early childhood services based on cooperative networks and public provision. We could abandon the language of 'customers' and consumption, and choose instead the language of citizens and rights, conceiving (to quote Rose's description from Chapter 1 of the 19th century turn towards the 'social state') 'human beings as citizens of a wider collectivity who did not merely confront one another as buyers and sellers on a competitive market', and recognising 'the right to education [as contained in the UN Convention on the Rights of the Child] during early childhood as beginning at birth' (United Nations Committee on the Rights of the Child, 2005, para. 28). We could turn away from the market values of competition and individual choice, and the accompanying pitting of autonomous consumers against each other, substituting in their place the mutual benefits of solidarity and cooperation and the collective choice of democracy. With critical thinking, we could choose to deconstruct what we are expected to accept uncritically and construct in its place something new, different and better.

Who do you think you are?

We can develop this theme of resistance, drawing further on the work of Michel Foucault, something that sociologist Stephen Ball has translated to the field of education, and with a particular focus on contesting neoliberal subjectivities, indeed the whole process of subjectification. Ball and his colleague Antonio Olmedo have written that '[t]o the extent that neoliberal governmentalities have become increasingly focused on the production of subjectivity, it is logical to think about subjectivity as a site of struggle and resistance' (Ball and Olmedo, 2013, p. 85). Ball has added, subsequently, that '[s]ubjectivity is now a key site of political struggle – not a sufficient site perhaps, but a necessary one … it is here also, in "our relation to ourselves", that we might begin to struggle to think about ourselves differently' (Ball, 2016, p. 1131).

Ball has described the evolution of Foucault's work. Especially in his middle period, Foucault was much concerned with power relations and oppression, exploring for example in education 'the processes of schooling, or the experience of teaching and learning, in terms of surveillance, classification and exclusion' (Ball, 2019, p. 133). But a new theme emerges in his later period, after 1980, when he articulates a 'politics of the care of the self' and the concept of self-formation, ways in which subjectification, for example through neoliberalism, can be contested and different subjectivities constituted by the self. Foucault's intention, as Ball puts it, was

> to destabilise, to make things 'not as necessary as all that'. Foucault, as a philosopher of contestation and difference, seeks to undermine self-evidences and open up spaces for acting and thinking differently about our relation to ourselves and to others and identify and refuse and transgress the horizon of silent objectification within which we are articulated. Such critique enables us to recognise that the things, values, and events that make up our present experience 'have been constituted historically, discursively, practically' (Mahon, 1992: 14), and indeed that the self, our subjectivity, is historically produced in and through technologies and relations of power.
>
> *(ibid.)*

Or put succinctly, in Foucault's own words, 'My role – and that is too emphatic a word – is to show people that they are much freer than they feel' (Foucault, in Martin, Gutman and Hutton, 1988, p. 9).

Following Foucault's argument, Ball starts from the view that the subject is governed by others, but at the same time by the self, that concept of governmentality – and it is the governing of the self via the embodying of neoliberal subjectivities that can be resisted. It is, Ball writes, in '"our relation to ourselves", that we might begin to struggle to think about ourselves differently…. In arguing against truth, an opportunity for the rearticulation of self is created' (Ball, 2016b, pp. 1134, 1135). In this struggle, through acts of 'voluntary inservitude, of reflective indocility' (terms that, by now, the reader will have gathered we find especially resonant), we can withhold our consent to the subjectivity that neoliberalism seeks from us, and work instead 'to define ourselves according to our own judgments' (Ball, 2016a, p. 1056).

In fact, Ball suggests that we might describe such contestation of neoliberalism and its work of subjectification not as resistance, but as refusal: for as Foucault says, '[m]aybe the target nowadays is not to discover what we are but to refuse what we are' (Foucault, 2000, p. 336).

> [I want to explore] a little more some forms of resistance to, or what I shall call the refusal of, neoliberalisation.... I want to see how far we might get in outlining instead, or rather in addition, a politics of refusal. In part, the use of refusal – rather than resistance – serves to highlight the specifics of my analysis, but it also enables some distancing from the more orthodox ontologies of resistance, which as Rose puts it are 'too simple and flattening' as 'merely the obverse of a one-dimensional notion of power as domination'.
>
> *(Ball, 2016b, pp. 1129–1130)*

Ball is particularly interested in how such refusal might work for school teachers who wish to contest a neoliberal subjectivity saturated with performativity, a self image that is dominated by the necessity to perform well through achieving externally imposed standards and targets – that is, the subjectification of the teacher as a technician and a bundle of skills and competencies (Ball, 2016a). Instead, he proposes re-imagining the teacher as an intellectual in a politics of refusal, the starting point for which is 'the site of subjectivity' and which involves 'a struggle over and against what it is we have become, what it is that we do not want to be' (ibid., p. 1143). In all cases the struggle is to change our understanding of what being a teacher – or a child, or a parent, or an early childhood centre – is all about. Or putting it more simply, refusing what seems to be expected of us, and working instead on creating a different subjectivity. This is subjectivity, in Ball's words, as 'a key site of political struggle.'

How might people enact this political struggle, this politics of refusal, once that is they have decided they need to engage in this struggle? How to refuse neoliberal subjectivity, but also how to engage in the work of constituting the self as a different subjectivity? How can one work on oneself, how can one practice self formation? Ball draws on Foucault's concept of 'care of the self', which he describes as

> a continuous practice of introspection, which is at the same time attuned to a critique of the world outside.... This is a form of ethics and a set of techniques of living, a concrete practice of freedom. Established patterns are to be challenged in order to ascertain what it is that is no longer indispensable for the constitution of the self: 'The ethical project which emerges is to envision one's self constitution as an on going task, an achievement requiring artistry in the face of the looming, omnipresent threats to our freedom to invent ourselves' (Pignatelli 1993, 165).
>
> *(Ball, 2016b, p. 1136)*

This 'care of the self', in order to criticize and free the self from embodied subjectivities and produce new ones, this struggle to constitute ourselves and our images of others, calls for (Foucault again) 'technologies of the self', tools to work with in this process of resistance or refusal. Reading is one such technology, providing the reader with invaluable ammunition for critical thinking, including the struggle against imposed subjectivities and for practicing self formation. In a vivid example, the director of an Australian early childhood centre has described the impact of reading on her work:

> Reading Foucault's book 'Discipline and punish: the birth of the prison' was a catalytic moment in bringing the critical to my reflection. This was when I began to weave theory and practice together to illuminate my subjectivities and consider what I bring to bear on my gaze of others.... Using Foucault's challenging idea that 'observation is a disciplinary apparatus' I began to question my right to know the child.... I began to consider how I might see my practice differently by turning the gaze within to illuminate my subjectivities and their effects for children, parents and colleagues.
>
> *(MacNaughton, 2005, pp. 57, 58)*

Writing is another technology of the self. For Foucault, 'self writing' offered 'a deliberate, self-conscious attempt to explain and express oneself to an audience within which one exists and from whom one seeks confirmation' (Ball, 2013, p. 152). This technology or technique goes back to the ancient Greeks and their *hypomnemata*, notebooks used for constituting a permanent relationship to oneself.

Ball, influenced as he is by Foucault, discusses writing as having an important role to play in working on the self. Such writing may take various forms, not just notebooks. Ball and Olmedo take the example of communications they have received from school teachers to exemplify and discuss the possibilities of emails as

> part of the process of struggle against, of critique, of making things intolerable, of 'unsettling' and the struggle to be different.... The emails provide a way for these teachers to articulate themselves and their practice differently by opening up spaces of doubt. Foucault saw writing as a key technique of the 'arts of the self', and a means for exploring the 'aesthetics of existence' and for inquiring into the government of self and others (Foucault, 1997b). The email may be understood as both part of an attempt to 'mark out an ethical space' (Burchell, 1996, p. 34) within which the teacher might teach differently and ways of exploring the possibilities and impossibilities of transgression.
>
> *(Ball and Olmedo, 2013, pp. 93–94)*

Another example of the potential role of writing in care of the self involves the keeping of journals by students (Gore, 1993) or practitioners.

'Care of the self' can also be fostered and promoted with and by working with others. It need not be a solitary activity. Students or practitioners can come together in mutually supportive explorations of processes of subjectification and the possibilities of transgression. Karyn Callaghan, from the Ontario Reggio Association, puts this well when she says that

> [f]eminist scholars hold that we come to know ourselves through others. In a profession that must have relationship as a central foundation ... [c]ommunities of practice, study groups, reading groups, the sharing of documentation with colleagues, children and families [discussed further below] are all ways that we can come to see ourselves differently, and to become aware of our assumptions, and to accept responsibility to consider explicitly others' ways of thinking, seeking greater complexity and, as the Italians say, 'confronto'.
>
> *(personal communication to the authors)*

So far we have discussed contesting neoliberal subjectivities, to refuse what we are, and work to reconstitute or reform our subjectivity. But the same principles and processes could be applied to other subjectivities, such as we discussed in Chapter 4: the image of the child, the parent, the early childhood centre and the early childhood worker. We can ask, what images have been presented to us as if they are 'timeless, natural, unquestionable'? What images do we actually have? What other images might there be? And which images do we want to have?

Reading and writing have a part to play here, but so too might processes of group enquiry and debate, for example using 'pedagogical documentation' as a tool for deconstructing our embodied images and working on the construction of new ones. Pedagogical documentation can be described as a tool for making visible processes (such as learning) and practices (such as project work), but also dominant discourses and the images they construct, and consequently subject to reflection, dialogue, interpretation and critique. It involves, therefore, both documentation itself through the production and selection of varied material (e.g. photographs, videos, tape recordings, notes, children's work etc.) *and* analysis and interpretation of this documentation in a rigorous, critical and democratic way – always in relationship with others.

Swedish researcher Gunilla Dahlberg has described a project in which she worked with preschool teachers from a number of early childhood centres in Stockholm, and of how they used documentation as a critical tool

> to understand *how the child has been constructed in our early childhood institutions*. It has helped us to answer the question: Do we see the child? What do we mean by saying 'to see the child'? This can be seen as a form of deconstructive work in relation to pedagogical practice – [we have analysed] what constructions of the child are behind the way we talk about the child and what kind of constructions are behind our way of relating to the child in our practice. How have these constructions shaped how the environment has been ordered? How has the whole pedagogical space been constructed? Are there other constructions to be made? Is this a pedagogical space for the 'rich' child, pedagogue and parent? [...]
>
> When the pedagogues started to listen to the children, and changed their pedagogical relationship, a new construction of the child and the pedagogue appeared. It was a child that, for example, could concentrate on an activity much longer than the pedagogues' earlier constructions had said he or she

should be able to, and who was not as egocentric. The children in our project more and more start saying 'look what I can do and know', and the pedagogues are becoming more and more aware of the children's potentialities – what they actually can do and do do rather than what classificatory systems say they should do. The excitement that this has generated among the pedagogues is captured in this comment by one of them: 'I have been working with pre-school children for 20 years now and I never thought children know and can do that much. I now have got another child in front of me'.

It is astonishing how *changing the construction of the child has contributed to the production of a new practice*. Malaguzzi once said about such change: 'in fact this is very simple, but there is someone who has made us think it is so difficult'. Through troubling the dominant discourses and constructions of the child one can open up for 'another child' – a child with lots of capabilities and a child that has got thoughts and theories that are worth listening to both from the perspective of other children but also from the perspective of the adult.

(Dahlberg, Moss and Pence, 2013, pp. 143–144; emphasis added)

As this quotation indicates, deconstructing and reconstructing images or constructions of the child (but this applies equally to images of parents, early childhood centres or early childhood workers) has important implications for practice: for images, as we argued in Chapter 4, are productive, shaping not only what we think but also what we do and how we relate. This applies not only to the here and now, but to the future. For if we desire an early childhood education and care freed of neoliberalism's grasp, we must struggle to deconstruct and refuse neoliberalism's images and to construct new ones that we find satisfying and productive of alternative practices and better futures.

Transgressing policies and practices

In her book 'Movement and Experimentation in young children's learning', Swedish preschool and university teacher Liselott Marriett Olsson comments that

[e]ven the most rigid of governing systems is built upon a whole set up of micro movements. 'Hierarchy is not simply pyramidal; the boss's office is as much at the end of the hall as on the top of the tower' (Deleuze and Guattari, 2004: 231). Hierarchy is not functioning without the inventiveness and creation of a flow of micro-political movements. Even the most totalitarian and bureaucratic of organizations exhibits examples of suppleness and creativeness when facing administrative regulations (Deleuze and Guattari, 2004: 237). In this respect, a curriculum for instance is to be seen as a macro-political decision; but when it encounters preschool practices, an enormous creativity is released that completely and continuously transforms and defines the curriculum and its accompanying practices in a reciprocal relationship.

(Olsson, 2009, pp. 74–75)

Olsson here is drawing our attention to the spaces in everyday life that may exist for resisting neoliberal policies or practices, the example given being curriculum implementation. This, it could be said, is the potential for bringing micro-politics, those 'minor engagements' in the everyday to which Rose refers, to bear in order to contest, shape or interpret the purposes and prescriptions of macro-politics. Of course, the amount of space available for micro-politics, the micro-political movements that are possible, will vary being contingent on a variety of conditions, including the autonomy allowed to practitioners, their self-confidence and mutual support, the latitude allowed for local interpretation in policy or practice, and the intrusiveness and rigidity of management systems.

But even where conditions are least favourable to resistance and effective micro-politics, there is always some space left. We will offer two examples from early childhood services in England, a country as we saw in Chapter 5 where the early childhood sector is very closely governed and the low level of qualification and pay of many 'childcare workers' presumes limited autonomy. In the first, Nathan Archer describes what he calls 'stories of activism by early years professionals in response to political decisions', stories that emerge from research with 'early educators' in a variety of English services, all of whom experienced 'the tension between their personal beliefs and policy expectations … [and most of whom] were navigating, negotiating and mediating external expectations with strongly held values and beliefs.' Archer notes that the practitioners in his research showed passion and bravery in their activism for children and families, activism that took many forms, including lobbying, social media activity, petitions, engagement with policy makers and informing others. However, examples also included what might be called 'micro-resistances' when 'practitioners took a stand or advocated at a service level in the interests of children and families'. In a comment that connects with and adds to our earlier discussion of the importance of 'critical thinking', Archer concludes that:

> A key to this strength of the practitioners in the study, and, I believe, a pre-requisite for activism, appears to be their critical awareness, or critical 'literacy' about policy developments. Through engagement in consultations, sector discussions, online forums and network meetings, practitioners demonstrated a form of literacy in analysing and critiquing emerging policy. Critical literacy can be described in terms of recognising the power of dominant narratives and how these shape policy trajectories.
>
> *(Archer, 2019, np)*

'Critical literacy', then, as an important facet of 'critical thinking;'.

The second example involves resistances by teachers and schools to a new form of governance, first mentioned in Chapter 5: proposals by the English government to introduce a system of national assessment for 4-year olds, to be conducted shortly after entry to reception class, the first year of primary school. To recap: this 'Reception Baseline Assessment' (RBA) is a standardised test of 'attainment in early literacy, communication and language and early mathematics skills', intended to enable the measurement and comparison of progression rates for children through primary schools. It represents a new tool for stronger management of these schools.

The RBA was first introduced to schools on a voluntary basis in September 2015, with the stated intention of the English Department for Education (DfE) that it was to become statutory for all 20,000 English primary schools in Autumn 2016 (Department for Education (England), 2015b, p. 4). However, this initial piloting of RBA was met with resistance from many early years teachers, supported by early years organisations and teaching unions (Bradbury and Roberts-Holmes, 2016). The renowned head-teacher Dame Alison Peacock, who was also one of the DfE's key advisers, stated bluntly that 'we are not doing baseline' (Ward, 2015), and in total nearly 5,000 English primary schools refused to introduce the test. This forced the DfE to retreat, announcing that the RBA would remain voluntary in Autumn 2016 (Department for Education (England), 2016). Subsequently only 4,000 schools applied the RBA in 2016, and the RBA was not funded or recommended by the DfE at all in 2017. Undeterred, however, the DfE returned with a second attempt to introduce RBA in 2019. Once again, this was met with widespread resistance, with over 7,000 schools deciding not to participate in that year's initial optional pilot study (Ward, 2019b).

This mass refusal was based upon an understanding by many teachers of RBA as 'exhibiting contempt for teachers and distrust of parents, [as it] represses creative teaching, destroys challenging and imaginative programs of study, and treats children as mere inputs on an assembly line' (Giroux, 2019, p. 508). RBA was widely seen as an affront to early childhood education's pedagogic principles of caring respectful relationships built upon meaningful dialogue and play, and as part of a strategic policy attempt to repurpose early childhood education in the service of primary school performance.

If implemented as planned, RBA will routinise and normalise the standardised assessment of 4-year-old children, using a tightly scripted computer-generated maths and literacy test. Many early years teachers have not been prepared to accept this, with its negative consequences for children.

> They [4-year-olds] need to be able to sit for twenty minutes, at least. They need to be able to maintain their attention; they need to be able to listen to adults and follow instructions; they need to know their letter sounds, that's what they're [RBA] trying to find out.
>
> *(Deputy Head teacher, cited in Roberts-Holmes et al., 2020, p. 27)*

> They were intimidated and scared. They knew they were being assessed and many were scared of 'getting it wrong'. They are 4 YEARS OLD! When there have been reports out recently about older children feeling so much stress and anxiety about tests, education and learning I do not think this is a wise move which will positively change the tragedies we are already seeing. It is simply embedding it earlier. We are going in the wrong direction here!
>
> *(Questionnaire response in Roberts-Holmes et al., 2020, p. 27)*

Many schools refused to participate from the onset. Others, 178 schools, originally signed up to the voluntary RBA pilot, only to withdraw after they experienced its damaging impacts (Ward, 2019c).

> Our school stopped the trial half-way through due to its tremendously negative affect on pupils, teacher workload and overall setting of the child.
>> *(Reception class teacher, cited in Roberts-Holmes et al., 2020, p. 27)*

> We withdrew from the baseline pilot as we felt it unnecessary to put so much pressure on our youngest learners. We feel there are better, more human ways, of getting to know the whole child. Children do not learn in a linear way and using the baseline to track progress would put further stress on children and teachers which is completely unnecessary.
>> *(Reception class teacher, cited in Roberts-Holmes et al., 2020, p. 27)*

Dame Alison Peacock has gone further in her opposition, arguing that it is a teacher's professional responsibility to advocate for new forms of democratic accountability.

> As teachers we have the opportunity (and *responsibility*) to make a difference for those within our own learning sphere today. *We can make the decision to listen, to trust, to work collaboratively and most importantly, to believe that there is another way.*
>> *(Peacock, 2016, p. 132; original emphasis)*

This other way would be very different to RBA, involving teachers and families taking democratic responsibility for the assessment of children's learning rather than relying on 'outside experts' with their supposedly objective indicators and standardised performance measures. Such a co-operative and democratic accountability is a moral and political process that involves a shared, mutual trust and responsibility from teachers, families, children and local early years' advisors (Fielding and Moss, 2011).

This example of passionate and brave critical policy literacy demonstrates Foucault's axiom that 'where there is power there is resistance' (Foucault, 1998, p. 95). Such resistance in the face of government power is politically and ethically inspiring. At the same time the determination of neoliberal policy makers should not be underestimated as they

> attempt to undermine all forms of solidarity capable of challenging market-driven values and social relations, promoting [instead] the virtues of an unbridled individualism almost pathological in its disdain for community, social responsibility, public values and the public good.
>> *(Giroux, 2014, p. 2)*

The Covid-19 crisis has, for the moment, put the RBA on hold. Confronted by young children's prolonged absence from nurseries and schools and the need to prioritise their care and well-being, the English Department for Education (2020) has announced that 'due to the challenging circumstances faced by schools in the context of the Covid-19 pandemic, statutory introduction of the RBA has been postponed to Autumn 2021'. Despite this, the schools minister Nick Gibb remains 'committed to introducing the new assessment' (Gaunt, 2020d) so that 'schools will have the option to sign up to the RBA "Early Adopter" year [applying the RBA on a voluntary basis] to familiarise themselves with assessment materials before the RBA becomes statutory in September 2021' (Department for Education (England), 2020). It remains to be seen how many schools will accept this invitation.

Words and stories

Couze Venn, in his book *After Capital*, highlights the importance of vocabulary: 'The attitudes, values and understandings inscribed in the discourse of neoliberalism are revealed in its watchwords such as value for money, competition, targets, audit, "the market", compliance, resilience and other incantations of management-speak' (Venn, 2018, p. 8).

To these neoliberal watchwords we might add others particularly common in early childhood education and care, a sample of which we started this book with: 'outcomes' and 'quality', 'testing' and 'assessment', 'interventions' and 'programmes', 'evidence-based' and 'best practice', 'investment' and 'human capital', 'preparation' and 'readiness'. Being choosey about words is not being faddy: language matters, the words we use are essential to the discourses that govern us or the stories we choose to tell. If you work with the vocabulary above, you will soon become ensnared in highly instrumental, managerial and economistic neoliberal stories about early childhood education and care – for example, what have been termed the 'story of quality and high returns' and 'the story of markets', discourses that offer impoverished ('poor') images of children and early childhood centres alike, the former being subjected to the application of human technologies by the latter in order to achieve predetermined and standardised outcomes in the interests of gaining supposedly high returns on investment.

But try adopting another vocabulary, for example using words such as 'projects', 'potentialities' and 'possibilities'; 'uncertainty', 'wonder' and 'surprise'; 'in-between', 'lines of flight' and 'rhizomes'; 'images', 'interpretations' and 'meaning making'; 'rich child' and 'hundred languages'; 'encounters' and 'dialogue'; 'democracy' and 'experimentation'. These are words that foreground relationships and responsibility, unpredictability and emergence, diversity and complexity, the ethical and political. Such words not only reflect and express another way of thinking about early childhood education and care; they open up to different discourses, to creating and telling new stories – and '[s]tories are the means by which we navigate the world…. The only thing that can displace a story is a story' (Monbiot, 2017), a rich story that can displace the impoverished story of neoliberalism. For example, 'the story of democracy, experimentation and potentiality', which is about an education built upon and inscribed with two fundamental values – democracy and experimentation – and a belief in the endless and unknowable possibilities of people and the institutions they create (see Moss, 2013 for the full telling of this story, as well as the story of quality and high returns and the story of markets).

Once again, practitioners and others may vary in how much space is allowed them to express different language and stories. But even in the most constrained environment, it is possible to use critical thinking to question the language being used: Why these words? What images or rationales do they produce? What words might I want to use instead? And there is always the outlet of reading and writing, of dialogue with colleagues and friends, where different vocabularies and different stories can be accessed and expressed.

Neoliberalism: eventually replaceable

Resistance and refusal are important parts of a strategy to contest neoliberalism: but they are not, we would argue, enough. As we said in Chapter 3, markets (strongly managed or otherwise) are just one way of organising and developing early childhood services. There are alternatives! Equally important, therefore, is looking ahead to what might replace neoliberalism, as it goes the way of all hegemonic projects, descending into crisis and eventually losing power.

The importance of thinking ahead and preparing for the future is captured in these famous words:

> Only a crisis – actual or perceived – produces real change. When that crisis occurs the actions that are taken depend on the ideas that are lying around. That, I believe, is our basic function: to develop alternatives to existing policies, to keep them alive and available until the politically impossible becomes politically inevitable
>
> *(Friedman, 1962/1982, p. ix)*

These words were written by Milton Friedman, a key player in the rise of neoliberalism, a founder member of the Mont Pelerin Society, but at a time before that rise took off and when another regime – social democratic or Keynesian – was dominant in many parts of the post-war world. Not liking the results of Friedman's strategy is no reason for ignoring his strategic advice.

For following this advice, neoliberals were ready when the crisis of social democracy/Keynesianism set in during the 1970s – ready with ideas, ready with new ways of looking at things, ready with alternatives to existing policies. Working away in networks and think tanks, discussing their ideas in meetings and publications, the disciples of neoliberalism were doing their homework in the 1950s and 1960s, biding their time, thinking the unthinkable, proposing the apparently inconceivable, preparing for when the politically impossible would become politically inevitable. Following this example, it is incumbent on those of us who believe neoliberalism will be replaced, and should be, to do our homework: to put forward new ideas, new ways of looking at things, as well as new ways of doing things, alternative policies.

The immanent crisis of neoliberalism

But before developing this theme of new ideas, we want to emphasise that time is short, for the crisis of neoliberalism is, it seems to us, already in sight, if not already upon us. It may be that neoliberalism remains deeply embedded in many societies, and is still a force to be reckoned with – so much of life today depends on institutions, practices and subjectivities that neoliberalism has shaped over recent decades, while the winners from neoliberalism, especially the top 1%, constitute a formidable vested interest wielding great political influence. Yet despite this, there are reasons to think that neoliberalism is vulnerable and its future uncertain.

Its damaging consequences have bred disenchantment and opposition, even though it benefits from the world being full of 'people who believe neoliberalism doesn't really exist'; it is hard to oppose something whose existence you don't believe in, the danger being that instead you turn your anger with how things are on something or somebody you do believe in as the real source of present misfortunes – and there are scapegoats a-plenty to fit this bill. But for those who do believe in the existence of neoliberalism, who have some familiarity with its story and the claims it makes and who have some understanding of its dire consequences, it is possible to detect how that story has had its legitimacy badly dented by events, in particular the 2008 financial crisis and its grim continuing aftermath, a traumatic event that can be seen as a

> forewarning of the dangers inherent in the witches' brew concocted from the rapacious plunder of the earth, the degradation of the environment, the pollution of the environment, the pollution of habitats, the massive increase in inequality worldwide and the assimilation of the state within capital. The destructive consequences have brought into focus the fragility of much that the dominant orthodoxy thought solid and enduring, exposing the illusion of a triumphant and benign capitalism.
>
> *(Venn, 2018, p. 1)*

For many, events such as 2008 have helped remove the scales from their eyes, and what appears is not a pretty sight.

Neoliberalism is vulnerable today for another reason: because, like all dominant ideologies or discourses, it is not immortal but subject to a natural life cycle, a rise and eventual fall, just as previous dominant ideologies before it, for example communism or social democracy.

This sense of flux has been captured by the Hungarian-American political economist Karl Polanyi, author of 'The Great Transformation' in which he develops his concept of the 'double movement' in capitalism; by which he refers to the tension and shifts between marketization, a push to commodify everything and make everything subject to market relations, and social protection, a reaction against that marketization through the provision of a strong welfare state (Polanyi, 1944/2001). The rise of neoliberalism from the 1970s brought a shift from social protection (and the social state) to marketization; but arguably we are now on the brink of a reverse movement, away from untrammelled marketization back to more social protection, spurred on by recognition of the damage caused by the former.

But neoliberalism's mortality also resides, as we have suggested, in its unsustainability: humankind and the planet cannot afford it. The 'witches' brew' of dangers that neoliberalism has helped concoct adds up to converging crises – environmental, but also political and social – that can only be ameliorated if we turn away from neoliberalism and 'seek drastic transformations in practices, ways of life and expectations that underlie the problems' (Venn, 2018, p. 1). Focusing on the environmental crisis, Klein asks if it is possible to turn things round and answers 'absolutely' – but goes on to further ask if this is possible 'without challenging the fundamental logic of deregulated capitalism' and answers bluntly: 'not a chance' (Klein, 2015, p. 24). In short, more of the same is neither desirable nor feasible.

There are, though, differences of view about how drastic the transformations need to be. For some, what is needed is not to ditch capitalism altogether, but a major reform of capitalism, purging it of its 'free market' obsessions and bringing it back under stronger political and social regulation. Thus Ha-Joon Chang argues that to be

> critical of free-market ideology is not the same as being against capitalism. Despite its problems and limitations, I believe that capitalism is still the best economic system that humanity has invented. My criticism is of a particular version of capitalism that has dominated the world in the last three decades, that is, free-market capitalism. This is not the only way to run capitalism, and certainly not the best, as the record of the last three decades shows ... there are ways in which capitalism should, and can, be made better.
>
> *(Chang, 2011, p. 3)*

Paul Collier admits that present-day capitalism is 'generating divided societies in which many people lead anxious lives', but believes that '[w]hat has happened recently is not intrinsic to capitalism; it is a damaging malfunction that must be put right'. For, he argues, capitalism is 'the only system that has proved to be capable of generating mass prosperity.... [Putting it right though] is not a simple matter, but, guided by prudent pragmatism, evidence and analysis that fit our current context [we] can shape policies that would gradually be effective' (2018, pp. 201–202).

Nobel prize-winning economist Joseph Stiglitz is another reformer. He is a strong critic of neoliberalism for its damaging effects on equality, democracy and the environment:

> The credibility of neoliberalism's faith in unfettered markets as the surest road to shared prosperity is on life-support these days. And well it should be. The

simultaneous waning of confidence in neoliberalism and in democracy is no coincidence or mere correlation. Neoliberalism has undermined democracy.... [A]fter 40 years, the numbers are in: growth has slowed and the fruits of that growth went overwhelmingly to a very few at the top. As wages stagnated and the stock market soared, income and wealth flowed up, rather than trickling down.... *If the 2008 financial crisis failed to make us realise that unfettered markets don't work, the climate crisis certainly should: neoliberalism will literally bring an end to our civilisation.*

(Stiglitz, 2019a; emphasis added)

But while scathing about the consequences and credibility of neoliberalism, Stiglitz retains a belief in the future of capitalism, distinguishing between good or 'progressive capitalism', which he calls 'wealth creation', and the bad capitalism exemplified by neoliberalism, which he calls 'wealth grabbing' from rent extraction, and that prevails today especially in the United States. The former benign version of capitalism involves channelling

the power of the market to serve society … [and is] based on an understanding of what gives rise to growth and societal well-being.… Progressive capitalism is based on a new social contract between voters and elected officials, between workers and corporations, between rich and poor, and between those with jobs and those who are un- or underemployed.

(Stiglitz, 2019b, np)

The philosopher Michael Sandel also believes in the possibilities of reforming a system that has taken marketisation to excess. In his book *What Money Can't Buy: The Moral Limits of Markets* (Sandel, 2012), he argues that there are many goods for which markets are unexceptionable and provide an efficient mechanism for pricing and distribution, for example groceries or entertainment. But then there are other goods (products or services) which should not be put on the market, because we value them in ways that cannot be reduced to a price tag. Put another way, he poses the question: what things should we relate to as consumers and what relate to as citizens, what should be determined by economics and what by politics?

Nancy Fraser, critical theorist and feminist, is uncertain about the possibilities for reform. She argues that the erosion of social bonds and an attendant 'crisis of care', as capacities to care are squeezed by the demands of production, are recurring tendencies in capitalism. Her claim, she writes, is that

every form of capitalist society harbours a deep-seated social-reproductive 'crisis tendency' or contradiction: on the one hand, social reproduction is a condition of possibility for sustained capital accumulation; on the other, capitalism's orientation to unlimited accumulation tends to destabilize the very processes of social reproduction on which it relies. This social-reproductive contradiction of capitalism lies at the root of the so-called crisis of care.

(Fraser, 2016b, p. 100)

Under today's financialised or neoliberal capitalist regime, this 'crisis tendency' has become acute and manifests in a distinctive way, elements of which appeared in Chapter 3 when we discussed the marketisation and commodification of early childhood education and care:

> Globalizing and neoliberal, this regime promotes state and corporate disinvestment from social welfare, while recruiting women into the paid workforce – externalizing carework onto families and communities while diminishing their capacity to perform it. The result is a new, dualized organization of social reproduction, commodified for those who can pay for it and privatized for those who cannot, as some in the second category provide carework in return for (low) wages for those in the first.
>
> *(ibid., p. 104)*

The resolution of the crisis of care requires deep structural transformation, to 'overcome financialized capitalism's rapacious subjugation of reproduction to production', including re-inventing the relationship between production and reproduction, between the economic and the social, and 'reimagining the gender order'. But that scale of transformation begs a larger question: will the result be compatible with capitalism at all (ibid., p. 117).

Others, however, are unequivocal about the coming transformation. They have no doubt that capitalism itself, not just its neoliberal manifestation, can and should be replaced, pointing to fundamentally new conditions that make this both necessary and possible. For Paul Mason in his 2015 book *Postcapitalism*, a fundamentally new condition is the digital revolution, which he argues poses an existential threat to capitalism (Mason, 2015). He concludes that the digital revolution has the potential to reshape utterly our familiar notions of work, production and value; and to destroy an economy based on markets and private ownership. In fact, he contends, this is already happening: he points to parallel currencies, co-operatives, self-managed online spaces, even Wikipedia as examples of what the postcapitalist future might look like. So from the ashes of the global financial crisis, we have the chance to create a more socially just and sustainable global economy. The postcapitalism thesis, Mason writes,

> suggests a different route beyond the market, premised on the decisive automation of productive activity, the delinking of work from wages, the leveraging of the network effect and the democratisation of data. States need to:
>
> - enable the emergence of a non-market sector of the economy, consisting of mutuals, co-operatives and pools of relative abundance;
> - expand the state sector to provide universal basic services and a basic income;
> - enhance network effects, to create free utility not captured by private ownership and market exchange; and

- enact laws to break up tech monopolies and discourage rent-seeking business models, including more traditional rent-seekers such as property and financial speculators.

(Mason, 2019, np)

The parlous state of the environment is one of the most pressing of the new conditions that, it is argued, are game changers. Novelist and commentator John Lanchester recognises this, both in his novel *The Wall* and in an article on the case for a Universal Basic Income (UBI), in which he suggests that

stimulus for change could come in the form of the climate crisis.... [T]he fact is that warming of a few degrees Celsius by the end of the century – the most likely version of the trajectory we are currently on, according to the Intergovernmental Panel on Climate Change – will overturn many aspects of the current order. In a world facing floods, droughts, storms, heatwaves, unprecedented winters, and mass migration on a never before seen scale, will people be content with the current winner takes all version of capitalism? Will we be fine with the rich taking a bigger and bigger share of total income, until the end of time, as the world drowns and burns and starves? Will we succumb to what's now being called 'climate apartheid', with the rich world cutting itself off from the poor and entrenching itself behind barriers and walls, and letting the poor world die? On current form, you would have to say that is not an unlikely version of future events. If we are to avoid going down that route, we will need to have some different, better ideas; we will need to have some ideas about shared responsibility, shared security and shared prosperity. The left will need a new toolkit. It will need to have done its intellectual prep. That, more than anything, is what this new wave of work on UBI represents.

(Lanchester, 2019, p. 8)

Couze Venn identifies the perfect storm of environmental problems as an important part of the case for transformation and moving to (the title of his book) *After Capital*. He contends that 'the correlated crises can be seen to be the culmination of tendencies in process for at least two hundred years'. In other words, from his perspective, while neoliberalism may be an extreme case of capitalism, it is capitalism itself, and all that underlies it, that 'is fundamentally destructive, undemocratic and unethical; it is incapable of resolving the crises that now beset it' (Venn, 2018, p. 121).

Environmentalist George Monbiot has changed his position, from the reformist to the abolitionist camp, in recognition of capitalism's addiction to endless growth:

For most of my adult life I've railed against 'corporate capitalism', 'consumer capitalism' and 'crony capitalism'. It took me a long time to see that the problem is not the adjective but the noun. While some people have rejected capitalism gladly and swiftly, I've done so slowly and reluctantly. Part of the reason was that I could see no clear alternative: unlike some anti-capitalists, I have never been an enthusiast for state communism. I was also inhibited by its religious status. To say 'capitalism is failing' in the 21st century is like saying 'God is dead' in the 19th: it is secular blasphemy. It requires a degree of self-confidence I did not possess.

But as I've grown older, I've come to recognise two things. First, that it is the system, rather than any variant of the system, that drives us inexorably towards disaster. Second, that you do not have to produce a definitive alternative to say that capitalism is failing. The statement stands in its own right. But it also demands another, and different, effort to develop a new system.

(Monbiot, 2019, np)

While admitting he does not have a 'definitive alternative' to hand, nor does he think any one person does, Monbiot argues it is possible to see the outline of an alternative emerging from the collective work of many people and disciplines.

Part of it is provided by the ecological civilisation proposed by Jeremy Lent, one of the greatest thinkers of our age. Other elements come from Kate Raworth's doughnut economics and the environmental thinking of Naomi Klein, Amitav Ghosh, Angaangaq Angakkorsuaq, Raj Patel and Bill McKibben. Part of the answer lies in the notion of 'private sufficiency, public luxury'. Another part arises from the creation of a new conception of justice based on this simple principle: every generation, everywhere, shall have an equal right to the enjoyment of natural wealth.

I believe our task is to identify the best proposals from many different thinkers and shape them into a coherent alternative. Because no economic system is only an economic system but intrudes into every aspect of our lives, *we need many minds from various disciplines – economic, environmental, political, cultural, social and logistical – working collaboratively to create a better way of organising ourselves that meets our needs without destroying our home.*

(ibid.; emphasis added)

The work of sociologist Erik Olin Wright provides a final example of writers who see capitalism as needing to be replaced, since 'it generates and perpetuates unjust forms of economic inequality; it narrows democracy and restricts the freedom of many while enormously enhancing the freedom of some; and it cultivates cultural ideas that endorse individual competitive success over collective welfare' (Wright, 2019, p. 35). He also considers it inimical to the environment. But he goes beyond critique to set out strategies for transformative change, arguing not only that 'another world is indeed possible', but that 'elements of the new world are already being created in the world as it is' and that 'there are ways to move from here to there' (ibid., p. 3). While he dismisses revolutionary attempts to 'smash the state', he offers a strategy of 'eroding capitalism', proposing a mix of

'dismantling' capitalism (installing elements of socialism from above) and 'taming capitalism' (neutralizing its harms). These strategies from above are complemented by strategies from below: 'resisting' capitalism and 'escaping' capitalism. It is the articulation of these four strategies that brings about the 'eroding' of capitalism – his reformulation of the transition to democratic socialism.

(Buraway, in Wright, 2019, p. 54)

Wright still sees a place for markets in democratic socialism, but is clear that 'non-market-oriented economic activity in a variety of forms would play a much more important role than in contemporary capitalism' (ibid., p. 85). In this nonmarket sphere, he envisages a major role for 'state provision' across a wide range of activities including 'caregiving services' and 'education at all levels'. Under the heading of 'state provision' he includes both direct public provision and indirect provision via public funding of cooperatives and other non-profit providers. While sketching the broad forms of transformation, Wright also emphasises the importance of experimentation and democratic deliberation in the design of specific components of change – what Unger calls 'democratic experimentalism', which he defines as 'the organisation of a collective experimental practice from below' (Unger, 2004, p. civ).

It is beyond the scope of this book or the capacities of its authors to offer a comprehensive and credible account of the future; all we can do is indicate that many thinkers and writers believe that neoliberalism is already in, or entering, crisis – and that this calls for transformative change. What we take from Milton Friedman's strategy and the work we refer to above is that criticism, though important, is not enough; there is urgent need to develop ideas for a post-neoliberal and possibly, too, a post-capitalist world. As political scientist Sheri Berman puts the matter,

A broad appreciation that many ideas and policies advocated by neoliberals since the 1970s are responsible for the economic, social and political mess in which the west finds itself has opened a political space for transformation. But for that to occur, the left would need to be ready with an alternative – not just criticisms.

(Berman, 2019, np)

If a 'political space for transformation' has indeed opened up in the wake of neo-liberalism's failings, the task before us is to widen that space and fill it with other possibilities, throwing off the dictatorship of no alternative to explore the potential of transformative change.

Transforming early childhood education and care

The development of new ideas, of alternatives, of transformative change applies to early childhood education and care. But it should not take place in isolation, rather as part of wider thinking and debate about education as a whole and, indeed, about societies that in the future are built on democracy, social justice, solidarity and sustainability – and education's contribution to that future. As Monbiot says, we need many minds and various disciplines working collaboratively. Those of us in the early childhood field need to be able to understand and relate to the transformative ideas emerging in many other fields, including economy, environment, equality, welfare state, health, democracy and social justice; while those working on these broad subjects need to be aware of what early childhood education and care could contribute to them.

There are already hopeful signs, for example around the relationship between early childhood education and care and the development of more environmentally sustainable forms of living. Education for sustainability has emerged in recent years, becoming a global movement (Tilbury, 2013), and that educational engagement has included early childhood. Ryan and Tilbury (2013) note how Early Childhood Education for Sustainability (ECEfS) grew out of practitioner networks, mainly in Australia, since when the field has developed rapidly, including the establishment of a UNESCO Chair for Early Childhood and Sustainable Development; the organisation of international meetings; the forming of cross-national networks (e.g. Teacher Education for Equity and Sustainability; Transnational Dialogues in Research in Early Childhood Education for Sustainability); and a growing body of research, publications and teaching resources. As an example of the latter, the Early Childhood Education for Sustainability Framework (www.ljmu.ac.uk/microsites/early-childhood-education-for-sustainability) provides a pedagogical toolkit that supports and challenges early years practitioners to understand how they can embed crucial ecological values into their practice.

This desire to commit ECEC to a transformative environmental agenda is also apparent in the field's growing engagement with post-humanism (e.g. Taylor, 2013; Murris, 2016; Hackett and Somerville, 2017), in which

> [t]he central, privileged and autonomous position of human (adult) beings, lording it over all else from on high, along with the belief in their superiority and separateness from all else, is superseded: the world is no longer centred on human beings and their affairs (Prout, 2004). Instead, the place of human beings in the world is de-centred, with the focus moving to inter-dependence within what has been termed 'more than human worlds', a term that encompasses a wide range of constituents: 'things, objects, other animals, living beings, organisms, physical forces, spiritual entities, and humans'. The term 'entanglements' is often used to convey a sense of the multiplicity, complexity and inescapability of the relationships involved.
>
> From this new, posthuman perspective, old boundaries, especially those that sustain a distinct and privileged position for human beings, have begun to break down and blur, to be replaced by an attention to inter-dependencies, interconnections and (shades of the rhizome) entanglements.
>
> *(Moss, 2019, pp. 143–144)*

This example illustrates a fundamental point about change. Change will require new structures, new ways of doing things, but these practical concerns must emerge from new thinking and new relationships that replace the dominant ideas and relationships produced by neoliberalism. Such new thinking and new relationships should be open and transparent, the product of democratic political processes, where political questions are put forward and alternative answers are advocated, argued over and chosen between, with no pretence that there is only one right way. Such a politics of education will range over many areas, including images, purposes, values, ethics and pedagogies – and only then consider structures and systems, the best ways in which to organise early childhood services to meet the political choices that have been made. 'Where to?' and 'why?' should always precede 'how?', but all must be considered.

At the heart of our own political choices is the image of an early childhood centre that is fit for the image of a 'rich' child: a child born with a hundred languages, a citizen with rights, a protagonist who is 'active in constructing the self and knowledge through social interactions and inter-dependencies' (Malaguzzi, cited in Cagliari et al., 2016, p. 377), a human being living an important part of their life, here and now, not just readying themselves for a later stage. This is the image of the early childhood centre as a public space or forum, a place of encounter for all citizens, young and old, and capable of many projects, social, cultural, political, aesthetic, economic and more beside. This is a centre inscribed with values of democracy, solidarity, cooperation, inter-connectedness, experimentation, uncertainty and surprise; enacting relational ethics of care and encounter; and employing democratic professionals, whose work is valued and trusted and who are supported by a 'competent system.' This is a centre that is accountable to the society that has taken responsibility for its provision – accountable not in the sense of meeting performance targets but rather in the sense of being transparent, having public visibility, and being subject therefore to public scrutiny of and deliberation about its everyday life and work.

This image of the centre-as-public-space is the very antithesis of the neoliberal early childhood centre, with its accompanying images, purposes, values, ethics and pedagogies. It rejects the commodification and privatisation of early childhood centres, their reduction to businesses trading and competing in a market place to sell a product or commodity to individual consumers. Instead our image of the early childhood centre is as a public service available as of right to all citizens and serving its local community, responsive to that community's needs and desires – the early childhood centre as the collective provision of a public good. Rather than being expected to compete with each other, we would expect cooperation and solidarity to infuse networks of such community-based centres; rather than private businesses, we would expect early childhood centres to be provided either by democratically elected public bodies (such as local authorities) or by non-profit private organisations (such as cooperatives and community groups), answerable to such public bodies and committed to politically agreed and common values and ethics.

The early childhood centre, so imagined, could be one of the free, publicly-funded 'universal basic services', available as of right to all citizens, that some are today arguing should form the basis for a transformed society (cf. Social Prosperity Network, 2017; Coote and Percy, 2020). It is one of the shared spaces that constitute the 'social infrastructure', a vital element of society that allows people to make connections, form networks and find ways to know and help one another (Moore, 2018). Put a slightly different way, the early childhood centre, co-produced by the public for the public, is part of the commons, alongside other collectively owned amenities, institutions and services, such as schools, libraries, museums, public galleries, parks and playgrounds, 'a common treasury to enrich the quality of life of all irrespective of personal means, creating a sense of belonging to a common space, and sustaining social cohesion and solidarity' (Venn, 2018, p. 119). Often described in today's neoliberal language in economic terms of creating social or cultural 'capital', Venn insists such places are 'in truth a common inheritance'. We should, therefore,

> shun the term capital when applied to such commons because it converts these forms of public goods into the categories that belong to the conceptual structure of liberal capitalism and thus already corrupts and commodifies them within the sphere of calculation of value consistent with the interest of 'enterprise' and the accounting practices of business.
>
> *(ibid., p. 122)*

As we have already said, being choosey about the words you use matters.

There is clearly much work to be done in elaborating new ideas and developing alternative policies that would enable these ideas to be enacted in practice: to make the move from utopias to (in the words of Erik Olin Wright) 'real utopias', in which desirability is important but must be partnered by viability and achievability. What form or forms would centres take? How exactly would they be run and by whom? What profession(s) would work in these centres, and how would they be educated? What support would be needed to form a 'competent system', that system of 'reciprocal relationships between individuals, teams, institutions and the wider socio-political context … [that provides] support for individuals to realise their capability to develop responsible and responsive practices that respond to the needs of children and families in ever-changing societal contexts' (Urban, Vandenbroeck, Lazzari, Van Larer and Peeters, 2012, p. 21)? What would this early childhood service cost and how would it be funded? What would be the relationship between early childhood and compulsory education, and what conditions would be needed to create and sustain this relationship? What forms of management, evaluation and accountability would be commensurate with and supportive of such a system? How, for example, might democratic accountability work in practice? These are complex, difficult but also exciting questions to answer, but answered they can be once the initial step is taken of re-imagining the early childhood centre and opening up for democratic deliberation of alternative possibilities.

Last, but by no means least, is the question of what happens within such centres, what are they for and what do they do. As we have said, we see this public space, this basic service, this part of the social infrastructure, as a place of encounter for citizens with the potential for many projects – social, cultural, political, economic and more besides, projects emerging from the needs and desires of local children, families and communities. Among these projects would be education, though an education very different to the narrow, target-driven and strongly managed education of neoliberalism. It is an education in which

> cooperation and participation, democracy and listening are central pedagogical values and ethics, informing our way of being with and relating to young children. It is an education that slows down, adopting notions of slow knowledge and slow thinking and slow pedagogy, notions that value lingering, revisiting, reflection, and that lead to deep learning and rich meaning-making. It is an education that is comfortable with uncertainty and unpredictability, and so opens up to the unexpected and the surprising, to re-discover and to express wonder about the immediate and abstract world. It is an education that understands the importance of context and interpretation, and is sceptical of attempts to apply, unquestioningly, universal standards. It is an education in which observation and documentation, and in particular pedagogical documentation, enable all learning of all children, in its full diversity and complexity, to become visible and valued, and which understands assessment as a cooperative and dynamic process embedded in everyday educational experience. It is an education that will enable a turning away from the current demand for managerial accounting, towards a search for democratic, participatory and meaningful accountability. It is an education that recognises the importance of skilled and trusted practitioners, able to co-construct both curriculum and learning with children understood to be valued protagonists in education. Last but not least, it is an education based on trust in and respect for the agency, capabilities and potentialities of all involved, whether children, practitioners, parents or others.
>
> *(Moss and Cameron, 2020, p. 232)*

But there is a further challenge. Not only where do we want to be going, but also how do we get there from the current situation? For instance, how might we get from a marketized and privatised system of early childhood education to one that is democratic, collaborative and public, from competitive markets to cooperative networks? How do we decommodify? This will mean, certainly in some countries, taking up the challenge of de-marketising and de-privatising the early childhood system, and in the process contesting entrenched assumptions and interests – though again such tasks will not be confined to early childhood education and care, since the reaction to neoliberalism also entails contesting the marketisation and privatisation of other important services and utilities, and evolving new forms of public ownership and control that do not attempt a reversion to older forms of nationalisation.

In broad terms, what we envisage is using public funding as a lever of change, redirecting it from one system to another. This would involve the consolidation of all types of public funding for early childhood education and care, whether payments to services or parents, and over a transition period of some years moving this 'Consolidated Fund' away from supporting private for-profit services and towards the direct funding of a public system of services, a mix of public provision and private non-profit provision, all working towards and all committed to shared goals, principles and values. All, also, cooperating together in a system committed to the common good and universal access. Private, for-profit services will continue to exist and can continue to compete with each other, but will do so without the benefit of public money or public encouragement; workers in these services who want to move will be welcomed into the public system.

So we end this book with a hope and a plea. Hope that the neoliberal narrative can be pushed back until it becomes just one of many narratives told about early childhood education and care, no longer claiming the privilege of necessity and monopoly. And a plea that the early childhood community takes up the challenge of engaging in a vibrant politics of resistance and refusal, as well as joining in the wider project of transformation through building alternatives, both of ideas and of practical policies.

That way we can be ready for when 'the politically impossible becomes politically inevitable'.

A PANDEMIC POSTSCRIPT

As we neared the completion of this book, the world was engulfed in the Covid-19 pandemic. This has not only brought suffering to many and death to some, but caused massive dislocation to everyday life and economies, and imposed unprecedented demands on governments and public services – all on a global scale. While children have not borne the main brunt of the disease itself, they are 'emerging as the unforeseen – and, until very recently, largely unseen – victims of Covid-19' (Nolan, 2020, np), with all the disruption, fear and confinement it has brought. Caught up in the midst of this frightening and terrible event, we felt unable to end our work without a brief and very provisional reflection on this extraordinary and overwhelming crisis and its possible longer-term consequences.

The pandemic is the latest in a series of global shocks, following the gathering storm of environmental crises and the financial disaster of 2008 and its aftermath. Despite their disparate natures, these events have cumulative effects. All expose the falsity of neoliberalism's core claim that markets know best and government is the problem; as the Earth heats and is polluted, when the banking system tottered on the edge of complete collapse, and when Covid-19 struck, no one has said or is saying 'leave it to the market'. All have required or will require immense collective effort and strong state action, yet all have also revealed populations and societies that have been weakened by growing inequality, spreading precarity and the deterioration of public services and the rest of the social infrastructure – as the President of the Republic of Ireland writes, we have been confronted by 'the impact decades of unfettered neoliberalism have had on whole sectors of society and economy, left without protection as to basic necessities of life, security and the ability to participate' (O'Higgins, 2020, np). All reveal how the poor, the insecure and the otherwise vulnerable always pay the highest price in times of crisis. All call for solutions based on values of democracy, solidarity and equality, especially at the intersections of gender, race and class where the highest price is paid in times of neoliberal capitalist crises, for example the disproportionate impact of Covid-19 on

Black, Asian and minority ethnic communities and, more generally, more deprived areas has brought the racialised and classed nature of neoliberalism into stark relief (Lawrence, 2020; Marmot and Allen, 2020; PHE, 2020; Saad-Filho, 2020).

Such reflections provoked by the current pandemic have brought home to both of us how neoliberalism has become a zombie ideology. This was perhaps evident after the 2008 financial crisis, but the pandemic has made the evident blindingly obvious. Unable to contribute to the resolution of the crises we are living through or to offer us hope for a better, healthier and more sustainable future, neoliberalism lurches onwards waiting to be finished off if only we have the imagination, creativity and determination to put something better in its place. As outlined in Chapter 6, that something may involve a less rapacious and more responsible variant of capitalism, expected to contribute to the greater good and not just to maximise returns to shareholders and managers. Or it may involve something more radical.

That 'something better' will certainly require a reprioritising, refinancing and rebuilding of the public sphere, a public sphere built on every citizen's right to a good life, the importance of the public good, and a commitment to democracy, equality and solidarity. Ireland's President Michael O'Higgins (ibid.) has further written of the urgent need for such renewal of the public sphere, built on revived values:

> On the most basic level, we should recover and strengthen instincts which we may have suppressed, which the lure of individualism may have driven out, displacing a sense of the collective, of shared solidarity – allowing the state's value and contribution to be derided and disregarded, so that a narrow agenda of accumulation could be pursued.

The coronavirus, he argues, 'has highlighted the unequivocal case for a new eco-social political economy', including 'universal basic services that will protect us in the future'.

Writing about the coronavirus crisis, Matteo Lucchese and Mario Pianta (2020, np) also argue the case for renewal of the public sphere, in particular of the welfare state:

> Three decades of neoliberal policies have seriously reduced the welfare state: privatizations and cuts in public budgets have forced public agencies to downsize their activities, sometimes losing universality, effectiveness and quality of services [...] The welfare state is not a 'cost' for the private economic system. It is a parallel system that produces public goods and services and ensures the reproduction of society based on rights and needs of citizens, rather than on the ability to spend of customers. ... .
> [...]
> [W]e should massively refinance – through a more progressive taxation of income and wealth and through deficit spending – the whole range of public activities – health, education, universities, research, pensions, social assistance,

the environment. The welfare state could become the engine of a new model of development, with high social quality and environmental sustainability.

An essential part of this renewed public sphere, and part of its system of universal basic services, must be education, built on every citizen's right to lifelong learning from birth and on public schools that are open to everyone, vital public institutions in and of their local communities and essential constituents of a renewed welfare state. And early childhood must be an important and equal partner in this public education and the system of public schools.

Of course, the neoliberal zombie may stagger on. After the pandemic, people and societies may be too fatigued, too stressed and too preoccupied to undertake the hard and uncertain work of building a better world; the desire to 'get back to normal', to the way things were before Covid-19, may overwhelm voices calling for profound change. Such exhaustion may grant reprieve to a neoliberalism that had seemed finished, just as it did after the financial crisis.

The zombie may even seek new life, battening onto opportunities for profit afforded by the pandemic. In May 2020, we find EducationInvestor Global, the company we met in Chapter 3, advertising a webinar titled 'Shelter from the storm: Investing in education amid the Covid-19 pandemic'. This event, for 'investors and stakeholders worldwide in education', promises a panel drawn from private equity, corporate finance and strategic consulting, who will 'explore the future of education investment in the UK and elsewhere against a backdrop of unprecedented economic turbulence.... [and] identify opportunities in education markets, considering the perspectives of trade, private equity and overseas investors, while assessing the impact of Covid-19 on deal flow, pricing, due diligence and more' (https://mailchi.mp/educationinvestor/ei-webinar-shelter-from-storm-investment-covid-19?e=776e51d517). Old habits die hard!

This latest crisis could, the pessimists argue, even make things worse: '[f]or governments looking to monitor their citizens even more closely, and companies looking to get rich by doing the same, it would be hard to imagine a more perfect crisis than a global pandemic' (Baker, 2020, np). Developing this pessimistic possibility in the field of education, the pandemic opens up the prospect of new business opportunities and stronger governance possibilities, through the extension of digital technologies, including enhanced data collection and expanded use of data analytics, personalized learning software and artificial intelligence – 'the dream of a perfect education delivered by machine' (Beard, 2020, np).

Ben Williamson (2020, np) has described how, with hundreds of millions of children unable to attend school,

> [p]owerful networks, consisting of big tech companies such as Google, Microsoft and Facebook, international organizations including the OECD and UNESCO, as well as a global education industry of edu-businesses, consultancies, investors and technology providers, are coming together to define how education systems should respond to the crisis.

These 'pandemic power networks', Williamson argues, have their sights firmly set on the post-pandemic world, 'seizing the opportunity [of the health emergency] to project their longer-term objectives for large-scale educational adaptation and change ... seeking to build a private infrastructure on which public education will depend'. The ambition of organisations forming these networks is to 'embed digital technologies in education at very large scale, not just to assist in human capital development as the OECD explicitly states it, but in some cases to generate commercial advantage and market share too'. Neoliberals have always been accomplished at taking advantage of disasters – Naomi Klein's Shock Doctrine, and the pandemic is a disaster of unparalleled scale and scope.

But not everyone is a pessimist. The optimists believe that the shock to the system delivered by the pandemic, following the slow-burn of environmental decay and the sudden discovery of the financial system's instability, will give added momentum to a ground-swell of opinion and hope already manifest. An opinion that we cannot continue as we are, that 'there can be no return to normal because normal was the problem in the first place' (graffiti in Hong Kong, cited by Wintour, 2020). A hope, too, expressed by the Indian author and political activist Arundhati Roy when she writes of the choice, a political and collective choice, confronting us:

> Nothing could be worse than a return to normality. Historically, pandemics have forced humans to break with the past and imagine their world anew. This one is no different. It is a portal, a gateway between one world and the next. We can choose to walk through it, dragging the carcasses of our prejudice and hatred, our avarice, our data banks and dead ideas, our dead rivers and smoky skies behind us. Or we can walk through lightly, with little luggage, ready to imagine another world. And ready to fight for it.
>
> *(Roy, 2020, np)*

It may be that the difficult but exhilarating choice 'to walk through lightly ... ready to imagine another world' will come to seem more necessary and urgent as assumptions widely held for years, the accepted wisdom for a generation or more, those neoliberal axioms that we have been falsely told are self-evident and inevitable, begin to crumble faster, leaving the way open for new ideas, new thinking, new ways of seeing things.

> Maybe we can view our problems as shared, and society as more than just a mass of individuals competing against each other for wealth and standing. Maybe, in short, we can understand that the logic of the market should not dominate as many spheres of human existence as we currently allow it to.
>
> *(Baker, 2020, np)*

The British novelist and journalist James Meek, writing during the Covid-19 pandemic about the plague pandemic in the 1340s (the 'Black Death'), also sees such openings as a possible consequence of huge social, economic and cultural shocks:

Just as medieval peasants wondered whether the world would end if they refused to give their lord their labour for free, we might find ourselves wondering why, if the world is capable of mustering so much financial and material firepower to fight Covid-19 and save businesses from going under, it can't muster it for other purposes.

(Meek, 2020)

Environment, finance, disease: these shocks should propel all of us to ask first 'why?', then 'where to?' and 'how?' Education should engage in this questioning, for now is the time for a radical re-thinking of education freed from the constraints imposed by neoliberalism, a 'Great Reset' that starts with deliberating on the purposes of education. Such deliberation must bring to the fore the part education can and should play in securing children's and families' well-being, including their physical and mental health, as well as giving priority to ecological projects (Monbiot, 2020). It must lead to local democratic control of education, including the creation of localised democratic accountability systems, and the creation of co-operative communities of learners, including teachers, children and families – transformations that open up many exciting possibilities. Early childhood education and care can and should take its part in this 'Great Reset', no longer dominated by the logic of the market but firmly situated in the public domain, a public service taking its rightful place in a renewed public education.

We leave the final word to the American writer Rebecca Solnit (2020, np):

Ordinary life before the pandemic was already a catastrophe of desperation and exclusion for many human beings, an environmental and climate catastrophe, an obscenity of inequality. It is too soon to know what will emerge from this emergency, but not too soon to start looking for chances to help decide it. It is, I believe, what many of us are preparing to do.

REFERENCES

Acton, R. and Glasgow, P. (2015) 'Teacher wellbeing in neoliberal contexts: A review of the literature', *Australian Journal of Teacher Education*, 40 (8), 99–114.

Adams, R. (2019) 'One in four teachers say pupils are being forced out to boost school rankings', *The Guardian*, 10 May. (www.theguardian.com/education/2019/may/10/one-in-four-teachers-in-england-say-they-have-witnessed-off-rolling).

Adams, R. and Barr, C. (2019) 'British schoolchildren among least satisfied, says OECD report', *The Guardian*, 3 December. (www.theguardian.com/education/2019/dec/03/british-schoolchildren-among-least-satisfied-with-their-lives-says-oecd-report).

Adriany, V. (2019) 'Negotiating local and glocal discourses in kindergarten: Stories from Indonesia', *Journal of Pedagogy*, 10 (1), 77–93.

Allen, A., Benhenda, A., Jerrim, J. and Sims, S. (2019) *New Evidence on Teachers' Working Hours. An Empirical Analysis of Four Datasets.* (https://johnjerrim.files.wordpress.com/2019/09/working_paper_teacher_hours.pdf).

Alvarado, F., Chancel, L., Piketty, T., Saez, E. and Zucman, G. (2018) *World Inequality Report 2018: Executive Summary.* (https://wir2018.wid.world/files/download/wir2018-summary-english.pdf).

Akgunduz, Y. and Plantenga, J. (2014) 'Childcare in the Netherlands: Lessons in privatisation', *European Early Childhood Education Research Journal*, 22 (3), 379–385.

Amoore, L. and De Goede, M. (2005) 'Governance, risk and dataveillance in the war on terror', *Crime, Law and Social Change*, 43 (2–3), 149–173.

An, M. Y. (2013) 'Childcare expansion in East Asia: changing shape of the institutional configurations in Japan and South Korea', *Asian Social Work and Policy Review*, 7 (1), 28–43.

An Oifig Buiséid Pharlaiminteach (The Parliamentary Budget Office, Republic of Ireland) (2019) *Childcare in Ireland: An Analysis of Market Dynamics, Public Programmes and Accessibility.* (https://data.oireachtas.ie/ie/oireachtas/parliamentaryBudgetOffice/2019/2019-11-14_childcare-in-ireland-an-analysis-of-market-dynamics-public-programmes-and-accessibility_en.pdf).

Andrews, P. et al. (2014) 'Letter to The Guardian', *The Guardian*, 6 May. (www.theguardian.com/education/2014/may/06/oecd-pisa-tests-damaging-education-academics).

Archer, N. (2019) 'Hope and resilience in testing times'. (https://medium.com/childrens-centre/hope-and-resilience-in-testing-times-22d37b8c6af7).

Asthana, A. and Boycott-Owen, M. (2018) '"Epidemic of stress" blamed for 3,750 teachers on long-term sick leave', *The Guardian*, 11 January. (www.theguardian.com/education/2018/jan/11/epidemic-of-stress-blamed-for-3750-teachers-on-longterm-sick-leave).

ASX (Australian Stock Exchange) (nd) *A-REITs*. (www.asx.com.au/products/managed-funds/areits.htm).

Auld, E. and Morris, P. (2016) 'PISA, policy and persuasion: Translating complex conditions into education "best practice"', *Comparative Education*, 52 (2), 202–229.

Auld, E. and Morris, P. (2019) 'The OECD and IELS: Redefining early childhood education for the 21st century', *Policy Futures in Education*, 17 (1), 11–26.

Azmanova, A. (2019) 'The big Green New Deal and its little red social question', blog for *Social Europe*, 30 October. (www.socialeurope.eu/the-big-green-new-deal-and-its-little-red-social-question).

Baker, P. (2020) 'We can't go back to normal', *The Guardian*, 31 March. (www.theguardian.com/world/2020/mar/31/how-will-the-world-emerge-from-the-coronavirus-crisis).

Ball, S. J. (1998) 'Big policies/small world: An introduction to international perspectives in education policy', *Comparative Education*, 34 (2), 119–130.

Ball, S. (2003) 'The teacher's soul and the terrors of performativity', *Journal of Education Policy*, 18 (2), 215–228.

Ball, S. (2012) *Global Education Inc.: New Policy Networks and the Neo-Liberal Imaginary*. London: Routledge.

Ball, S. (2013) *Foucault, Power and Education*. London: Routledge.

Ball, S. (2016a) 'Neoliberal education? Confronting the slouching beast', *Policy Futures in Education*, 14 (8), 1046–1059.

Ball, S. (2016b) 'Subjectivity as a site of struggle: refusing neoliberalism?', *British Journal of Sociology of Education*, 37 (8), 1129–1146.

Ball, S. (2017) *The Education Debate* (3rd edn). Bristol: Policy Press.

Ball, S. (2018a) 'Commercialising education: Profiting from reform!' *Journal of Education Policy*, 33 (5), 587–589.

Ball, S. (2018b) 'The tragedy of state education in England: Reluctance, compromise and muddle – a system in disarray', *Journal of the British Academy*, 6, 207–238.

Ball, S. (2019) 'A horizon of freedom: Using Foucault to think differently about education and learning', *Power and Education*, 11 (2), 132–144.

Ball, S. and Olmedo, A. (2013) 'Care of the self, resistance and subjectivity under neoliberal governmentalities', *Critical Studies in Education*, 54 (1), 85–96.

Ball, S. and Vincent, C. (2006) *Childcare, Choice and Class Practices: Middle-class Parents and their Children*. London: Routledge.

Ball, S., Junemann, C. and Santori, D. (2017) *Edu.net: Globalisation and Education Policy Mobility*. London: Routledge.

Ball, S., Maguire, M., Braun, A., Perryman, J. and Hoskins, K. (2012) 'Assessment technologies in schools: "Deliverology" and the "play of dominations"', *Research Papers in Education*, 27 (5), 513–533.

Banerjee, A. and Duflo, E. (2020) 'How poverty ends: The many paths to progress – and why they might not continue', *Foreign Affairs*, 99 (1), 22–29.

Barber, M. (2007) *Instruction to Deliver: Tony Blair, the Public Services and the Challenge of Delivery*. London: Methuen.

Barnett, A. (2020) 'Out of the belly of hell: COVID-19 and the humanisation of globalisation', *openDemocracy*, 21 May. (www.opendemocracy.net/en/opendemocracyuk/out-belly-hell-shutdown-and-humanisation-globalisation/).

Beach, J. and Ferns, C. (2015) 'From child care market to child care system', *Policy Alternatives*, Summer, 53–61. (www.policyalternatives.ca/sites/default/files/uploads/publications/National%20Office/2015/09/OS120_Summer2015_Child_Care_Market_to_Child_Care_System.pdf).

Becker, G. (2002) *Human capital*. Paper given at the University of Montevideo. (www.um.edu.uy/docs/revistafcee/2002/humancapitalBecker.pdf).

Beer, D. (2017) *The Data Gaze*. London: Sage.

Beer, D. (2018) 'Data and political change', blog for *Towards Data Science*, 20 September. (https://towardsdatascience.com/data-and-political-change-f4679c86f3d8)

Benn, M. (2011) *School Wars: The Battle for Britain's Education*. London: Verso.

Berman, S. (2019) 'Interregnum or Transformation', blog for *Social Europe*, 9 December. (www.socialeurope.eu/interregnum-or-transformation).

Biesta, G. (2007) 'Why "What works" won't work: Evidence-based practice and the democratic deficit in educational research', *Educational Theory*, 57 (1), 1–22.

Biesta, G. (2010) *Good Education in an Age of Measurement: Ethics, Politics, Democracy*. Boulder, CO: Paradigm Publishers.

Bjørnholt, B. and Larsen, F. (2014) 'The politics of performance measurement: Evaluation use as mediator for politics', *Evaluation*, 20 (4), 400–411.

Blades, R., Greene, V., Wallace, E., Loveless, L. and Mason, P. (2014) *Implementation study: Integrated Review at 2–2/12; Years – Integrating the Early Years Foundation Stage Progress Check and the Healthy Child Programme Health and Development Review*. (https://assets.publishing.service.gov.uk/government/uploads/system/uploads/attachment_data/file/376698/DFE-RR350_Integrated_review_at_age_two_implementation_study.pdf).

Boaler, J. (2005) 'The "psychological prisons" from which they never escaped: The role of ability grouping in reproducing social class inequalities', *FORUM*, 47 (2 & 3), 125–134.

Boaler, J. (2013) 'Ability and mathematics: The mindset revolution that is reshaping education', *FORUM*, 55 (1), 143–152.

Bonetti, S. (2018) *The Early Years Workforce: A Fragmented Picture*. London: Education Policy Institute. (https://epi.org.uk/wp-content/uploads/2018/03/EPI_-Early-Years-Workforce.pdf).

Bonetti, S. (2019) *The Early Years Workforce in England*. London: Education Policy Institute. (https://epi.org.uk/publications-and-research/the-early-years-workforce-in-england/).

Bradbury, A. (2013) 'Education policy and the "ideal learner": Producing recognisable learner-subjects through early years assessment', *British Journal of Sociology of Education*, 34 (1), 1–19.

Bradbury, A. (2019) 'Pressure, anxiety and collateral damage: The Headteachers' verdicts on SATS'. (www.morethanascore.org.uk/wp-content/uploads/2019/09/SATs-research.pdf).

Bradbury, A. and Roberts-Holmes, G. (2016) '"They are children … not robots, not machines". The introduction of Reception Baseline Assessment'. (www.betterwithoutbaseline.org.uk/uploads/2/0/3/8/20381265/baseline_assessment_2.2.16-_10404.pdf).

Bradbury, A. and Roberts-Holmes, G. (2018) *The Datafication of Primary and Early Years Education: Playing with numbers*. London: Routledge.

Brannen, J. and Moss, P. (1998) 'The polarisation and intensification of parental employment in Britain: consequences for children, families and the community', *Community, Work & Family*, 1 (3), 229–247.

Breakspear, S. (2012) *The Policy Impact of PISA: An Exploration of the Normative Effects of International Benchmarking in School System Performance* (OECD Education Working Papers, No. 71). Paris: OECD Publishing.

Brennan, D., Cass, B., Himmelweit, S. and Szebehely, M. (2012) 'The marketisation of care: Rationales and consequences in Nordic and liberal care regimes', *Journal of European Social Policy*, 22 (4), 377–391.

Brighouse, T. (2019) 'A hopeful Labour future for our education system', interview in *The Morning Star*, 29 October. (https://morningstaronline.co.uk/article/f/hopeful-labour-future-our-education-system).

Bright Horizons (2019) *Expanding our Portfolio Development*. (www.brighthorizons.co.uk/about/expanding-our-portfolio).

Brown, C. and Carr, S. (2018) 'Education policy and mental weakness: a response to a mental health crisis', *Journal of Education Policy*, 34 (2), 242–266.

Brown, W. (2015a) 'Booked #3: What Exactly Is Neoliberalism?', interview in *Dissent*, 2 April. (www.dissentmagazine.org/blog/booked-3-what-exactly-is-neoliberalism-wendy-brown-undoing-the-demos).

Brown, W. (2015b) *Undoing the Demos: Neoliberalism's Stealth Revolution*. New York, NY: Zone Books.

Brown, W. (2016) 'Sacrificial citizenship: Neoliberalism, human capital and austerity politics', *Constellations*, 23 (1), 3–14.

Bukodi, E. and Goldthorpe, J. (2018) *Social Mobility and Education in Britain: Research, Politics and Policy*. Cambridge: Cambridge University Press.

Burchell, G. (1996) 'Liberal government and techniques of the self', in A. Barry, T. Osborne and N. Rose (eds), *Foucault and Political Reason*. London: UCL Press.

Business Buyers (2018) 'Attenborough Day Nursery sold to ambitious buyer', item on Business Buyers website, 12 April. (https://businessbuyers.co.uk/2018/04/12/attenborough-day-nursery-sold-ambitious-buyer/).

Cagliari, P., Barozzi, A. and Giudici, C. (2004) 'Thoughts, theories and experiences: For an educational project with participation', *Children in Europe*, 6, 28–30.

Cagliari, P., Castagnetti, M., Giudici, C., Rinaldi, C., Vecchi, V. and Moss, P. (2016) *Loris Malaguzzi and the Schools of Reggio Emilia: Selected Writings and Speeches 1945–1993*. London: Routledge.

Camehl, G., Schober, P. and Spiess, K. (2017) *Information Asymmetries between Parents and Educators in German Childcare Institutions* (DIW Berlin Discussion Paper No. 1693). (https://ssrn.com/abstract=3056210 or http://dx.doi.org/10.2139/ssrn.3056210).

Carney, S. (2012) 'Imagining globalisation: Educational policyscapes', in G. Steiner-Khamsi and F. Waldow (eds), *World Yearbook of Education 2012: Policy Borrowing and Lending in Education*. London: Routledge.

Case, A. and Deaton, A. (2020) *Deaths of Despair and the Future of Capitalism*. Princeton, NJ: Princeton University Press.

Castañeda, L. and Selwyn, N. (2018) 'More than tools? Making sense of the ongoing digitizations of higher education', *International Journal of Educational Technology in Higher*, 15. (https://link.springer.com/article/10.1186/s41239-018-0109-y).

Chang, H-J. (2011) *23 Things They Don't Tell You About Capitalism*. London: Penguin Books.

Chon, Y. (2018) 'The marketization of childcare and elderly care, and its results in South Korea', *International Social Work*, 62 (4). (https://doi.org/10.1177/0020872818796123).

Christie and Co. (2018) *Business Outlook 2018*. (www.christie.com/christieMediaLibraries/christie/PDFs-Publications/Christie-Co-Business-Outlook-2018.pdf).

Christie and Co. (2019) *Child Centric Sectors*. (www.christie.com/sectors/childcare-education/overview/).

Cleveland, G., Forer, B., Hyatt, D., Japel, C. and Krashinsky, M. (2008) 'New Evidence about child care in Canada: Use patterns, affordability and quality', *IRPP Choices*, 14 (12). (https://pdfs.semanticscholar.org/fec2/a14182c3cffa41c17518827d49274de4bc9e.pdf).

Cleveland, G. and Krashinsky, M. (2003) *Financing ECEC Services in OECD Countries*. Paris: OECD.

Cleveland, G. and Krashinksy, M. (2004) *Financing early learning and child care in Canada*, Discussion paper prepared for the Canadian Council on Social Development's National Conference on Child Care in Canada, Winnipeg, 12–14 November 2004.

Coffield, F. (2019) 'OFSTED's worst practice – its four-grade scale – undermines the real advances in its new draft framework', blog for UCL Institute of Education, 31 January. (https://blogs.ucl.ac.uk/ioe/2019/01/31/ofsteds-worst-practice-its-four-grade-scale-undermines-the-real-advances-in-its-new-draft-framework/).

Collet-Sabé, J. and Ball, S. (2020) 'Revolting families: The Catalan "opt out" movement and practices of resistance against Standard Assessment Test (SAT). Some exploratory research', *Power and Education*, 12 (1), 123–136.

Collier, P. (2018) *The Future of Capitalism: Facing the New Anxieties*. London: Allen Lane.

Connell, R. (2013) 'The neoliberal cascade and education: An essay on the market agenda and its consequences', *Critical Studies in Education*, 54 (2), 99–112.

Coote, A. and Percy, A. (2020) *The Case for Universal Basic Services*. Cambridge: Polity.

Curtis, P. (2008) 'SATs for 14-year-olds are scrapped', *The Guardian*, 14 October. (www.theguardian.com/education/2008/oct/14/sats-scrapped).

Dahlberg, G. and Moss, P. (2005) *Ethics and Politics in Early Childhood Education*. London: Routledge.

Dahlberg, G., Moss, P. and Pence, A. (2013, 3rd edn) *Beyond Quality in Early Childhood Education and Care: Languages of Evaluation*. London: Routledge.

Dao, M. C., Das, M., Koczan, Z. and Lian, W. (2017) *Drivers of Declining Labor Share of Income*. (https://blogs.imf.org/2017/04/12/drivers-of-declining-labor-share-of-income/).

Davies, B. and Bansel, P. (2007) 'Neoliberalism and education', *International Journal of Qualitative Studies in Education*, 20 (3), 247–259.

Davies, W. (2015a) *Review of 'Undoing the Demos' by Wendy Brown*. (www.perc.org.uk/project_posts/review-of-undoing-the-demos-by-wendy-brown/).

Davies, W. (2015b) *The Happiness Industry: How the Government and Big Business Sold Us Well-being*. London: Verso.

Davies, W. (2016) *The Difficulty of 'Neoliberalism'*. (www.perc.org.uk/project_posts/the-difficulty-of-neoliberalism/).

Davis, J. and Elliott, S. (eds.) (2014) *Research in Early Childhood Education for Sustainability: International Perspectives and Provocations*. London: Routledge.

Davis, J. and Muzumder, B. (2017) *The Decline in Intergenerational Mobility after 1980* (www.chicagofed.org/~/media/publications/workingpapers/2017/wp2017-05-pdf.pdf).

Deleuze, G. and Guattari, F. (2004) *A Thousand Plateaus: Capitalism and Schizophrenia* (trans. B. Massumi). London: Continuum.

Department for Children, Schools and Families (England) (2008) *Statutory Framework for the Early Years Foundation Stage. Setting the Standards for Learning, Development and Care for Children from Birth to Five*. (https://dera.ioe.ac.uk/6413/7/statutory-framework_Redacted.pdf).

Department for Children, Schools and Families (2010) *The Improving Schools Programme Handbook* (https://dera.ioe.ac.uk/2428/7/pri_isp_handbook_0031409_Redacted.pdf).

Department for Education (England) (2012) *Statutory Framework for the Early Years Foundation Stage. Setting the Standards for Learning, Development and Care for Children from Birth to Five*. (www.foundationyears.org.uk/files/2014/05/eyfs_statutory_framework_march_2012.pdf).

Department for Education (England) (2015a) *Review of Childcare Costs: the analytical report. An economic assessment of the Early Education and Childcare Market and Providers' Costs*. (https://assets.publishing.service.gov.uk/government/uploads/system/uploads/attachment_data/file/479659/151124_Analytical_review_FINAL_VERSION.pdf).

Department for Education (England) (2015b) *2010 to 2015 Government Policy: School and College Funding and Accountability.* (www.gov.uk/government/publications/2010-to-2015-government-policy-school-and-college-funding-and-accountability/).

Department for Education (England) (2016) *Reception Baseline Comparability Study.* (www.gov.uk/government/news/reception-baseline-comparability-study-published).

Department for Education (England) (2017a) *Statutory Framework for the Early Years Foundation Stage. Setting the Standards for Learning, Development and Care for Children from Birth to Five.* (www.foundationyears.org.uk/files/2017/0).

Department for Education (England) (2017b) *Supporting Early Years Providers to Run Sustainable Businesses: Summary.* (www.gov.uk/government/publications/supporting-early-years-providers-to-run-sustainable-businesses/supporting-early-years-providers-to-run-sustainable-businesses-summary).

Department for Education (England) (2017c) *Expressions of Interest for a National Centre to Administer the Organisation for Economic Cooperation and Development's (OECD) International Early Learning Study (IELS).*

Department for Education (England) (2019a) *Assessment Framework: Reception Baseline Assessment.* (https://assets.publishing.service.gov.uk/government/uploads/system/uploads/attachment_data/file/781766/Reception_baseline_assessment_framework.pdf).

Department for Education (England) (2019b) *Early Years Foundation Stage Profile Results in England, 2019.* (https://assets.publishing.service.gov.uk/government/uploads/system/uploads/attachment_data/file/839934/EYFSP_2019_Main_Text_Oct.pdf).

Department for Education (England) (2019c) *Implementing your School's Approach to Pay: Advice for Maintained Schools, Academies and Local Authorities.* (https://assets.publishing.service.gov.uk/government/uploads/system/uploads/attachment_data/file/786098/Implementing_your_school_s_approach_to_pay.pdf).

Department for Education (England) (2020) *Guidance: Reception Baseline Assessment, 25 June 2020.* (https://www.gov.uk/guidance/reception-baseline-assessment).

Department of Health (England) (1997) *Children's Day Care Facilities at 31 March 1997.* London: Department of Health.

Desilver, D. (2018) 'For most U.S. workers, real wages have barely budged in decades', Pew Research Center Fact Tank, 7 August. (www.pewresearch.org/fact-tank/2018/08/07/for-most-us-workers-real-wages-have-barely-budged-for-decades/).

Dickens, J. (2016) 'Philanthro-philes – meet the donors propping up our education system', *Schools Week*, 17 June. (https://schoolsweek.co.uk/the-rise-and-rise-of-the-philanthro-philes/).

Dixon, A. (2002) 'Editorial', *FORUM*, 44 (1), 1.

Dunleavy, P. J. and Hood, C. (1994) 'From Old Public Administration to New Public Management', *Public Money and Management*, 14 (3), 9–16.

Dunn, I. (2010) '"The Centre is My Business": neo-liberal politics, privatisation and discourses of professionalism in New Zealand', *Contemporary Issues in Early Childhood*, 11 (1), 49–60.

Dunne, M., Humphreys, S., Dyson, A., Sebba, J., Gallannaugh, F. and Muijs, D. (2011) 'The teaching and learning of pupils in low-attainment sets', *Curriculum Journal*, 22 (4), 485–513.

Early Education (2012) *Development Matters in the Early Years Foundation Stage (EYFS).* (www.foundationyears.org.uk/files/2012/03/Development-Matters-FINAL-PRINT-AMENDED.pdf).

EducationInvestor Global (2019a) *Investment Opportunities in ASEAN Early Years Education, a Conference to be held in Singapore in February 2019.* (www.ipevents.net/education-asia/early-years/).

EducationInvestor Global (2019b) *Panel Discussion: Early Doors: Establishing a Niche Nursery Proposition in the Middle East.* (https://events.bizzabo.com/216174/agenda/session/132678).

Eisenstadt, N. (2011) *Providing a Sure Start: How Government Discovered Early Childhood.* Bristol: Policy Press.

Elliott, L. (2019) 'Inequality is ripping Britain apart. Is it about to be addressed', *The Guardian*, 16 May. (www.theguardian.com/commentisfree/2019/may/15/inequality-britain-social-injustice-beveridge-report).

Esping-Andersen, G. (1990) *The Three Worlds of Welfare Capitalism.* Princeton, NJ: Princeton University Press.

Eubanks, V. (2019) *Automating Inequality: How High-Tech Tools Profile, Police and Punish the Poor.* New York, NY: Picador.

Fendler, L. (2001) 'Educating Flexible Souls: The construction of subjectivity through developmentality and interaction', in K. Hultqvist and G. Dahlberg (eds), *Governing the Child in the New Millennium.* London: Routledge.

Fielding, M. and Moss, P. (2011) *Radical Education and the Common School: A Democratic Alternative.* London: Routledge.

Flewitt, R. and Roberts-Holmes, G. (2015) 'Regulatory gaze and "non-sense" phonics testing in early literacy', in M. Hamilton, R. Heydon, K. Hibbert and R. Stooke (eds), *Negotiating Spaces for Literacy Learning: Multimodality and Governmentality.* London: Bloomsbury, 95–113.

Fortunati, A. (2006) *The Education of Young Children as a Community Project: The Experience of San Miniato.* Azzano San Paolo, Brazil: Edizioni Junior.

Foucault, M. (1988a) *Politics, Philosophy, Culture: Interviews and Other Writings 1977–1984* (trans. A. Sheridan et al.). London: Routledge.

Foucault, M. (1988a) 'Truth, power, self', in L. Martin, H. Gutman and P. Hutton (eds), *Technologies of the Self*, Amhurst, MA: University of Massachusetts Press.

Foucault, M. (1997) *Ethics, Subjectivity, and Truth* (edited by Paul Rabinow). New York, NY: The New Press.

Foucault, M. (1998) *The History of Sexuality: The Will to Knowledge.* London: Penguin.

Foucault, M. (2000) *The Essential Works of Michel Foucault, 1954–1984, Volume 3: Power.* (edited by J. D. Faubion). New York NY: Free Press.

Foucault, M. (2008) *The Birth of Biopolitics; Lectures at the Collège de France, 1978–79* (trans. G. Burchell). New York NY: Palgrave Macmillan.

Foundation Years (nd) *Marketing.* (www.foundationyears.org.uk/business-sustainability/marketing/).

Francis, B., Archer, L., Hodgen, J., Pepper, D., Taylor, B. and Travers, M.-C. (2017) 'Exploring the relative lack of impact of research on "ability grouping" in England: a discourse analytic account', *Cambridge Journal of Education*, 47 (1), 1–17.

Fraser, N. (2016a) 'Capitalism's crisis of care', *Dissent*, Fall. (www.dissentmagazine.org/article/nancy-fraser-interview-capitalism-crisis-of-care).

Fraser, N. (2016b) 'Contradictions of Capital and Care', *New Left Review*, 100 (July Aug), 99–117. (https://newleftreview.org/issues/II100/articles/nancy-fraser-contradictions-of-capital-and-care.pdf).

Friedman, M. (1962/82) *Capitalism and Freedom* (1982 edn). Chicago, IL: University of Chicago Press.

Friendly, M., Larsen, E., Feltham, L., Grady, B., Forer, B. and Jones, M. (2018) *Early Childhood Education and Care in Canada 2016.* Toronto: Childcare Research and Resource Unit. (www.childcarecanada.org/sites/default/files/ECEC-in-Canada-2016.pdf).

Fuller, B. C., Livas, A. and Bridges, M. (2005) *How to Expand and Improve Pre-school in California: Ideals, Evidence, and Policy Options* (PACE Working Paper 05–1). Berkeley, CA: Policy Analysis for California Education (PACE).

Gallagher, A. (2017) 'Growing pains? Change in the New Zealand childcare market 2006–2016', *New Zealand Geographer*, 73 (1), 15–24.

Gambaro, L., Stewart, K. and Waldfogel, J. (eds) (2014) *An Equal Start? Providing Quality Early Education and Care for Disadvantaged Children*. Bristol: Policy Press.

Gaunt, C. (2020a) 'Ofsted annual report highlights changing childcare market', *Nursery World*, 22 January. (www.nurseryworld.co.uk/news/article/ofsted-annual-report-highlights-changing-childcare-market).

Gaunt, C. (2020b) 'Busy Bees drives expansion in US with acquisition of EduKids', *Nursery World*, 6 February. (www.nurseryworld.co.uk/news/article/busy-bees-drives-expansion-in-us-with-acquisition-of-edukids).

Gaunt, C. (2020c) '30 hour childcare key to getting the country back to work, says nursery market report', *Nursery World*, 15 May. (www.nurseryworld.co.uk/news/article/30-hour-childcare-key-to-getting-the-country-back-to-work-says-nursery-market-report).

Gaunt, C. (2020d) 'Reception Baseline on hold until September 2021', *Nursery World*, 25 June. (www.nurseryworld.co.uk/news/article/reception-baseline-on-hold-until-september-2021).

George, S. (1999) *A Short History of Neoliberalism: Twenty Years of Elite Economics and Emerging Opportunities for Change*, paper presented at conference Economic Sovereignty in a Globalising World, Bangkok, Thailand, 24–26 March 1999. (www.tni.org/en/article/short-history-neoliberalism).

Gibson, M., McArdle, F. and Hatcher, C. (2015) 'Governing child care in neoliberal times: Discursive constructions of children as economic units and early childhood educators as investment brokers', *Global Studies of Childhood*, 5 (3), 322–332.

Gilbert, J. (2020) *Twenty-First Century Socialism*. Cambridge: Polity Press.

Gillborn, D. and Youdell, D. (2000) *Rationing Education: Policy, Practice, Reform and Equity*. Buckingham: Open University Press.

Gillies, D. (2011) 'State education as high-yield investment: Human Capital Theory in European policy discourse', *Journal of Pedagogy*, 2 (2), 224–245.

Gillies, D. (2015) 'Human Capital Theory in Education', in M. Peters (ed.), *Encyclopedia of Educational Philosophy and Theory*. Singapore: Springer.

Giroux, H. (2004) 'Public Pedagogy and the Politics of Neo-liberalism: making the political more pedagogical', *Policy Futures in Education*, 2 (3–4), 494–503.

Giroux, H. (2014) *Neoliberalism's War on Higher Education*. Chicago, IL: Haymarket Books.

Giroux, H. (2019) 'Neoliberal fascism as the end point of casino capitalism', *Fast Capitalism*, 16 (1), 7–23.

Giugale, M. (2009) 'Foreword' to R. Paes de Barros, F. Ferreira, J. Molinas Vega and J. Saavedra Chanduvi, *Measuring Inequality of Opportunities in Latin America and the Caribbean*. Washington, DC and New York, NY: World Bank and Palgrave MacMillan.

Glazzard, J. (2019) 'Mistrust of new teachers leads to poor mental wellbeing', *Times Educational Supplement*, 19 March. (www.tes.com/news/mistrust-new-teachers-leads-poor-mental-wellbeing).

Goldstein, H., Moss, G., Sammons, P., Sinnott, G. and Stobart, G. (2018) *A Baseline Without Basis: The Validity and Utility of the Proposed Reception Baseline Assessment in England*. London: British Educational Research Association. (www.bera.ac.uk/researchers-resources/publications/a-baseline-without-basis).

Gore, J. (1993) *The Struggle for Pedagogics: Critical and Feminist Discourses as Regimes of Truth*. New York, NY: Routledge.

Gormley, K. (2018) 'Neoliberalism and the discursive construction of "creativity"', *Critical Studies in Education*, doi:10.1080/17508487.2018.1459762.

Greany, T. and Higham, R. (2018) *Hierarchy, Markets and Networks. Analysing the 'Self-Improving School-Led System' Agenda in England and the Implications for Schools*. London: Trentham Books.

Gu, L. (2006) 'Chinese early childhood education in transition', *Wingspan*, 16 (1), 30–41.

Gupta, A. (2018) 'How neoliberal globalization is shaping early childhood education policies in India, China, Singapore, Sri Lanka and the Maldives', *Policy Futures in Education*, 16 (1), 11–28.

Hackett, A. and Somerville, M. (2017) 'Posthuman literacies: Young children moving in time, place and more-than-human worlds', *Journal of Early Childhood Literacy*, 17 (3) 374–391.

Hallam, S. and Ireson, J. (2007) 'Secondary school pupils' satisfaction with their ability grouping placements', *British Educational Research Journal*, 33, 27–45.

Hallam, S., Ireson, J. and Davies, J. (2004) 'Primary School Pupils' Experience of Different Types of Grouping in Schools', *British Educational Research Journal*, 30 (4), 515–534.

Hammersley, M. (2013) *The Myth of Research-Based Policy and Practice*. London: Sage.

Hanushek, E. and Woessmann. L. (2010) *The High Cost of Low Educational Performance: The Long-Run Economic Impact of Improving PISA Outcomes*. Paris: OECD.

Hanushek, E. and Woessmann, L. (2015) *Universal Basic Skills: What Countries Stand to Gain*. Paris: OECD.

Harbach, M. (2015) 'Childcare market failure', *Utah Law Review*, 2015 (3), 659–720.

Harris, J. (2018) 'Can Labour forge a new, 21st century socialism?', *The Guardian*, 24 September. (www.theguardian.com/commentisfree/2018/sep/24/can-labour-forge-socialism-21st-century-conference-liverpool).

Harvey, D. (2005) *A Brief History of Neoliberalism*. Oxford: Oxford University Press.

Hatch, J. A. (1995) 'Studying childhood as a cultural invention: A rationale and framework', in J. A. Hatch (ed.), *Qualitative Research in Early Childhood Settings*, Westport, CT: Praeger.

Held, V. (2002) 'Care and the extension of markets', *Hypatia*, 17 (2), 19–33.

Hill, E. and Wade, M. (2018) 'The "radical marketization" of early childhood education and care in Australia', in D. Cahill and P. Toner (eds), *Wrong Way: How Privatization and Economic Reform Backfires*. Carlton, VIC: La Trobe University Press.

Holborow, M. (2012) 'Neoliberalism, human capital and the skills agenda in higher education: The Irish case', *Journal for Critical Education Policy Studies*, 10 (1), 93–111.

Holloway, J. and Brass, J. (2018) 'Making accountable teachers: the terrors and pleasures of performativity', *Journal of Education Policy*, 33 (3), 361–382,

HolonIQ (2018) '$10 trillion global education market by 2030'. (www.holoniq.com/2030/10-trillion-global-education-market/).

Hood, C. (1991) 'A public management for all seasons?', *Public Administration*, 69 (Spring), 3–19.

House of Commons Treasury Committee (2018) 'Childcare'. (https://publications.parliament.uk/pa/cm201719/cmselect/cmtreasy/757/757.pdf).

Hursh, D. (2016) *The End of Public Schools: The Corporate Reform Agenda to Privatize Education*. New York, NY: Routledge.

Hutchings, M. (2015) *Exam Factories? The impact of accountability measures on children and young people*. London: National Union of Teachers.

Hutchinson, J. (2016) *School Inspection in England: Is There Room to Improve?* London: Education Policy Institute. (https://epi.org.uk/wp-content/uploads/2018/01/school-inspection-in-england-web.pdf).

Hutchinson, J., Reader, M. and Akhal, A. (2020) *Education in England: Annual Report 2020*. London: Education Policy Institute. (static1.squarespace.com/static/543e665de4b0fbb2b140b291/t/5f3f9a353e183776e6f0cb4a/1598003777133/2020_ReportCard_FEA.pdf).

IBISWorld (2019) *Day Care in Canada – Market Research Report*. (www.ibisworld.ca/industry-trends/market-research-reports/healthcare-social-assistance/day-care.html).

Institute for New Economic Thinking (2016) 'Heckman Study: Investment in Early Childhood Education Yields Substantial Gains for the Economy', blog for Institute for New

Economic Thinking, 12 December. (www.ineteconomics.org/perspectives/blog/heckman-study-investment-in-early-childhood-education-yields-substantial-gains-for-the-economy).

Jackson, T. (2009) *Prosperity without Growth*. (www.sd-commission.org.uk/data/files/publications/prosperity_without_growth_report.pdf).

Jarvis, P. (2016) 'Developmentally informed teaching: Challenging premature targets in early learning', in NUT (ed.), *The Mismeasurement of Learning: How Tests are Damaging Children and Primary Education*. London: National Union of Teachers.

Jerrim, J. (2019) 'How do headteachers in England use test data, and does this differ from other countries?' blog for UCL Institute of Education, 15 October. (https://blogs.ucl.ac.uk/ioe/2019/10/15/how-do-headteachers-in-england-use-test-data-and-does-this-differ-from-other-countries/).

Jones, K. (2016) *Education in Britain: 1944 to the Present* (2nd edn). Cambridge: Polity Press.

Jones, K. (2018) *Baseline – The Test That Nobody Wants*. (https://neu.org.uk/assessment/baseline-test-nobody-wants).

Joshi, H. and Davies, H. (1993) 'Mothers' Human Capital and Childcare in Britain', *National Institute Economic Review*, 146 (1), 50–63.

Judt, T. (2010) *Ill Fares the Land*. London: Allen Lane.

Keddie, A. (2016) 'Children of the market: performativity, neoliberal responsibilisation and the construction of student identities', *Oxford Review of Education*, 42 (1), 108–122.

Kenway, J. (1990) 'Education and the right's discursive politics: Private versus state schooling', in S. Ball (ed), *Foucault and education: Disciplines and knowledge*. London: Routledge, 167–200.

Kitchin, R. (2014) *The Data Revolution: Big Data, Open Data, Data Infrastructures and Their Consequences*. London: Sage.

Klees, S. (2018) 'Capitalism and global education reform', in K. Saltman and A. Means (eds), *The Wiley Handbook of Global Educational Reform*. Hoboken, NJ: John Wiley, 11–26.

Klein, N. (2008) *The Shock Doctrine: The Rise of Disaster Capitalism*. London: Penguin Books.

Klein, N. (2015) *This Changes Everything*. London: Penguin Books.

Komatsu, H. and Rappleye, J. (2017) 'A new global policy regime founded on invalid statistics? Hanushek, Woessmann, PISA, and economic growth', *Comparative Education*, 53 (2), 166–191.

Labaree, D. (2017) 'Futures of the field of education', in G. Whitty and J. Furlong (eds), *Knowledge and the Study of Education: An International Exploration*. Oxford: Symposium Books, 277–283.

LaingBuisson (2019) *Childcare UK Market Report: Fifteenth Edition*. (www.laingbuisson.com/shop/childcare-uk-market-report/).

LaingBuisson (2020) *Childcare UK Market Report: Sixteenth Edition*. (www.laingbuisson.com/shop/childcare-uk-market-report-16ed/).

Lanchester, J. (2019) 'Good new idea', *London Review of Books*, 41 (14). (www.lrb.co.uk/the-paper/v41/n14/john-lanchester/good-new-idea).

Lawrence, D. (2020) *An Avoidable Crisis: The disproportionate impact of Covid-19 on Black, Asian and minority ethnic communities*. (www.lawrencereview.co.uk).

Lazzarato, M. (2009) 'Neoliberalism in action: inequality, insecurity and the reconstruction of the social', *Theory, Culture and Society*, 26 (6), 109–133.

Leary, J. P. (2019) *Keywords: The New Language of Capitalism*. Chicago, IL: Haymarket Books.

Lee, S-F. (2020) 'Governing "disadvantage" through funded early years places and reconfigured spaces', *Journal of Early Childhood Research*. (https://journals.sagepub.com/doi/full/10.1177/1476718X20971322).

Lennard, N. (2018) 'The kids aren't alright', *Dissent*, Winter. (www.dissentmagazine.org/a rticle/malcolm-harris-kids-these-days-review-millennials-capitalism).

Lentzos, F. and Rose, N. (2009) 'Governing insecurity: Contingency planning, protection, resilience', *Economy and Society*, 38 (2), 230–254.

Levin, S. (2018) 'Jeff Bezos to fund schools where "child will be the customer" with new charity', *The Guardian*, 13 September. (www.theguardian.com/technology/2018/sep/13/amazon-jeff-bezos-philanthropy-day-one-fund).

Lightfoot-Rueda, T. and Peach, R. L. (2015) 'Introduction and historical perspective', in T. Lightfoot-Rueda and R. L. Peach (eds), *Global Perspectives on Human Capital in Early Childhood Education*. New York, NY: Palgrave Macmillan, 3–26.

Lim, S. (2017) 'Marketization and corporation of early childhood care and education in Singapore', in M. Li, J. Fox and S. Grieshaber (eds), *Contemporary Issues and Challenge in Early Childhood Education in the Asia-Pacific Region*. Singapore: Springer, 18–32.

Lingard, B. (2009) 'Testing times: The need for new intelligent accountabilities for schooling', *QTU Professional Magazine*, 24 (November), 13–19.

Lingard, B., Sellar, S. and Savage, G. (2014) 'Re-articulating social justice as equity in schooling policy, the effects of testing and data infrastructures', *British Journal of Sociology of Education*, 35 (5), 710–730.

Lloyd, E. (2010) *Comparing Childcare Market Developments in England and the Netherlands*, Social Policy Association Conference, Lincoln University, 5–7 July.

Lloyd, E. (2019) 'Reshaping and reimagining marketised early childhood education and care systems – Challenges and possibilities', *Zeitschrift für Pädagogik*, 65 (3), 89–106.

Lloyd, E. and Penn, H. (2014) 'Childcare markets in the age of austerity', *European Early Childhood Education Research Journal*, 22 (3), 386–396.

Lupton, D. and Williamson, B. (2017) 'The datafied child: The dataveillance of children and implications for their rights', *New Media & Society*, 19 (5), 780–794.

MacNaughton, G. (2005) *Doing Foucault in Early Childhood Studies: Applying Poststructural Ideas*. London: Routledge.

Mahon, M. (1992) *Foucault's Nietzschean Genealogy: Truth, Power and the Subject*. Albany, NY: State University of New York Press.

Mahony, P., Menter, I. and Hextall, I. (2004) Building dams in Jordan, assessing teachers in England: A case study in edu-business', *Globalisation, Societies and Education*, 2 (2), 277–296.

Male, T. (2019) *Governance in Multi-Academy Trusts (MATs). Evidence from the Field*, paper presented at ECER 2019 Conference, Hamburg, September 2019. (https://discovery.ucl.ac.uk/id/eprint/10080922/1/2019%20Governance%20in%20multi-academy%20trusts%20-%20evidence%20from%20the%20field%20-%20Trevor%20Male.pdf).

Marangos, A. and Plantenga, J. (2006) 'Introducing market forces', *Children in Europe*, 11, 18–19.

Marks, R. (2012) '"I get the feeling that it is really unfair": educational triage in primary mathematics', *Proceedings of the British Society for Research into Learning Mathematics*, 32, 58–63.

Marmot, M. and Allen, J. (2020) 'COVID-19: Exposing and amplifying inequalities', *Journal of Epidemiology and Community Health*, 74, 681–682. (http://dx.doi.org/10.1136/jech-2020-214720).

Marquand, D. (2004) *The Decline of the Public: The Hollowing-Out of Citizenship*. Cambridge: Polity Press.

Martin, L., Gutman, H. and Hutton, P. (eds) (1988) *Technologies of the Self: A Seminar with Michel Foucault*. London: Tavistock.

Mason, P. (2015) *Postcapitalism: A Guide to our Future*. London: Allen Lane.

Mason, P. (2019) 'Time for postcapitalism', blog for *Social Europe*, 1 July. (https://www.socialeurope.eu/time-for-postcapitalism).

Mathers, S. and Smee, R. (2014) *Quality and Inequality. Do Three- and Four-year-olds in Deprived Areas Experience Lower Quality Early Years Provision?*London: Nuffield Foundation. (www.nuffieldfoundation.org/sites/default/files/files/Quality_inequality_childcare_mathers_29_05_14.pdf).

Mathers, S., Sylva, K. and Joshi, H. (2007) *Quality of Childcare Settings in the Millennium Cohort Study* (Research Report SSU/2007/FR/022). London: Department for Children, Schools and Families.

McKinsey (2007) *How the World's Best Performing School Systems Come Out on Top*. Dubai: McKinsey & Company.

Meek, J. (2020) 'In 1348', *London Review of Books*. (https://www.lrb.co.uk/the-paper/v42/n07/james-meek/in-1348).

Melhuish, E. and Gardiner, J. (2017) *Study of Early Education and Development (SEED): Study of Quality of Early Years Provision in England* (DFE-RR706). London: Department for Education.   (www.gov.uk/government/uploads/system/uploads/attachment_data/file/665077/SE ED_Quality_Report_December_2017.pdf).

Millar, F. (2018) *The Best for My Child. Did the Schools Market Deliver?*Woodbridge: John Catt Educational.

Mirowski, P. (2013a) *Never Let a Serious Crisis go to Waste: How Neoliberalism Survived the Financial Meltdown*. London: Verso.

Mirowski, P. (2013b) 'The thirteen commandments of neoliberalism', *The Utopian*, 19 June. (www.the-utopian.org/post/53360513384/the-thirteen-commandments-of-neoliberalism).

Mirowski, P. (2014) *The Political Movement that Dared not Speak its own Name: The Neoliberal Thought Collective Under Erasure* (Institute for New Economic Thinking Working Paper No. 23). (www.ineteconomics.org/uploads/papers/WP23-Mirowski.pdf).

Mitchell, L. (2012) 'Markets and childcare provision in New Zealand: Towards a fairer alternative', in E. Lloyd and H. Penn (eds), *Childcare Markets: Can They Deliver an Equitable Service?* Bristol: Policy Press, 97–114.

Mitchell, L. (2019) 'Turning the tide on private profit-focused provision in early childhood education', *New Zealand Annual Review of Education*, 24, 75–89.

Monbiot, G. (2016a) *How Did We Get into this Mess?: Politics, Equality, Nature*. London: Verso.

Monbiot, G. (2016b) 'Neoliberalism – the ideology at the root of all our problems', *The Guardian*, 15 April. (www.theguardian.com/books/2016/apr/15/neoliberalism-ideology-problem-george-monbiot).

Monbiot, G. (2017) *Out of the Wreckage: A New Politics for an Age of Crisis*. London: Verso.

Monbiot, G. (2019) 'Dare to declare capitalism dead – before it takes us all down with it', *The Guardian*, 25 April. (www.theguardian.com/commentisfree/2019/apr/25/capitalism-economic-system-survival-earth).

Moore, R. (2018) 'Palaces for the people: How to Build a More Equal and United Society by Eric Klinenberg – review', *The Guardian*, 8 October. (www.theguardian.com/books/2018/oct/08/palaces-for-people-how-build-more-equal-united-society-eric-klinenberg-review).

Morabito, C., Vandenbroeck, M. and Roose, R. (2013) '"The greatest of equalisers": A critical review of international organisations' views on early childhood care and education', *Journal of Social Policy*, 42 (03), 451–467.

Morin, E. (2001) *Seven Complex Lessons in Education for the Future*. Paris: UNESCO.

Morris, P. (2016) *Education Policy, Cross-National Tests of Pupil Achievement, and the Pursuit of World-Class Schooling*. London: IOE Press.

Morrison, N. (2020) 'The truth about education policy is that it's based on a myth', *Forbes*, 29 July. (www.forbes.com/sites/nickmorrison/2020/07/29/the-truth-about-education-policy-is-that-its-based-on-a-myth/#189e849a3e52).

Morton, K. (2019a) 'Busy Bees buys its first nurseries in the US and Italy', *Nursery World*, 13 September. (www.nurseryworld.co.uk/news/article/busy-bees-buys-its-first-nurseries-in-the-us-and-italy).

Morton, K. (2019b) 'More than 5600 childcare settings closing each month', *Nursery World*, 30 October. (www.nurseryworld.co.uk/news/article/more-than-500-childcare-settings-closing-each-month).

Moss, P. (2013) *Transformative Change and Real Utopias in Early Childhood Education: A Story of Democracy, Experimentation and Potentiality*. London: Routledge.

Moss, P. (2019) *Alternative Narratives in Early Childhood*. London: Routledge.

Moss, P. and Cameron, C. (2020) 'From the state we're in to what do we want for our children', in C. Cameron and P. Moss (eds), *Transforming Early Childhood in England: From Childcare to a Democratic Education System*. London: UCL Press.

Muller, J. (2018) *The Tyranny of Metrics*. Princeton NJ: Princeton University Press.

Murgatroyd, S. J. and Sahlberg, P. (2016) 'The two solitudes of educational policy and the challenge of development', *Journal of Learning for Development*, 3 (3), 9–21.

Murris, K. (2016) *The Posthuman Child: Educational Transformation through Philosophy and Picturebooks*. London: Routledge.

National Audit Office (England) (2018) *Converting Maintained Schools to Academies*. (www.nao.org.uk/wp-content/uploads/2018/02/Converting-maintained-schools-to-academies.pdf).

National Center for Education Statistics (US) (2019) *Public Charter School Enrollment*. (https://nces.ed.gov/programs/coe/indicator_cgb.asp).

National Institute of Drug Abuse (US) (2019) *Opioid Overdose Crisis*. (www.drugabuse.gov/drugs-abuse/opioids/opioid-overdose-crisis).

New Zealand Educational Institute (2019) *Turning the Tide Away from a Privatised, Profit-Focused Education System*. (https://campaigns.nzei.org.nz/wp-content/uploads/2019/01/Turning-the-Tide-FINAL-20190109.pdf).

Noailly, J. and Visser, S. (2009) 'The impact of market forces on childcare provision: Insights from the 2005 Child Care Act in the Netherlands', *Journal of Social Policy*, 38 (3), 477–498.

Nolan, A. (2020) 'A Child Rights Crisis', *London Review of Books*. (https://www.lrb.co.uk/blog/2020/may/a-child-rights-crisis).

Norris, N. and Kushner, S. (2007) 'The new public management and evaluation', in S. Kushner and N. Norris (eds), *Dilemmas of Engagement: Evaluation and the New Public Management. Advances in Program Evaluation*. Oxford: Elsevier, 1–16.

Nóvoa, A. (2018) 'Comparing Southern Europe: The difference, the public, and the common', *Comparative Education*, 54 (4), 548–561.

NUEPA (National University for Educational Planning and Administration) (2016) *Elementary Education in India: Trends 2005–06 to 2015–16*. New Delhi: NUEPA.

Nursery World (2018a) 'Busy Bees expanding in China', *Nursery World*, 6 February. (www.nurseryworld.co.uk/News/article/busy-bees-expanding-in-china).

Nursery World (2018b) 'Busy Bees buys Australian nursery group', *Nursery World*, 1 May. (www.nurseryworld.co.uk/news/article/busy-bees-buys-australian-nursery-group).

Nursery World (2019a) 'French nursery group La Maison Bleue seals first UK deal', *Nursery World*, 19 February. (www.nurseryworld.co.uk/news/article/french-nursery-group-la-maison-bleue-seals-first-uk-deal).

Nursery World (2019b) 'Busy Bees buys first Irish nursery group', *Nursery World*, 11 February. (www.nurseryworld.co.uk/news/article/busy-bees-buys-first-irish-nursery-group).

Nursery World (2019c) 'Appetite for nursery deals remains high – market report', *Nursery World*, 5 July. (www.nurseryworld.co.uk/news/article/appetite-for-nursery-deals-remains-high-market-report).

O'Connor, S. (2018) 'Millennials poorer than previous generations, data show', *The Financial Times*, 23 February. (www.ft.com/content/81343d9e-187b-11e8-9e9c-25c814761640).

OECD (Organisation for Economic Cooperation and Development) (2006) *Starting Strong II*. Paris: OECD.

OECD (Organisation for Economic Cooperation and Development) (2014) *Lessons from PISA for Korea, Strong Performers and Successful Reformers in Education*. Paris: OECD.

OECD (Organisation for Economic Cooperation and Development) (2015) *Call for Tenders. International Early Learning Study*. (www.oecd.org/callsfortenders/CfT%20100001420% 20International%20Early%20Learning%20Study.pdf).

OECD (Organisation for Economic Cooperation and Development) (2017) *How Does United States Compare on Child Well-Being?* (www.oecd.org/els/family/CWBDP_Factsheet_ USA.pdf).

OECD (Organisation for Economic Cooperation and Development) (2020) *Education at a Glance*. (www.oecd.org/education/education-at-a-glance/).

Office for Public Management (2011) *Improving Business Skills in the Early Years and Child-care Sector* (Research report for 4Children and the Department for Education). (http:// flourishingpeople.co.uk/wp-content/uploads/2014/01/Improving-busi ness-skills-in-the-childcare-sector.pdf).

Ofsted (2017) *Bold Beginnings: The Reception Curriculum in a Sample of Good and Outstanding Primary Schools*. (https://assets.publishing.service.gov.uk/government/uploads/system/ uploads/attachment_data/file/663560/28933_Ofsted_-_Early_Years_Curriculum_Report_ -_Accessible.pdf).

Ofsted (2019) *Education Inspection Framework*. (www.gov.uk/government/publications/educa tion-inspection-framework).

O'Higgins, M. (2020) 'Out of the tragedy of coronavirus may come hope of a more just society', blog for *Social Europe*, 22 April. (www.socialeurope.eu/out-of-the-tragedy-of-coronavirus-may-come-hope-of-a-more-just-society).

O'Kelly, E. (2018) 'Increase in numbers attending Catholic primary schools', *RTE*, 27 February. (www.rte.ie/news/education/2018/0227/943832-primary-education/).

Olsson, L. M. (2009) *Movement and Experimentation in Young Children's Learning: Deleuze and Guattari in Early Childhood Education*. London: Routledge.

Olssen, M. and Peters, M. (2005) 'Neoliberalism, higher education and the knowledge economy: From the free market to knowledge capitalism', *Journal of Education Policy*, 20 (3), 313–345.

Onaron, Ö. (2018) *The Causes of Falling Wage Share: Sectoral and Firm Level Evidence from Developed and Developing Countries – What Have We Learned?* (http://gala.gre.ac.uk/19373/ 7/19373%20ONARAN_The_Causes_of_Falling_Wage_Share_2018.pdf).

Ong, A (2006) *Neoliberalism as Exception: Mutations in Citizenship and Sovereignty*. Durham, NC: Duke University Press.

Osgood, J. (2003) *Developing the Business Skills of Childcare Professionals: An Evaluation of Business Support Programmes*. London: Department for Education and Skills.

Osgood, J. (2004) 'Time to get down to business? The responses of early years practitioners to entrepreneurial approaches to professionalism', *Journal of Early Childhood Research*, 2 (1), 5–24.

Osgood, J. (2009) 'Childcare workforce reform in England and the 'early years professional': A critical discourse analysis', *Journal of Education Policy*, 24 (6), 733–751.

Ostry, J., Loungani, P. and Furceri, D. (2016) 'Neoliberalism: Oversold?', *Finance and Development*, 53 (2), 38–41.

Oxfam (2019) *Public Good or Private Wealth?* (https://oxfamilibrary.openrepository.com/bitstream/handle/10546/620599/bp-public-good-or-private-wealth-210119-en.pdf;jsessionid=956D0BF0A3648E971409297DB33C3B91?sequence=23).

Owen, D. (2019) 'What is off-rolling, and how does Ofsted look at it on inspection?', blog for Ofsted. (https://educationinspection.blog.gov.uk/2019/05/10/what-is-off-rolling-and-how-does-ofsted-look-at-it-on-inspection/).

Ozanus, P. (2017) 'Early childhood as the foundation for tomorrow's workforce', blog for World Bank (Education for Global Development), 17 January. (https://blogs.worldbank.org/education/early-childhood-foundation-tomorrow-s-workforce).

Parramore, L. (2018) 'Meet the economist behind the one percent's stealth takeover of America', blog for Institute for New Economic Thinking, 30 May. (www.ineteconomics.org/perspectives/blog/meet-the-economist-behind-the-one-percents-stealth-takeover-of-america).

Pascal, C., Bertram, T. and Rouse, L. (2019) *Getting it Right in the Early Years Foundation Stage: A Review of the Evidence.* London: Early Education. (www.early-education.org.uk/sites/default/files/Getting%20it%20right%20in%20the%20EYFS%20Literature%20Review.pdf).

Patalay, P. and Fitzsimons, E. (2018) 'Development and predictors of mental ill-health and wellbeing from childhood to adolescence', *Social Psychiatry and Psychiatric Epidemiology*, 53, 1311–1323.

Paull, G. (2012) 'Childcare markets and government interventions', in E. Lloyd and H. Penn (eds), *Childcare Markets: Can They Deliver an Equitable Service?* Bristol: Policy Press, 227–256.

Paull, G. and Xu, X. (2019) *Early Years Providers Cost Study 2018.* (https://assets.publishing.service.gov.uk/government/uploads/system/uploads/attachment_data/file/782471/Frontier_-_Childcare_Cost_Study.pdf).

Peacock, A. (2016) *Assessment for Learning Without Limits.* Milton Keynes: Open University Press.

Pearson (2018) 'Pearson to develop PISA 2018 Student Assessment 21st Century Frameworks for OECD', press release, 10 December. (www.pearson.com/news-and-research/announcements/2014/12/pearson-to-develop-pisa-2018-student-assessment-21st-century-fra.html).

Peck, J. and Theodore, N. (2015) *Fast Policy. Experimental Statecraft at the Thresholds of Neoliberalism.* Minneapolis, MN: University of Minnesota Press.

Penn, H. (2014) 'The business of childcare in Europe', *European Early Childhood Education Research Journal*, 22 (4), 432–456.

Penn, H. (2018) 'Why parents should fear childcare going the way of Carillion', *The Guardian*, 14 May. (www.theguardian.com/commentisfree/2018/may/14/parents-carillion-childcare-collapse-nursery-provider).

Penn, H. (2019a) 'Understanding the contexts of leadership debates', *Contemporary Issues in Early Childhood*, 20 (1), 104–109.

Penn, H. (2019b) 'Putting childcare at the heart of the social market economy', *Wilfried Martens Centre for European Studies Policy Brief*, October. (https://martenscentre.eu/sites/default/files/publication-files/childcare-social-market-economy-europe.pdf).

Perryman, J. and Calvert, G. (2019) 'What motivates people to teach, and why do they leave? Accountability, performativity and teacher retention', *British Journal of Education Studies*. (https://doi.org/10.1080/00071005.2019.1589417).

Pignatelli, F. (1993) 'What can I do? Foucault on freedom and the question of teacher agency', *Educational Theory*, 43 (4), 411–432.

Plantenga, J. (2012) 'Local providers and loyal parents: Competition and consumer choice in the Dutch childcare market', in E. Lloyd and H. Penn (eds), *Childcare Markets: Can They Deliver an Equitable Service?* Bristol: Policy Press, 63–78.

Polanyi, K. (1944/2001) *The Great Transformation: The Political and Economic Origins of our Time*. New York, NY: Farrar & Rinehart.

Pratt, N. (2016) 'Neoliberalism and the (internal) marketisation of primary school assessment in England', *British Educational Research Journal*, 42 (5), 890–905.

Pre-School Learning Alliance (2018) *Minds Matter: The Impact of Working in the Early Years Sector on Practitioners' Mental Health and Wellbeing*. (www.eyalliance.org.uk/sites/default/files/minds_matter_report_pre-school_learning_alliance.pdf).

Press, F., Woodrow, C., Logan, H. and Mitchell, L. (2018) 'Can we belong in a neo-liberal world? Neo-liberalism in early childhood education and care in Australia and New Zealand', *Contemporary Issues in Early Childhood*, 19 (4), 328–339.

Prout, A. (2004) *The Future of Childhood*. London: Routledge.

Public Health England (PHE) (2020) *Beyond the Data: Understanding the impact of COVID-19 on BAME communities*. (https://assets.publishing.service.gov.uk/government/uploads/system/uploads/attachment_data/file/892376/COVID_stakeholder_engagement_synthesis_beyond_the_data.pdf).

Qualifications and Curriculum Authority (2008) *Early Years Foundation Stage Profile Handbook*. (dera.ioe.ac.uk/8221/13/Early_FS_Handbook_v11_WO_LR_Redacted.pdf).

Qualifications and Curriculum Authority/Department for Education and Employment (England) (2000) *Curriculum Guidance for the Foundation Stage*. (http://www.educationengland.org.uk/documents/foundationstage/index.html).

Ravitch, D. (2010) *The Death and Life of the Great American School System: How Testing and Choice are Undermining Education*. New York, NY: Basic Books.

Ravitch, D. (2012) 'Pearson's expanding role in education', blog for *The Washington Post*, 7 May. (www.washingtonpost.com/blogs/answer-sheet/post/ravitch-pearsons-expanding-role-in-education/2012/05/07/gIQApr4H8T_blog.html).

Ravitch, D. (2013) *Reign of Error: The Hoax of the Privatization Movement and the Danger to America's Public Schools*. New York, NY: Knopf.

Raworth, K. (2017) *Doughnut Economics: Seven Ways to Think Like a 21st Century Economist*. London: Random House Business Books.

Read, J. (2009) 'A genealogy of homo-economicus: Neoliberalism and the production of subjectivity', *Foucault Studies*, 6, 25–36.

RECE (Reconceptualising Early Childhood Education) (nd) *Reconceptualizing Early Childhood Education: A Brief Introduction*. (www.receinternational.org/about.html).

Richardson, H. (2019) 'School break times "cut short to cram in more lessons"', *BBC News*, 10 May. (www.bbc.co.uk/news/education-48203595).

Rizvi, F. and Lingard, B. (2009) *Globalizing Educational Policy*. London: Routledge.

Roberts-Holmes, G. (2015) 'The "datafication" of early years pedagogy: "If the teaching is good, the data should be good and if there's bad teaching, there is bad data"', *Journal of Education Policy*, 30 (3), 302–315.

Roberts-Holmes, G. (2020) 'Reception baseline assessment: A flawed and inappropriate test', blog for *More than a Score*, 30 April. (www.morethanascore.org.uk/reception-baseline-assessment-a-flawed-and-inappropriate-test/).

Roberts-Holmes, G. and Bradbury, A. (2016) 'Governance, accountability and the datafication of early years education in England', *British Educational Research Journal*, 42 (4), 600–613.

Roberts-Holmes, G., Lee., S-F. and Sousa, D. (2020) 'Covid-19 and early years education and care: Not the time for baseline assessment', blog for UCL Institute of Education, 25 June. (https://blogs.ucl.ac.uk/ioe/2020/06/25/covid-19-and-early-years-education-and-care-is-this-really-the-time-for-baseline-assessment/).

Roberts-Holmes, G., Lee., S-F., Sousa, D. and Jones, E. (2020) *Research into the 2019 Pilot of Reception Baseline Assessment (RBA)*. London: UCL IoE/National Education Union. (neu.org.uk/media/9116/view).

Roberts-Holmes, J. (2019) 'The securitization of everyday London life in the post 9/11 era'. School of Geography, Queen Mary University of London. Personal Correspondence.

Robyns, I. (2006) 'Three models of education: Rights, capabilities and human capital', *Theory and Research in Education*, 4 (1), 69–84.

Rose, N. (1998) *Inventing our Selves: Psychology, Power and Personhood*. Cambridge: Cambridge University Press.

Rose, N. (1999) *Powers of Freedom: Reframing Political Thought*. Cambridge: Cambridge University Press.

Rosen, M. (2018) 'The data have landed', blog, 8 February. (http://michaelrosenblog.blogspot.com/2018/02/the-data-have-landed.html).

Roy, A (2020) 'The pandemic is a portal', *Financial Times*, 3 April. (www.ft.com/content/10d8f5e8-74eb-11ea-95fe-fcd274e920ca).

Rudd, K. and Macklin, J. (2007) *New Directions for Early Childhood Education: Universal Access to Early Learning for 4 Year Olds*. (parlinfo.aph.gov.au/parlInfo/download/library/partypol/JRPO6/upload_binary/jrpo63.pdf;fileType=application%2Fpdf#search=%22library/partypol/JRPO6%22).

Ruitenberg, C. (2018) 'How much human autonomy can the planet afford?', *Theory and Research in Education*, 16 (1), 110–113.

Russell, M. (2020) 'Reception baseline: "Children scared of getting it wrong", say teachers', February 26. (www.nurseryworld.co.uk/news/article/reception-baseline-children-scared-of-getting-it-wrong-say-teachers).

Rustin, M. (2016) 'Alternatives to neoliberalism: A framing statement', *Soundings*, 62. (www.lwbooks.co.uk/sites/default/files/s62_02rustin.pdf).

Ryan, A. & Tilbury, D. (2013) 'Uncharted waters: Voyages for education for sustainable development in the higher education curriculum', *Curriculum Journal*, 24 (2), 272–294. doi:10.1080/09585176.2013.779287

Saad-Filho, A. (2020) 'From COVID-19 to the End of Neoliberalism', *Critical Sociology*, 46 (4-5), 477–485. (https://journals.sagepub.com/doi/full/10.1177/0896920520929966).

Sahlberg, P. (2011) 'The fourth way of Finland', *Journal of Educational Change*, 12 (2), 173–185.

Sahlberg, P. (2012a) 'Global Educational Reform Movement is here!', blog for *PasiSahlberg.com*. (https://pasisahlberg.com/global-educational-reform-movement-is-here/).

Sahlberg, P. (2012b) 'How GERM is infecting schools around the world', blog for *Pasi-Sahlberg.com*. (https://pasisahlberg.com/text-test/).

Sahlberg, P. (2016) 'The global educational reform movement and its impact on schooling', in K. Mundy, A. Green, B. Lingard and A. Verger (eds), *The Handbook of Global Education Policy*. Hoboken, NJ: John Wiley, 128–144.

St. Pierre, E. (2000) 'Poststructural feminism in education: An overview', *International Journal of Qualitative Studies in Education*, 13 (5), 477–515.

St. Pierre, E. (2012) 'Another postmodern report on knowledge: Positivism and its others', *International Journal of Leadership in Education*, 15 (4), 483–503.

Sandel, M. (2012) *What Money Can't Buy: The Moral Limits of Markets*. New York, NY: Farrar, Straus and Giroux.

Sands, G. (2017) 'Are the PISA education results rigged?', blog for *Forbes Opinion*, 4 January. (www.forbes.com/sites/realspin/2017/01/04/are-the-pisa-education-results-rigged/#203965e01561).

Santos, B. de S. (2004) 'Interview with Boaventura de Sousa Santos', *Globalisation, Societies and Education*, 2 (2), 147–160.

School Curriculum and Assessment Authority (SCAA) (1996) *Desirable Outcomes for Children's Learning on Entering Compulsory Education*. London: DfEE/SCAA. (https://eric.ed.gov/?id=ED433091).

Schultz, T. (1961) 'Investment in human capital', *The American Economic Review*, 51 (1), 1–17.

Schwandt, T. (2003) '"Back to the rough ground!" Beyond theory to practice in evaluation', *Evaluation*, 9 (3), 353–364.

Sellar, S., Thompson, G. and Rutkowski, D. (2017) *The Global Education Race: Taking the Measure of Pisa and International Testing*. Edmonton: Brush Education Inc.

Selwyn, N. (2016) *Is Technology Good for Education?* Cambridge: Polity.

Shamir, R. (2008) 'The age of responsibilitization: On market-embedded morality', *Economy and Society*, 37 (1), 1–19.

Sharp, A. (2013) 'Exam culture and suicidal behaviour among young people', *Education and Health*, 31 (3), 7–11.

Sharp, C., Nelson, J., Lucas, M, Julius, J., McCrone, T. and Sims, D. (2020) *Schools' Responses to Covid-19: The Challenges Facing Schools and Pupils in September 2020*. Slough: NFER. (www.nfer.ac.uk/media/4119/schools_responses_to_covid_19_the_challenges_facing_schools_and_pupils_in_september_2020.pdf).

Shaw, J. (nd) 'Public choice theory', in *The Concise Encyclopedia of Economics*. (www.econlib.org/library/Enc1/PublicChoiceTheory.html).

Shonkoff, J. (2010) *The Early Childhood Initiative*, keynote address Center on the Developing Child, Harvard University.

Shore, C. and Wright, S. (2015) 'Audit culture revisited', *Current Anthropology*, 56 (3), 421–444.

Simmie, G. (2014) 'The neo-liberal turn in understanding teachers' and school leaders' work practices in curriculum innovation and change: A critical discourse analysis of a newly proposed reform policy in lower secondary education in the Republic of Ireland', *Citizenship, Social and Economics Education*, 13 (3), 185–198.

Sims, M. (2017) 'Neoliberalism and early childhood', *Cogent Education*, 4 (1), (www.cogentoa.com/article/10.1080/2331186X.2017.1365411.pdf).

Sjøberg, S. (2019) 'The PISA-syndrome – How the OECD has hijacked the way we perceive pupils, schools and education', *Confero*, 7 (1), 12–65. (www.confero.ep.liu.se/issues/2019/v7/i1/a02/confero19v7i1a02.pdf).

Social Mobility Commission (2016a) *State of the Nation 2016: Social Mobility in Great Britain*. (https://assets.publishing.service.gov.uk/government/uploads/system/uploads/attachment_data/file/569410/Social_Mobility_Commission_2016_REPORT_WEB__1__.pdf).

Social Mobility Commission (2016b) *Ethnicity, Gender and Social Mobility*. (https://assets.publishing.service.gov.uk/government/uploads/system/uploads/attachment_data/file/579988/Ethnicity_gender_and_social_mobility.pdf).

Society of St Vincent de Paul (2016) *Current Shortcomings in Irish ECCE, Childcare and After School Care*. Policy Links No.4. (www.svp.ie/getattachment/eb127982-d19e-4b7e-8333-8335a6f572ba05b/Policy-Links-Current-Shortcomings-in-ECCE-Childca.aspx).

Social Prosperity Network (2017) *Social Prosperity for the Future: A Proposal for Universal Basic Services*. London: UCL IGP.

Solnit, R. (2020) '"The impossible has already happened": What coronavirus can teach us about hope'. *The Guardian*, 7 April. (www.theguardian.com/world/2020/apr/07/what-coronavirus-can-teach-us-about-hope-rebecca-solnit),

Sosinsky, L. (2012) 'Childcare markets in the US: Supply and demand, quality and costs, and public policy', in E. Lloyd and H. Penn (eds), *Childcare Markets: Can They Deliver an Equitable Service?* Bristol: Policy Press, 131–152.

Sriprakash, A., Maithreyi, R., Kumar, A., Sinha, P. and Prabha, K. (2020) 'Normative development in rural India: "School readiness" and early childhood care and education', *Comparative Education*, 56 (3), 331–348.

Standards and Testing Agency (2013) *Early Years Foundation Stage Profile Handbook*. (www.educationengland.org.uk/documents/pdfs/2013-eyfs-profile-handbook.pdf).

Statista (2019) *Incarceration Rates in OECD Countries as of 2019*. (www.statista.com/statistics/300986/incarceration-rates-in-oecd-countries/).

Stedman Jones, D. (2014) *Masters of the Universe: Hayek, Friedman, and the Birth of Neoliberal Politics*. Princeton, NJ: Princeton University Press.

Steele, A. (2000) *Understanding the Ofsted Schools Inspection Process*. (https://dera.ioe.ac.uk/4337/1/Understanding_the_Ofsted_schools_inspection_process.pdf).

Stevenson, H. and Wood, P. (2013) 'Markets, managerialism and teachers' work: The invisible hand of high stakes testing in England', *The International Education Journal: Comparative Perspectives*, 12 (2), 42–46.

Stiglitz, J. (2019a) 'The end of neoliberalism and the rebirth of history', blog for *Social Europe*, 26 November. (www.socialeurope.eu/the-end-of-neoliberalism-and-the-rebirth-of-history).

Stiglitz, J. (2018b) 'Progressive capitalism is not an oxymoron', *New York Times*, 19 April. (www.nytimes.com/2019/04/19/opinion/sunday/progressive-capitalism.html).

Stuart, M. (2011) *Cradle and All: Rocking the Cradle of Wealth*, doctoral thesis at Auckland University of Technology Department of Education. (https://openrepository.aut.ac.nz/bitstream/handle/10292/4452/StuartMJ.pdf?sequence=3&isAllowed=y).

Su, J. and Su, S. (2019) 'Why solving intergenerational injustice through education does not work', *On_Education*, 4 (April). (www.oneducation.net/no-04_april-2019/why-solving-intergenerational-injustice-through-education-does-not-work/).

Sumsion, J. (2006) 'The corporatization of Australian childcare: Towards an ethical audit and research agenda', *Journal of Early Childhood Research*, 4 (2), 99–120.

Sumsion, J. (2012) 'ABC Learning and Australian early childhood education and care: a retrospective ethical audit of a radical experiment', in E. Lloyd and H. Penn (eds), *Childcare Markets: Can They Deliver an Equitable Service?* Bristol: Policy Press, 209–226.

Swift, A. (2020) 'What's fair about that', *London Review of Books*, 42 (2). (www.lrb.co.uk/the-paper/v42/n02/adam-swift/what-s-fair-about-that).

TACTYC (Association for Professional Development in Early Years) (2019) *Young Children as Guinea Pigs: The Reception Baseline Assessment Framework*. (http://imx07wlgmj301rre1jepv8h0-wpengine.netdna-ssl.com/wp-content/uploads/2019/03/Young-children-as-guinea-pigs-TACTYC_.pdf).

Takayama, K. and Lingard, B. (2019) 'Datafication of schooling in Japan: an epistemic critique through the "problem of Japanese education"', *Journal of Education Policy*, 34 (4), 449–469.

Tan, E. (2014) 'Human capital theory: A holistic critique', *Review of Educational Research*, 84 (3), 411–445.

Taylor, A. (2013) *Reconfiguring the Natures of Childhood*. London: Routledge.

TechSci Research (2017) *India Preschool/Child Care Market by Facility (Full Day Care Vs After School Care), by Age Group (Less than 1Yr, 1–2Yrs, 2–4Yrs, etc.), by Location (Standalone, School Premises, & Office Premises), Competition Forecast & Opportunities, 2012–2022* (Press Release). (www.techsciresearch.com/news/3003-preschool-child-care-market-in-india-to-grow-at-23-through-2022.html).

Thompson, G. (2016) 'The life of data; Evolving national testing', in B. Lingard, G. Thompson and S. Sellar (eds), *National Testing in Schools: An Australian Assessment*. London: Routledge.

Thunberg, G. (2019) *Our House is on Fire*. Filmed 29 January 2019 at World Economic Forum in Davos. (www.fridaysforfuture.org/#greta_speech_jan25_2019).

Trades Union Congress (2017) 'Cost of childcare has risen four times faster than wages since 2008', *TUC news listing*, 20 October. (www.tuc.org.uk/news/cost-childcare-has-risen-four-times-faster-wages-2008-says-tuc).

Tronto, J. (2017) 'There is an alternative: *Homines curans* and the limits of neoliberalism', *International Journal of Care and Caring*, 1 (1), 27–43.

Truss, E. (2013) *More great childcare*, speech to a Policy Exchange meeting in London, 29 January. (www.policyexchange.org.uk/modevents/item/elizabeth-truss-mp-more-great-childcare).

Truss, L. (2014) *Elizabeth Truss: The global education race*, speech given at Oxford University, 3 January. (www.gov.uk/government/speeches/elizabeth-truss-the-global-education-race).

Urban, M. and Swadener, B. B. (2016) 'Democratic accountability and contextualised systemic evaluation', *International Critical Childhood Policy Studies*, 5 (1), 6–18.

Unger, R. M. (2004, 2nd edn) *False Necessity: Anti-necessitarian Social Theory in the Service of Radical Democracy*. London: Verso.

Unger, R. M. (2005) *What Should the Left Propose?* London: Verso.

UNICEF (2013) *Child Well-being in Rich Countries: A Comparative Overview*. (www.unicef-irc.org/publications/pdf/rc11_eng.pdf).

United Nations Committee on the Rights of the Child (2005) *General Comment No.7 on Implementing Child Rights in Early Childhood*. (www.refworld.org/docid/460bc5a62.html).

United Nations Committee on the Rights of the Child (2013) *General Comment No.16 on State Obligations Regarding the Impact of the Business Sector on Children's Rights*. (www2.ohchr.org/english/bodies/crc/docs/CRC.C.GC.16.pdf).

Urban, M., Vandenbroeck, M, Lazzari, A., Van Larer, K. and Peeters, J. (2012) *Competence Requirements in Early Childhood Education and Care: Final report*. (https://files.eric.ed.gov/fulltext/ED534599.pdf).

Vabø, M. (2009) *New Public Management: The Neoliberal Way of Governance*. (https://thjodmalastofnun.hi.is/sites/thjodmalastofnun.hi.is/files/skrar/working_paper_4-2009.pdf).

Venn, C. (2018) *After Capitalism*. London: Sage.

Verger, A., Parcerisa, L. and Fontdevila, C. (2019) 'The growth and spread of large-scale assessments and test-based accountabilities: A political sociology of global education reforms', *Educational Review*, 71 (1), 5–30.

Vintimilla, C. (2014) 'Neoliberal fun and happiness in early childhood education', *Journal of the Canadian Association for Young Children*, 39 (1), 79–87.

Ward, H. (2010) 'League tables for five year olds: Gove to publish school-by-school results after just a year of formal education', *Times Educational Supplement*, 3 December. (www.tes.com/news/league-tables-five-year-olds).

Ward, H. (2015) 'Superhead Dame Alison Peacock snubs baseline tests for four-year-olds', *Times Education Supplement*, 2 October. (www.tes.com/news/superhead-dame-alison-peacock-snubs-baseline-tests-four-year-olds).

Ward, H. (2019a) 'SATs create needless pressure for teachers and pupils, heads warn', *Times Educational Supplement*, 19 March. (www.tes.com/news/sats-create-needless-pressure-teachers-and-pupils-heads-warn).

Ward, H. (2019b) 'Baseline: Almost 200 schools drop out of pilot', *Times Educational Supplement*, 16 September. (www.tes.com/news/baseline-almost-200-schools-drop-out-pilot).

Ward, H. (2019c) 'Baseline pilot snubbed by more than 7,000 schools', *Times Educational Supplement*, 14 May. (www.tes.com/news/baseline-pilotsnubbed-more-7000-schools).

Weale, S. (2017) 'More primary school children suffering stress from SATs, survey finds', *The Guardian*, 1 May. (www.theguardian.com/education/2017/may/01/sats-primary-school-children-suffering-stress-exam-time).

Weale, S. (2018) '300 schools picked out in GCSE "off-rolling" investigation', *The Guardian*, 26 June. (www.theguardian.com/education/2018/jun/26/300-schools-picked-out-in-gcse-off-rolling-investigation).

Weale, S. (2019a) 'Mental health of pupils is "at crisis point", teachers warn', *The Guardian*, 17 April. (www.theguardian.com/society/2019/apr/17/mental-health-young-people-england-crisis-point-teacher-school-leader-survey).

Weale, S. (2019b) 'Fifth of teachers plan to leave profession within two years', *The Guardian*, 16 April. (https://www.theguardian.com/education/2019/apr/16/fifth-of-teachers-plan-to-leave-profession-within-two-years).

Whitaker, F. (2018) 'Ofsted annual report reveals plight of "stuck schools"', *Schools Week*, 4 December. (https://schoolsweek.co.uk/ofsted-annual-report-reveals-plight-of-stuck-schools/).

Whittaker, F. (2019) 'Schools losing teacher goodwill over performance-related pay', *Schools Week*, 19 October. (https://schoolsweek.co.uk/schools-losing-teacher-goodwill-over-performance-related-pay/).

White, S. (2015) *Speech given at Institute for Government*, 20 January. (www.globalgovernmentforum.com/uk-most-centralised-developed-country-says-treasury-chief/).

Whitty, G, (2000) *Education reform and education politics in England: A sociological analysis*, paper at a seminar on the theme Education at the Crossroads: Education Reform and Education Politics in Japan and England, organised by the Japan Foundation at the London Institute of Education, 24 October. (www.cddc.vt.edu/digitalfordism/fordism_materials/whitty.pdf).

Widmalm, S. (2016) 'After NPM, curb your enthusiasm for the Principal Agent theory', *Statsvetenskaplig tidskrift*, 118 (1), 127–143. (https://statsvetenskapligtidskrift.files.wordpress.com/2016/03/2016-nr-01-06-widmalm.pdf).

Wilkinson, R. and Pickett, K. (2009) *The Spirit Level: Why More Equal Societies Almost Always Do Better*. London: Allen Lane.

Will, M. (2018) '5 things to know about today's teaching force', *Education Week*, 23 October. (https://mobile.edweek.org/c.jsp?cid=25920011&item=http%3A%2F%2Fapi.edweek.org%2Fv1%2Fblogs%2F62%2F%3Fuuid%3D77760).

Williamson, B. (2016) 'Digital education governance: Data visualization, predictive analytics, and "real-time" policy instruments', *Journal of Education Policy*, 31 (2), 123–141.

Williamson, B. (2017) *Big Data in Education: The Digital Future of Learning, Policy and Practice*. London: Sage.

Williamson, B., Rensfeldt, A., Player-Koro, C. and Selwyn, N. (2018) 'Education recoded: Policy mobilities in the international "learning to code" agenda', *Journal of Education Policy*, 34 (5), 705–725.

Williamson, B. (2020) 'New pandemic edtech power networks', *Code Acts in Education*, 1 April. (codeactsineducation.wordpress.com/2020/04/01/new-pandemic-edtech-power-networks/).

Woodrow, C. and Press, F. (2018) 'The privatisation/marketisation of ECEC debate: Social versus neoliberal values', in L. Miller, C. Cameron, C. Dalli and N. Barbour (eds), *The SAGE Handbook of Early Childhood Policy*. London: Sage, 537–550.

Wolfowitz, P. (2006) 'Foreword', in *World Bank Report 2006: Equity and Development*. New York, NY: World Bank and Oxford University Press.

Worth, J. (2018) 'The UK's teacher supply is leaking … and fast', blog in *Times Educational Supplement*, 28 June. (www.tes.com/news/uks-teacher-supply-leaking-and-fast).

Wright, E. O. (2019) *How to be an Anti-capitalist in the 21st Century*. London: Verso.

Yoon, J. (2013) 'The characteristics and policy issues of the labor markets in childcare', *Labor Review*, 3, 18–30.

Yuen, G. and Lam, M. S. (2017) 'Mothers' experience of a voucher scheme within the context of Hong Kong's early education: Issues of affordability and justice', *Children and Youth Services Review*, 82, 185–194.

Zeng, G., Hou, H. and Peng, K. (2016) 'Effect of growth mindset on school engagement and psychological well-being of Chinese primary and middle school students: The mediating role of resilience', *Frontiers in Psychology*, 7, Article 1873.

Zhou, X. (2011) 'Early childhood education policy development in China', *International Journal of Child Care and Education Policy*, 5 (1), 29–39.

Zigler, E. (2003) 'Forty years of believing in magic is enough', *Social Policy Report*, 17 (1), 10.

Zuboff, S. (2019) *The Age of Surveillance Capitalism: The Fight for a Human Future at the New Frontier of Power*. London: Profile Books.

INDEX

Page numbers in *italics* indicate figures